Democracy Without Decency

WILLIAM M. EPSTEIN

Democracy Without Decency

Good Citizenship and the War on Poverty

The Pennsylvania State University Press
University Park, Pennsylvania

LIBRARY OF CONGRESS
CATALOGING-IN-PUBLICATION DATA

Epstein, William M., 1944–
Democracy without decency : good citizenship and the war on poverty / William M.
Epstein.
    p.   cm.
Includes bibliographical references and index.
Summary: "An analysis of social and economic policies in the United States, with
emphasis on the 1960s War on Poverty"—Provided by publisher.
ISBN 978-0-271-03633-5 (cloth : alk. paper) 978-0-271-03634-2 (pbk : alk. paper)
1. United States—Social policy.
2. United States—Economic policy.
I. Title.

HV95.E695   2010
362.50973—dc22
2009034708

CONTENTS

Acknowledgments vii

Preface ix

Introduction:
The Good Citizen and American Social Welfare 1

1 The Programmatic Precursors to the War on Poverty 19

2 The War on Poverty:
Programs of the Office of Economic Opportunity 55

3 Other War on Poverty Programs 111

4 The Social Insurances and Welfare 151

5 Charity and Community Organization 179

Conclusion: The Iron Sculpture 215

Tables 237

References 241

Index 259

ACKNOWLEDGMENTS

The book owes an immense debt to the wonderful librarians of the University of Nevada, Las Vegas—Susie Skarl, Michael Frazier, Marta Sorkin, and their colleagues. The staff extended themselves past any expectation of customary service to provide bibliographic support, ready access to journal articles, and material searches. The librarians softened the shortcomings of this beleaguered public university that lacks the resources even to sustain adequate research assistance. I am also grateful to the University of Nevada, Las Vegas, for a sabbatical term.

My first readers, advisors, scholarly colleagues, and occasional graduate assistants provided invaluable support and advice: Robert Dippner, Ronald A. Farrell, Erin Friedl, Gabriela Gandarilla, Carolyn V. Grossmann, Jorge V. Grossmann, Brij Mohan, Jennifer Nutton, Leroy H. Pelton, David Smail, Frank Stricker, and Joanne Thompson.

A special note of thanks for the attentiveness, wisdom, and gentle touch of the Penn State Press's former director, Sanford G. Thatcher.

Terence, this is stupid stuff . . .

—A. E. HOUSMAN

It is easy to fall into the trap of broad cultural condemnation—any society but this one, any age but the present—invoking superior conditions in other cultures as though the comparisons were informed or sensible. The critical observations in the present work are made entirely within the American tradition and loyal to the hope of social progress here at home. Other societies need to heed their own critics and their own traditions. The United States is a miracle of both achievement and disappointment and offers the eternal opportunity of an open society to reconcile the two.

The rules of good citizenship achieve mass consent in the United States through an ecology of detached role organizations rather than through deliberative democracy's boast of conscious reason. A few noble individuals may live lives of blessed rationality, but they are tortured, depressed, sometimes suicidal, and always obsessed with their behaviors—joyless narcissists. The rest of America has reached an enormous agreement over the priorities, rugged and durable through the centuries, that are embedded in the daily free choices of citizens. Planned change is improbable; the grave inadequacies of contemporary social welfare, endorsed with maddening regularity over the course of the nation's history, will likely persist.

The full history of domestic social welfare is not the current concern. Rather, the period beginning after World War II is the chunk of time in which contemporary social welfare policy has emerged, engendered by traditional values but worked out through updated arrangements. Perhaps the persistence of American indifference to deprivation and need—the knowing, accepted, and even intended failure of social welfare programs—might offer a small alert, but by no means any point of optimism. Poverty persists, and deep inequality slowly corrodes the American promise.

The Introduction opens the central theme—American social welfare policy as the consensual, mandated choice of the American people. The auxiliary themes—romanticism, social efficiency, welfare as patronage, the failure of the rational enterprise in social policymaking, and others—are developed throughout the chapters that analyze social welfare policy. The substance of the discussion involves the War on Poverty and its immediate programmatic precursors, similar programs that followed, old age insurance, public assistance, and the charitable sector. The War on Poverty, mainly conducted during the Johnson administration's Great Society of the 1960s, was the most focused effort during the contemporary period, and perhaps in American history, to address poverty. With few exceptions of limited influence, the War on Poverty and public policy in general have largely failed to reduce poverty or income inequality or to provide much income security. The charitable sector has been similarly unsuccessful, even disingenuous. The Conclusion, "The Iron Sculpture," reunites the material around the process of detached role organization as the mechanism of the pervasive American consensus. Rather than usurpations of power by illegitimate elites, autonomous government action, or factional politics, that is, pluralism, the American consensus accounts for the nation's institutionalized social welfare arrangements.

Many social welfare programs are covered, but some are not. Child welfare, formal public education, higher education, urban renewal and housing, most of the social insurances apart from old age insurance, among others, are redundant stories. The goal is not encyclopedic coverage but rather to lay out a theory of social welfare provision and decision making with ample evidence. The failure of social welfare policy to remedy poverty and America's growing inequality is the occasion for an extended meditation on American society.

Preference is best defined as uncoerced choice; enduring public and private policies thus become statements of enduring national priorities. The fundamental proposition that in a free society public and private policy reflects the social will allows American values to be illuminated through the choice of public policy rather than indirectly through devices such as surveys and less structured tools. Public and private policy is probably a more accurate and reliable statement of social preference than social science analyses and historical narratives that customarily build from impaired data to explain how apparent decision makers, tradition, intellectuals, autonomous actors, special interests, economic elites, social institutions, and others determine policy choice. The very choice of public policy defines American values, and the relationship of the individual to the state and the society defines, in a word, citizenship.

All theories of social decision making are bedeviled by the absence of proof. Without definitive tests of cause, any assumption of originating or determinitive power is speculative. Elites that seem to be the authors of events may be working from a popular consensus or within cultural bounds, neither of which they engendered; the relationship between the individual and the times is maddeningly difficult to sort out. The few must govern, since direct participatory democracy in a large, complex society is impossible; yet the question remains whether their decisions reflect sectarian preferences or broader permissions. True tests of power are usually impossible, as large entities such as nations do not lend themselves to randomized experimentation. Yet even a randomized trial identifies only one cause in what is usually a causal chain. This is not much of a problem when the issue is the effectiveness of a drug. However, it is an enormous problem when actors perform in a social context within a tradition.

Only in the event of a clear difference of self-defined preference between alternative actors—e.g., the masses pressing for one policy and elites for another—is it possible to declare a political victor. Yet a winner in one event that may not even endure is not a prototypical power. Differences need to be tracked through many issues and across time. However, deep differences among large groups—that is, deep social cleavages—rarely exist in contemporary American social politics; the very openness of the society that facilitates an ecology of detached role organizations creates enduring agreement over much of the policy terrain.

Without a credible process for testing theory, the identification of the motor of social decision making becomes arbitrary and ideological. The standard histories of contemporary American social welfare argue toward their embedded ideologies, frequently assuming what they hope to prove by selective use of the historical record. That record is infinite and impossible to sort through without initial assumptions. Institutional histories implicitly argue for the importance of the institutions they explore; biographies accord unique prowess to individual actors; histories of group competition assume a particular form and influence for social organization; belief in the influence of the good heart finds instances in which the moral will prevails. In this way, historical analysis is at best suggestive and at worst tendentious, either flattering the vanities of dominant society, playing to partisan stakes, or simply expressing the author's angst, disappointments, and hopes through tacit autobiography.

While the different theories of social decision making typically acknowledge some influence for mass preference, none accord it a determinative role. Except under the most coercive, authoritarian, and oppressive regimes, social policy and culture may well be the products of popular consent. In turn, a consensual social order is probably the most influential factor in determining events, according roles to all social actors that they depart from at their peril. In an open society, power is extremely diffuse, and the human vehicles of a popular will—the elites of politics, government, commerce, art, the professions, and intellect—embody that power rather than usurp it.

The theory of mass dominance cannot test its propositions any better than alternative explanations of social decision making can. It is usually possible to preserve the robustness and plausibility of a theory by isolating inconvenient events and data in special categories that accord them unique status, or that leave their true nature in doubt, or that reinterpret their essential meaning. Disconfirming data can be explained away as ambiguities that have yet to be understood, or as instances of values in transition, or, in rare cases that are relatively unimportant, as inexplicable. In other words, the ecology of detached roles can explain almost all social decision making, at least in retrospect. This is not a virtue, for the true test of theory lies in its predictive ability; no theory of social decision making has survived this level of sophistication. Instead, theories of social decision making reach conclusions through such devices as the consistency of findings, the balance of evidence, and informed guesses. These are troublingly weak substitutes for rigorous theory testing.

Without rigorous testing, the acceptance of any theory of social decision making becomes ideological, an instance of faith, convenience, and compatibility. In this way, the Left in the United States, with its theatrical sympathies for supposedly oppressed masses, has grasped theories of class dominance. Conservatives tend to justify the rule of enduring elites in terms of an "objective" national interest, national preference, the natural value of those who preside, even Darwinian survival and an overarching mystical belief in the virtues of tradition and stability. The patrician view of an autonomous and selfless class of decision makers legitimates the rational pretenses of philosopher kings. Most theories of social policymaking assume that democratic processes in the United

States have been subverted. Few accept that the system is true to its assumptions and rules, and therefore they avoid the consequent conundrum: a democracy that produces problematic policy raises fundamental questions about its own value.

For a theory of mass determination, such as the ecology of detached roles, to gain currency would require an almost unimaginable honesty—we are what we invest in; the failures of American social welfare are intentional—and perhaps an agreement to improve the conditions of American citizenship. But a revolution in consciousness is unlikely to occur within a complacent America or to be forced on the nation by crisis. Catastrophes such as the Great Depression and two world wars have been absorbed with little challenge to a traditional civic ethos that is as rigid as an iron sculpture.

INTRODUCTION:
THE GOOD CITIZEN AND AMERICAN SOCIAL WELFARE

It is a curiosity verging on the miraculous when inherently weak ideas enjoy enduring popularity. Form over substance, ritual without function, meaning deprived of value: empty notions, often clamoring with millenarian fervor, capture the civic imagination even as the ingenuous and well intended conspire with the practical. In just this way, the programs of the War on Poverty, Model Cities, the negative income tax (especially the attempts by the Nixon and Carter administrations), assets development, housing programs for the poor, near poor, and the homeless, No Child Left Behind, Just Say No to Drugs, the Peace Corps, VISTA, Americorps, affirmative action—including the Voting Rights Act and the Civil Rights Act—the Contract with America, notably welfare reform, faith-based programs, community organization, and community development, among others, have been largely ineffective. Even Social Security (old age, survivors, disability, and health insurance), Medicaid, and food stamps provide much less than meets the eye. The persistence of any social welfare program in the United States depends largely on its ritualistic reaffirmation of core American values, in particular an extreme form of individualism.

Social policymaking in America has been driven by the popular will, not by a conspiracy of predatory elites, the autonomous functionaries of government, or the vagaries of pluralism. The characteristic and embedded social welfare policies of the United States carry broad consent. They are probably the truest expressions of the popular will, more reliable and accurate than the most carefully conducted opinion poll. At the same time, their enduring indifference to social problems, notably inequality, poverty, and personal deviance, exposes the dilemmas of liberal, market-oriented democratic society: popular policies that are neither decent, nor generous, nor effective; the ascendency of spontaneous market orders over social planning; the small role of rationality, reason, public dialogue, or even coherence in a largely ungovernable, decentralized policy-making process that forms popular consent. Social reform is impeded little by the technical challenges of program development but constantly stymied by the monumental task of modifying established social priorities. Social reform programs, whether enacted or not, convey expectations for the role of the good citizen. They are sermons on the theme of the good citizen rather than substantial responses to social need.

The ideal of the good citizen consistently justifies social policy in the United States. Across decades, the enormous variety of programs, impressive in their total expenditures but superficial when viewed separately, annually, and against standards of need, all promised to create the good citizen. In turn, good citizenship offered a reciprocity with economic growth, political cohesion, social harmony, civility, courtesy, and even affection.

The substitution of form for substance in social welfare explains America's romances with heroic individualism, social capital, comity, communality, self-help, spirituality, and other concepts that inspired a social welfare strategy of preaching rather than material provision. Without rationality or even reasonability, each instance of American romanticism has fostered faith in its exceptional destiny. Yet few concrete goals if any were achieved by the major national reform efforts beginning with the War on Poverty and running through the rest of the post–World War II period coincidental with the ascendency of the modern American state. Nevertheless, the citizen preferences that construct America's myths of coherence and its cultural momentum prevail by creating their own social reality, perhaps a stronger force than economic self-interest. Political relevancy lies in social acceptance rather than objective truth.

Societal change is inevitably a narrative of tragedy, as ineluctable forces crush resistance, often at great human cost. Industrialization is the case in point. The American system has not faced an overpowering external threat to its complacency since World War II. In fact, only a catastrophe on the order of global warming, nuclear war, a devastating pandemic, or even uncaring social and economic dislocations created by newer revolutions in industrial production seems capable of moving traditional social institutions.

The persistence of heroic individualism and communal millenarianism in American ideology is a tribute to the strength and enduring preferences of the American people. Those preferences culminate in the principle of social efficiency, the demand that social welfare be minimal and conform to popular tastes. The controlling influence of social efficiency explains the persistence of inadequate and ineffective programs, even as the public presence in domestic policy has increased since the 1960s. The promise of big payoffs in good citizenship for small investments of actual resources has inspired the enormous range of personal social services, community organization, and community development that have been dedicated to reducing American poverty and inequality. Yet these programs have routinely failed to ameliorate social problems, even while they have persisted as morality plays, rites, rituals, totems, and ceremonies that endorse the society's values.

The romances of American civic faith, notably the possibility of socially efficient remedies for its problems, are ideological mantras, ineffable specters, sacred spirits, unimaginable and unweighable forces of underlying social beliefs in the good citizen that justify public and private actions. Thus reform efforts and enacted policies carry large ceremonial duties—ideological obligations—along with their concrete production functions in achieving specific social goals. American social welfare after World War II persisted for its expressive value more than for its success in reaching specified goals.

The United States has been surprisingly inept at fixing its social problems despite aggregating national wealth beyond the dreams of visionaries. The problems that have abated, most notably the conditions of abject economic poverty and even the illusory success of the welfare reforms of 1996, to take two examples, resulted from economic growth—the momentum of industrialization and technological innovation—more than from the planned efforts, either public or private, of philanthropy and public provision.

To be sure, the exquisitely engineered material infrastructure of modern society—sewerage, clean water, abundant food, and so forth—along with the bounty created by industrialization and technological innovation, has increased life expectancy and generally decreased morbidity. However, public and private efforts to ameliorate material inequality have been uniformly ineffective. Industrialization has certainly harmed many individuals and the environment, but the gain/loss ratio seems worse for recent reform programs: vast ineffectiveness and perhaps even actual harm associated with sporadic benefits that are often only coincidental with the program.

The precursors and the activities of the War on Poverty, as well as the enormous range of subsequent character-building programs underwritten by the public sector, testify to symbol over substance and the rejection by the American people of measurable public action against inequality. Few if any social welfare programs can put forward credible evidence that they did much to alleviate poverty, repair character flaws, improve education or employment, or provide jobs, except to staff. The income advances of poorer people are typically due to economic growth, not planned social welfare interventions, and notably not the welfare reforms of 1996. Nevertheless, contemporary economic growth, predicated on technology rather than labor, tends to exacerbate the divide between the poor, poorer groups, and lower-status people, on the one hand, and the well educated, on the other.

The programs of the War on Poverty and subsequent misadventures in reform were indentured to impossible values incapable of changing material circumstances, providing motivation, or repairing the inadequacies of the American system. They offered cheap, bogus compensations for prior deprivation that sidestepped customary participation in the core institutions of American society—family, education, employment, community, and so forth. Their mindless optimism about ersatz goods underscored the futility of America's faith in policy minimalism and the descendent approaches to social problems insistent on personal reformation.

The programs also failed because of huge administrative lapses, mistargeting, poor theoretical foundations, corrupt staff and boards, low recipient interest and superficial participation, incompetent organizers, and most notably the fact that few of the problems besetting poor neighborhoods are amenable to self-help and local resolution. Yet even with responsible administration and tactical astuteness the programs would probably not have overcome their essentially hollow inspirations. It is one of the grand hypocrisies of American social welfare that poor, problematic groups are often trapped in strategies of localism and self-invention by dominant groups whose hallmark successes emerged through geographic interdependence and after generous and sustained investments in their skills and socialization.

The romance of reform and its fantasies of social efficiency have prevailed over deep criticism, enduring to proselytize the American myth of progress and heroic individualism, abetting the American faith in the nation's exceptional destiny, and often pursuing a nostalgic dream of pastoral harmony. All would be well with social welfare as civic entertainment and binding ritual except that it endorses American inequalities, affirms socioeconomic stratification, encourages resistance to greater sharing, and ignores great need. Rituals of heroic individualism boost attention to America's problems that address character flaws at the price of structural approaches designed to handle the imperfections of the society itself.

The policy minimalism of social efficiency finds a ready audience among proponents of limited government, in particular those who rely upon free market solutions to economic and social growth. It also has enough charm to entrance sentimental liberals who yearn for a fellowship of noble, widespread volition. However, heroic individualism is a tyranny, although widely accepted, rather than a plan for either personal betterment or social progress. It takes literary inspiration from the empiricism of economics to justify a metaphysics of citizenship: mystical, unknowable, immeasurable, and ineffable—inner speech rather than whispering, the profoundly subjective and personal rather than an objective, concrete, and commonly shared human experience.

Yet the wonderment lies in the widespread and popular acceptance that the perilous condition of American society demanded a renewal of faith in civic voluntarism, the extension of heroic individualism to community problems. The wonderment is greatly enlarged in consideration of the absence of any credible or even systematic proof that voluntary charitable activities have in fact achieved any of their goals, including an increase in the nation's mystical store of conviviality and good will, let alone in their direct programmatic objectives. Similarly, the meaning of most social welfare programs and reform efforts lies in an affirmation of national values rather than in an ability to achieve direct service objectives; American social welfare programs often reprise a Puritan sermon on sin and redemption. Enacted policies, and especially the deep preferences that constitute the most enduring and powerful of the nation's social institutions, are windows into the American soul. The inspirations of many American welfare reforms, notably the War on Poverty, are grounded in a world that never was and can never be, rather than in the world that is. In this way the persistence of policy minimalism, embellished by the independence and self-invention of the good American citizen, denies the gravity of social problems and erects substantial barriers to change.

Even when a social welfare program transfers a substantial amount of money and service, as in the case of the social insurances, their benefits are typically inadequate for the most needy, while they maintain the reward hierarchy of American social stratification. Provisions for those outside the workforce—Medicaid, TANF, food stamps, SSI—are even more inadequate than provisions for those who work. Indeed, it is not at all obvious that old age insurance has done much more than simply routinize sharing within families through intergenerational transfers between the young and the old. The social preference for equity trumps concern for equality or adequacy; lower-paid workers still get very small benefits, while those with comfortable private retirement incomes enjoy the largest social security benefits. It takes quite the optimist to look at America's social insurance programs and come away with the confidence that they provide security. The vaunted success of Social Security is really very modest, adhering, just like the more obvious failures of reform, to central American preferences for individual responsibility over social responsibility—heroic individualism rather than the protections and supports of community.

Civilization as we know it, including the abundance of agriculture, is the product of the learning and commerce that attended urbanization. The broader forces that created the modern world were typically unplanned and perhaps even uncontrollable. It is laughable to place cries for social welfare reform and civic renewal alongside these forces and expect inherently weak volition to resolve society's material deficiencies. Yet constructs of social efficiency that inspire many American reform programs—the War on Poverty, Just Say No to Drugs, the Hinckley solution to mental health, twelve-step programs, psychotherapy, to name a few—deny the impelling forces of society. Indeed, American reform programs typically substitute symbolic affirmation for effectiveness and rarely extend the central institutions of society—quality education, nurturing families, adequate income, productive work, secure retirement, medical care, and the like—to the poor, the unemployed, the sick, and the disabled.

The call for a revolution in American consciousness, even a third Great Awakening, is very much in the American tradition of heroic individualism. These myths of self-invention have deep roots in American transcendentalism, which echoed the nineteenth-century European philosophies of Fichte, Hegel, and Nietzsche, with later imports from their philosophical offspring—the postmodernists and notably Freud. Indeed, the nation's fascination with psychotherapeutic solutions to social problems—voluntary individual perfectability as the building block of social progress—constitutes America's civil religion and its policy expression in social efficiency.

The deepest and most important community involvement is not in the town meeting's bogus concern with governance but rather in the day-to-day decencies of living that actually determine the moral climate of a society and provide its members with enduring satisfactions. Planned community involvement has largely failed to resolve social problems while nurturing small-minded neighborhood feudalism. Local problems are customarily too complicated and interconnected with the larger society to be resolved locally. The history of community organization and community development has been a series of sentimental forays into the problems of modernity using the tools of rustic nostalgia—small may be beautiful, but it is not noticeably effective or even satisfying. But these programs—epitomized by the Community Action Program of the Great Society, Alinsky-style organizing, earlier efforts at agricultural extension, and much more recent activities of ACORN, the Southern Christian Leadership Conference, and the specific organizations and projects that grew out of the social capital crusade—persisted because they posed little challenge to reigning social institutions. Indeed, they offered people with problems separate, far less costly systems of care, attacking problems with moral truisms rather than with material steps toward greater equality (e.g., education, family, work, and so forth). Most voluntary charitable organizations pass through time as denial, as diversions from substantive solutions.

Community development and even centrally planned changes have not offered workable substitutes for industrialization, migration, urbanization, and technological innovation, or even credible controls and compensations for their risks. They have been largely incapable of lubricating the tectonic plates of social and economic change. Indeed, the liberal state (including its American variant) cherishes the free market and picks up the tab for only a small amount of the damage it does. By contriving a sense of continuity, safety, progress, and control where little really exists, community development and community organization are apologists for the near-ungovernable forces of society. The

planned central programs of the liberal welfare state have largely ritual-
ized popular values realized in a bifurcated system—parsimony for
workers through the social insurances contrasted with a beggar's mite
for the dependent. This system institutionalizes American stratification
in defiance of repairing it with an adequate social provision.

American society refuses to put up sufficient resources to explore the
nature of social problems because it is largely uninterested in solutions,
especially if those solutions point to the endemic problems of the society
itself. Most social welfare programs are largely unevaluated, or they are
evaluated so poorly that only their failure to achieve stated goals seems
plausible. Mobilization for Youth and the Gray Areas Projects, as well as
the Community Action Program they preceded, were never put under a
credible microscope, except that they clearly did not cure poverty, urban
blight, or juvenile delinquency. The effects of faith-based initiatives remain articles of faith. The transition from Aid to Families with Dependent Children to Temporary Assistance for Needy Families and the
broader reforms of 1996 were occasioned by hardening social attitudes
toward the poor rather than by credible solutions to poverty.

Indeed, there is no scientific evidence that testifies to the benefits of
psychotherapy and counseling, their application to numerous personal
problems, or any of the other personal social services. The possibility
that psychotherapy works in the manner of the Catholic sacrament of
confession pays tribute neither to the church nor to talk therapy but
rather justifies little tyrannies of emotional blackmail and organizational
aggrandizement.

The public reform programs of modern America, even those with
intentions to change American policymaking processes, largely depended on individual initiative, minimal and usually temporary public
funding, and the assurance that the good citizen was largely a result of
an individual epiphany within a community of the like-minded—the
communality of individualism, a uniqueness that isn't. All largely de-
fended the American system, denying the possibility of any deep structural imperfections. Yet all failed for the same fundamental reason: the
costs of long-term repair exceeded the willingness of the American people to tax and spend or to pursue greater social and economic equality.
Americans have thwarted each epoch of reform with their fundamental
satisfaction.

Model Cities distinguished itself both for its extensive and persistent
efforts to develop a constituency for progressive urban reform and for

its thoroughgoing failure. Even the mass of people targeted as prime stakeholders in urban renewal and redistributive national welfare policy—the poor, the working class, people living in blighted areas, "urban villagers," and so forth—failed to come together in support of Model Cities' participatory plans. Indeed, their indifference was a choice to reject a progressive agenda and a larger government role. The rejection demonstrates more graphically and credibly than inherently ambiguous opinion polls the dominance of the pervasive culture of America, the perfusion of central cultural values throughout every organ of the body politic and every rung of American stratification.

The culture wars—fought largely over the body issues of abortion, teenage birth control, and gay rights—have been exaggerated to the point of French operas, when in fact they remain border issues and are far less intensely divisive than the combatants report. It is even surprising that the deeper conflict between traditionalists, literalists, and pietists, on the one hand, and progressives and liturgicals, on the other, has remained latent, without much influence on American political choices. The small differences between the major American parties, along with the absence of any serious third-party challenge, underscore the conservatism and contentment of Americans. Their classic liberalism and awe for tradition persist despite rapid changes of style in popular music, clothes, cars, architecture, literature, movies, art, and perhaps even body sculpting, skin ornamentation, and personal relations that offer a boost for the economy more than a challenge to cultural stability. Even the extraordinary depth and size of American high culture has not devised much of an appealing alternative to current policies.

Public discussions of social reform have been reluctant to grapple with the American people's satisfaction with their system and their participation in the metaphors and myths that justify the choices they have made. Theories of class dominance and even the autonomous state need a dissatisfied citizenry or, failing that, the assistance of false consciousness and imputed social need to maintain their independent sense of social reality, that is, a reality separate from the self-defined beliefs of citizens. Even the toughest critics of American society ignore the complicity of the American people in their own problems. By and large the American people do not feel that they are facing much peril, let alone any grave threat to their chosen way of life. They grouse about politics and society with recreational and artistic fervor in opinion polls, one of the culture's novel communication mediums. The grousing rarely leads to action.

An open political system in which citizen decisions are uncoerced, and in which stigma, isolation, and exile are rare, expresses the will of the people through public policy and social institutions, notably those outside government in both the private and civic spheres. Public policy becomes the pinnacle compromise among the infinitely complex differences of individual citizens. It is a better estimate of the national will than the most detailed survey of opinions and intentions or historical reconstructions of policymaking. Opinion surveys are bedeviled by response falsification, chief among many other problems (Epstein 2006b); they report verbal choices rather than actual choices—Monopoly investments rather than money investments, hypotheticals rather than actuals, Walter Mitty dreams rather than true risk taking. In their turn, historical analyses are inevitably compromised by missing and distorted data. Even if every citizen said that he rejected long-established social policy priorities, the fact of their persistence in an open society proves the negotiated, balanced correctness of the priorities in mirroring the popular will. Uncoerced choice defines preference.

Through an ecology of independent roles that become detached from individuals through role organizations in an open political system, public policy summates the collective preferences of the people as a behavior—the choice of specific action among alternatives. In this way the reform programs of the United States—its periodic, coherent, coordinated choices of specific programs to handle social problems, including the definition of those problems as well as the inadequacies of the responses—actually represent the nation's meaning, purpose, intentions, preferences, values, and, most important, its balanced judgment of the correct, the appropriate, the just, and, tellingly, the esthetics and ethics of the good citizen. Thus the enduring themes of social reform in the United States—a near monomania for individual responsibility, applied with a consistency so uniform as to be definitive—represent a continuing, freely chosen sanction for the United States as it is. This stability of choice is the nut of the problem for reformers. A system so satisfied with itself does not change easily, even as a result of cherished public dialogue and town meetings. The United States is, and things happen, both rebukes to reason.

Is America open and free, or are citizen behaviors actually coerced by a subversive conspiracy of elites? Do powerful elites, for their own predatory advantage, mesmerize the masses through the media and through an exquisite ability to maintain social obedience by way of small economic and status reinforcements?

An open society abjures coercion, not influence, a subtle distinction. That individuals are forced bodily or through dire threat to make an unwanted choice is different from the situation in which a person chooses because of a preference dictated by culture. Socialization is not coercion but the shared process through which a people integrates its members and achieves consensus. Presumably, if socialization failed, people would change. Yet when they maintain tradition in the face of enormous abuse—Gypsies, Jews, Native Americans, Hutterites, Amish, and so on—they are making a profound and conscious choice. At least formally, the person who chooses conformity is free to disobey. Of course social institutions and the momentum of tradition guide individual choices, but so too individuals' consumption of reality collectively shapes social structures. Third forces—e.g., crowding, instinct, predestination, alien influence (from space, not from Europe), competition, unseen hands, unseen strings, chemical and biological infestations, momentum, progress, technological innovation—may even sidestep consciousness to dominate individual choice and the subsequent creation of tradition. However, it is impossible to separate these influences rationally.

Indeed, even high-minded and seemingly neutral arguments for particular causal agents—theories of social decision making—inevitably degrade into ideological positions. The fateful ignorance of cause cannot be overcome by a series of assumptions, inadequate proofs, and conclusions, even when drawn from carefully compared historical re-creations. Yet even the most detailed and compulsive descriptions of policymaking do not constitute proof, let alone wisdom, but tend to confuse detail with explanation. The closest approximations to defensible political understanding are inevitably flawed, despite their satisfying tendency to sustain cultural belief. Erudition and the best available evidence may fail both as rationality and as reason: inadequate to provide scientifically credible answers to social problems and insufficient to loosen the ideological commitments that determine social decision making.

The fact that policymaking takes place over time does not imply that each succeeding event is the result of its predecessor and the cause of the next. Rather, the cultural envelope of role organizations expressing a consistency of social preference customarily predetermines each element in the choice of a social policy. A policy is truly considered only when social preferences are ambiguous and traditional supports erode. The causes of such erosion are rarely if ever a product of the human will and planning but rather of the impersonal, unimaginably powerful factors that define epochs in human history, the revolutions of agriculture, commerce, and industrialization that continue through technological change and through calamities on the order of war, famine, pestilence and pandemic, natural catastrophes, and the like.

The political system of the United States has matured into a "hyperdemocracy," a system so enfranchised and driven by a mass will that even gray privilege pays homage to the consent of the people in order to maintain itself. Despite many recriminations and much caterwauling about the imperfections of the culture—hedonism, anomie, isolation, crime, corruption, and materialism, to name a few—it is most likely that social conditions exist and persist because they are on balance satisfying. They are not perceived as sufficiently threatening or severe to justify changing American priorities. In an open society, the acceptance of social conditions expresses a balance between benefits and costs that are the result of widely chosen priorities, in spite of the inevitable displeasure attending any distribution of scarce resources. But the expression of displeasure as a verbal response to a survey question does not by itself necessarily invalidate choice or deprive it of a deep social mandate; true displeasure is expressed as alternative choices and notably as disruptive and destructive behavior. The most feasible series of priorities for the most people, especially if consistent over time and even if not their individual first preference, cements a very powerful détente among citizens of an open society.

The communitarian concern with a moral consensus and not just quality bonding, and its belief in the persuasive influence of "moral dialogues," assumes at least a protorational process of social decision making: "New norms must be formulated by building on, or revising or even rebelling against old ones, a rebelling still affected by what is being rebelled against. Traditions cannot be ignored. . . . Much more generally, all moral revivals draw on values people already have, on a cultural repertoire of known and shared moral symbols and narratives" (Etzioni 2001, 368). The enduring ethos of the United States developed through the formal and informal negotiation of role organizations. A broad and deep consensus has developed slowly around a series of consistent choices that constitute a moral order, although one that many disparage. Democracy, and notably hyperdemocracy, assures popular choices but not an extracultural morality, not the rule of Heaven or Reason but rather the rule of the national will.

The hope for a reflective policymaking process—moral dialogues of one sort or another that involve sorting through values, experiences, and social conditions—while very satisfying for the vanity of patriots in a democracy, ignores the degree to which actual preferences, more populist than progressive, determine policy choices. Social dialectics are motored by individual role preferences more than by reasoned choice. People's daily choices—market behavior, intimate behavior, family patterns, and so forth—provide both informal and formal sustenance for some roles more than others. Individual roles become detached from the individual as they are represented in numerous role organizations: religious organizations that press for the interest of the religious roles; consumer organizations that press for ascendency for consumerism; and, in the same manner, role organizations for politics, recreation, employment, tax policy, conservation, the environment, and a near infinity of others that impose on public and private choices for particular ends. Even the simplest informal organizations state preferences that boost particular roles: standing in line states a preference for particular ordering, chitchat at bars defines one of the roles of affability, spontaneous courtesies ("bless you" after a sneeze) express a preference for a role of courtesy, and so forth.

Roles are organized through spacial hierarchies—e.g., block associations, citywide tenant and homeowner associations, state and national associations—that at succeeding levels digest ever more sophisticated information and endorse ever more powerful policy options in furthering the interests of their particular roles. At every level they vie against and negotiate with other role organizations. They draw their influence from the degree to which citizens participate in or conform to their agendas. The process operates without the obligation of a generally informed citizenry. All that is necessary is that role organizations inform their choices and that the political and social systems are open and uncoerced, permitting the individuals to change behaviors and allowing the role organizations to compete against each other on grounds of satisfying mass preferences (again, as expressed in role hierarchies). Role organizations build on the informal and formal microchoices of individuals rather than through a time-ordered and consecutive process of objective choice.

By giving "astonishingly little weight to economic change, social movements, or public policies" that constitute the milieu of the citizen's role choices, progressive reformers typically fail to appreciate the intricacies of citizen consent in crafting the contemporary society of the United States. Role organizations that represent flagging citizen choices lose power. They are accountable to citizens weakly, through rare elections and plebiscites, but powerfully through their conformity with emerging and institutionalized preferences. Thus the process of consent remains largely informal—private preferences preceding public policy— ensuring that enduring power carries the consent of the masses. In this way, the immense power of the petroleum industry is maintained by the centrality of oil and energy in American life—the near-ubiquitous American insistence on individual transportation and spacious homes— rather than by a conspiracy of oil barons and insidious corporate control.

In an open society such as the United States, notions of class dominance or even class independence (e.g., the autonomous state) are illusory. That policy innovation comes from government is not proof of autonomy but rather of a free but circumscribed space permitted to employed and controlled specialists. Elites and the powerful maintain their position through consent, despite widespread envy and popular fascination with conspiracy. Curiously, the tradition of deriving American public policy from mass attitudes (e.g., Dahl 1976; Key 1961) developed during a period when elites probably did in fact exert enormous influence for their own benefit.

The business community in the United States has come to enjoy a special position not because of any flummery in controlling the citizen but rather because the citizen's many roles conform to the interests of largely unregulated free markets. Becoming increasingly unequal over the past thirty-five years or so, American socioeconomic stratification results from role trade-offs that have cemented a special cachet for the wealthy, including the widespread belief that their private wealth produces a general public benefit. The stable conditions of the United States, however distasteful to the liberal and radical sensibilities, are nevertheless the intricately negotiated concrete manifestations of a national ethos. There is more of a culture war among intellectuals than among the masses. But again, the plausibility of inferring social intention from cultural choices and institutions, notably public policy, depends profoundly on the openness of the system and the absence of coercion—the ability of citizens to change role preferences.

Social critics who define social conditions as problematic often fail to accept the amoral functionality of enduring social arrangements and the profound degree to which the culture has reached a satisfying consensus. All too frequently the critic and the committed reformer dismiss evidence of mass acceptance as a "potentially reactionary" form of false consciousness or delusion (DeFillipis 2002, 791). The recourse to nostalgia is not merely polemic but active fable, a summary of American preference as myth that reconciles desire with reality. To stop at the imperfections of myth as social science is to miss the point. Myth is not reactionary; its believers are.

The dominant attempts at social reform of the past fifty years or so have drawn on enduring myths, notably the benefits of social cohesion that arise from communal self-invention, the oxymoron of community as heroic individualism. The contemporary romantic imagination refreshes Emersonian ideals—a transcendentalist faith in introspection, self-invention, and rustic retreats, a moral superiority over commerce, the affection for rural and communal innocence, fierce patriotism, ingenuity, and optimism.

Power in the United States is largely exercised legitimately with the consent of the masses. Indeed, class dominance as an explanation for current inequalities falls apart when presented with a different reality: America has largely fulfilled its democratic obligations in creating a society that in fact reflects the preferences of its members, even while those preferences result in deplorable policies from an egalitarian perspective. Even worse, from this point of view, the presumed victims of the predatory system largely support the system and its values, notwithstanding the Stockholm syndrome (identification with the oppressor) to preserve the innocence of the masses. The insistence on a moral order, especially one that is somehow to emerge spontaneously from the goodness of the people and their public intellectuals but without any great public expenditure, does not create one.

In the same manner as competitive theories, detached role organization is at best a hypothetical construct that defies easy testing. Yet it has a number of virtues compared with other theories that posit even the semblance of linear social decision making, grand conspiracies, or an independent, controlling source of power. Detached role organization is vested in the characteristics of an open culture; it sidesteps the problem of information; and, most important, it seems to explain the immense stability of the United States by locating changes in national preferences rather than in hidden processes.[1] It fulfills the logic of democracy and provides an attractive although not compelling explanation of social reality: we have what we want.

In the end, its explanation of the failure of American reforms such as the War on Poverty in terms of national preferences rejects notions of technical failure, class dominance, and the rest, including the momentum of history and its metaphysical imperatives, whatever they are. It also sees the principal barrier to reform not in political competition or in more rational forms but in terms of the principal institutions of the society—its preferences—while providing a mechanism by which to infer those preferences: the conditions of public and private policies. It also leads to a variety of empirical tests of its value: the expressions of citizens through their own behavioral choices and through detached role organization that suggest contentment or discontentment, acceptance or rejection, obedience or dissent. In an open society, the actual mundane choices of people going about their daily lives and coming to accept their own customs take on a received inevitability and momentum after generations of acceptance.

Reform efforts in general, as well as regnant social policy, yearn for the cachet of rationality. They even assume rationality in their selection of goals, the preferred policies to achieve, and the processes by which to evaluate them, i.e., the social sciences. Nevertheless, the social policy-making process remains profoundly political, with only the rarest evidence that rationality has ever modified social dialectics. Stable public policy represents a national consensus. Certainly the pursuit of rational goals was abandoned at the outset by the social imagination that chose democratic decision making. Democracy is a process that shares risk

1. This might pose the problem of an apparent circular logic, since the actual policy changes seem to be the same as the preferences that create them. This apparent tautology might be addressed by an analysis of consistency, that is, an analysis of the degree to which consent in a culture is consistent across its many expressions. The problem remains, however, of defining national preference apart from its expression in policy choice, which may be difficult without reliable verbal reports or the ability to test the causal relationship between a preference and the implementation of a policy. Such a test may defy practical, legal, and ethical considerations: it is impossible to randomly assign free citizens to different conditions of living. The theory of detached role organization predicts that public and private policies in a democracy are established through mass consent. But the prediction is difficult to test without a way to measure mass consent independent of actual policy choices. Nevertheless, as noted just below, consent can in fact be estimated as a behavioral choice and through detached role organizations that suggest contentment or discontentment, acceptance or rejection, obedience or dissent from social policies.

precisely because rational information is typically absent, and probably too because of the impossibility of defining rational goals, or at least of imposing any version of them on a complex culture. Especially in the realm of social welfare, broadly conceived, the means of achieving political goals—in this case, social welfare programs—have rarely been tested rationally. In the narrower sense of social welfare as public and private charity for the needy, and also covering the multitude of social programs designed to treat individual deviance, there has rarely if ever been a credible application of rationality to test outcomes, to test, that is, whether the programs were effective or not. In the end, goal rationality has eluded the most brilliant minds, while instrumental rationality remains an Enlightenment hope.

Despite the many informed and coherent attempts to objectify and concretize the social policymaking process—to identify the determinants of policy choices, let alone to attribute demographic conditions to specific policies or even to identify the actual events that the policies uniquely produce—the social policymaking process remains impenetrable, a deficit of analysis obscured by the endless number of post hoc descriptions of policymaking that can never be tested rationally, that is, through randomized designs. Decisive tests of policy influence (of instrumental rationality) are largely impossible to conduct—extraordinarily expensive, impractical, illegal, and often unethical. Thus, in the absence of definitive information, theories of policymaking—usually bouncing between the determinative influence of elites or masses—boil down to metaphysics and ideology rather than even nascent or immature scientific theories of collective behavior. They boldly justify enumerated causes of social problems in the style of the rationalist, but they invariably lack the ability to test their propositions. Theories of policymaking are uninhibited by the fact of citizen ignorance, while efforts to educate the public are largely futile, naive tributes to a rational national will. The collectivity knows what the individual cannot.

All would be well with the organic and mystical policy process of an open society, except that the outcomes frequently frustrate humanitarian expectations. The democratic tradition, appropriating Adam Smith's mysticism of liberal spontaneous orders, assumed that the unseen hand in politics would be gentle and kind. Yet the United States and other democracies are frequently cruel. The broad and deep consent of a society does not assure equality, decency, comity, or even a satisfying life.

That the Unites States does not slaughter imperfect citizens or maintain slaves anymore is hardly ennobling in the face of large numbers of needy citizens in a nation of immense wealth. The nation does not have the excuse of Chad's, Haiti's, or Bangladesh's poverty in ignoring illiteracy, ignorance, incapacity, and disease. Long-standing social need in the United States is social policy, a statement of what private and civil society endorses and public policy ignores. In this sense, social problems are intended.

The tragedy of autocratic state domination—the classic hubristic failure to control destiny and to realize the perfect society through centralized power—was marked by the disasters of the twentieth century in Russia, China, Nazi Germany, and their client states. State-sanctioned slaughter and state-induced poverty refute the notion of planned change. Grand planning is an illusion. Indeed, personal control is often an illusion. Similarly, America's welfare provisions (broadly conceived) have also failed in their defining objectives. Indeed, they convey more of a symbolic meaning than any impressive movement toward decency, adequacy, or social progress.

Devoid of central planning and committed to an open society, America's social welfare initiatives define the nation, the popular sense of what needs to be done and what should not be done. They continue to fail not because of technical ignorance or enduring administrative inefficiencies but because the nation has opted for a shriveled sense of citizenship. The story of American social welfare is told not in chapters of innocent good will and unintended failure but rather in the rituals of social value—the myths of the American consensus made live in its social welfare programs.

1

THE PROGRAMMATIC PRECURSORS TO THE WAR ON POVERTY

The true hypocrite is the one who ceases to perceive his deception, the one who lies with sincerity.
—ANDRÉ GIDE

It is clear from the evidence, such as it is, that the War on Poverty was largely unsuccessful. Its personal service approach to need—Head Start, Job Corps, employment training, neighborhood health centers—and its local citizen organizing strategies, carried out through the Community Action Program and Model Cities, fell flat on their faces. Moreover, the nation's burgeoning wealth was not applied equitably to reduce economic deprivation. Still, the inadequacies of public policy probably reflected a national consensus. The War on Poverty's failure to recruit an effective constituency for broad and deep change reflected an enduring national consensus that has consistently been expressed in minimalist social welfare policies throughout the nation's history.

The underlying ideal of the good citizen, and the actual values pursued during the period, were characteristically Puritanical and stingy. The electoral franchise expanded, but the quality of citizenship did not. The civil rights legislation of the period—the Voting Rights Act and the Civil Rights Act—was procedural, not substantive, lacking the concrete resources to remedy historical deprivation. Minority voting increased, but still not to the levels of middle-class or majority turnouts. Middle-class white women were the principal beneficiaries of affirmative action, while the nation has been retreating from substantive equality since the early 1970s.

The gains of the 1960s were due largely to economic growth rather than public interventions. The poor were handled through separate organizations outside mainline social structures. Perhaps the initial intent was to organize the poor into a politically influential interest group through these separate institutions. But even after it became apparent that this reform strategy could not work and was not working, it was still pursued, largely because of its appeal as patronage. The War on Poverty provided payoffs for blacks and perhaps other minorities in jobs through the Office of Economic Opportunity (OEO), and for the middle class in education programs; but the programs themselves failed either to reduce poverty or to achieve other important social goals.

The intellectual community has provided two basic types of analysis of the War on Poverty period—the 1960s to mid-1970s, covering the New Frontier, the Great Society, and the Nixon aftermath. Conservatives, pressing a theory of pauperization, blame the War on Poverty itself for increasing public dependency. Presumably, welfare that does not require a quid pro quo from recipients undercuts their initiative and actually exacerbates the hardships it intends to relieve. The conservative critique, typically offered with affection for the private market, regulated lightly if at all, blames the liberal interventions for undermining basic American values and the obligations of citizenship and thus increasing the problems of dependency.[1]

The liberal analysis concedes problems with some of the War on Poverty programs but claims considerable gains against poverty and inequality. In a continuation of Enlightenment optimism, the liberals use the Great Society programs as evidence that planned, rational interventions are possible and even see some of the programs as socially efficient victories.[2]

It is obvious that the conservative critique relies heavily on the improbable notion of American exceptionalism and the virtues of unfettered markets and natural man. Yet American liberalism is no less misguided. As it is argued and practiced in real, live politics, American liberalism contains frankly ideological and metaphysical notions, start-

---

1. Murray's very influential *Losing Ground* (1983) updated the long conservative tradition of contemporary social welfare. For more on the contemporary conservative tradition, see also George Gilder (1981), Lawrence Mead (1986, 1997), and the many authors associated with the Heritage Foundation and the American Enterprise Institute.

2. See especially the publications of the Institute for Research on Poverty. This is American liberalism with a preference for regulatory reform and social welfare programs, as very distinct from democratic socialism and its competition with market institutions. For a fuller discussion of modern liberal and conservative thought, see Epstein (2002), O'Connor (2004), and O'Connor (2001).

ing with Keynesian constructs but also extending to the virtues of planned, minimal social interventions and the virtues of the helping professionals. Reflecting an underlying American consensus, both liberal and conservative ideologies have converged on the good citizen as fundamentally volitional, even heroic. Despite engaging in the theater of bold creativity and fearless reform, President Kennedy's New Frontier embraced self-help, one of the most conventional dictates of the American experience, and then followed up with a program package that departed little from embedded notions of assistance.

American conservatism and American liberalism both accept the underlying assumption that civic choices are largely free; thus individual responsibility lies at the heart of both ideologies. American liberalism's weak affection for structural explanations of social need places itself closer to conservative thought than to traditional progressivism, while democratic socialism sits a long distance away at the other end of the political continuum. Their differences over the period's social welfare programs lie in the conservative's claim that the War on Poverty undercut the ideal of the independent, autarkic citizen, and the liberal's insistence that it was promoted—that the variety of programs and their more systemic consequences enhanced participation in the American experience. Neither side mounted an assault or even offered a serious alternative to the nation's civil religion of heroic individualism, the core of its ideal of citizenship.

Yet neither camp can sustain its assertions with credible empirical evidence. Indeed, the basic data necessary for even rudimentary attempts at reasonable and objective decision making, let alone rational decision making, were simply absent from policy deliberations during the period (and largely since then as well). The compromise of the period that expresses the classic American response to need extended the franchise in the spirit of formal equality but largely denied public remedies for social inequality and for prior deprivation. Economic expansion, a very unheroic and structural consideration, rather than public intervention, remains the principal vehicle of social change and social adaptation. The gains in income and wealth were largely the result of a buoyant economy, with an assist from the concrete cash and in-kind transfer programs. But even here the extent of long-term poverty in the absence of these programs, notably the social insurances, remains an open question, and necessarily so.

The policy decisions of the period followed a political logic far more than a service imperative to measure progress against the remission of social problems. The programs handled political problems; and many of them are better understood as ethnic, racial, and regional patronage than as planned interventions engineered to reduce poverty and its associated problems. The War on Poverty reflected Jacksonian democracy rather than Enlightenment rationalism, populist romance rather than progressivism, the fantasy of egalitarian innovation rather than the virtues of bureaucratic rationality—the curse of bigness fearful of the tyranny of goodness. The War on Poverty emerged from a consistent and broad cultural preference for solutions to social problems that are participatory, self-inventive, and localized rather than centralized—the symbols of decentralized republicanism rather than effective remedies for want.

Despite the detailed preferences of the policy experts and their elegant narratives of national progress, public policies may well have reflected popular sentiments. Policies that were ambiguous or contradictory usually indicated a divided nation rather than the intellectual confusion of policymakers. Moreover, the experts themselves most frequently lacked any sort of rational justification for their cherished advice. To read the period through "the social thought of experts on poverty and welfare"—the natural fallback position in the absence of good program information—is to confuse intellectual history with lived experience (Patterson 1981, x).

It is intriguing that even the incomplete evidence of the period often contradicts both liberal and conservative positions and often suggests that democracy was working itself out in its usual unruly way, although with an unfortunate disregard for decency and generosity. Social welfare policy then and now remains largely political, responding to popular values rather than material programmatic goals. Even the most fundamental questions—the contribution of War on Poverty initiatives to alleviating poverty and want—remain largely unanswered. Where the record should have good information, there is silence. In the end, there is little if any credible evidence that the programs themselves contributed to the reduction of poverty, but considerable evidence for their programmatic irrelevance.

The Programmatic Precursors to the War on Poverty

The precursors to the programs of the War on Poverty, funded principally by the Ford Foundation and President Kennedy's Committee on

Delinquency and Youth Crime, were more symbolic than substantive, more political than rational. Each of them—Mobilization for Youth and the related initiatives of Ford Foundation's Gray Areas Projects—was deeply flawed as an instrument to achieve its goals. The precursors embodied the belief in social efficiency, the delusion that deep prior deprivation can be addressed cheaply and compatibly, that is, without disrupting contemporary social, political, and economic relations. The nation wished to address its problems with good will rather than ample resources and with the settled assumption that the responsibility for advancement rested on the deprived themselves.

Social scientists, notably through opportunity theory and then through scholarly debates over social decision making and thus strategies of reform, sustained the fiction of social efficiency. The social sciences were pushing their rational abilities, although without much evidence, on a citizenry all too ready to believe that American ingenuity could solve social problems in the same way that its engineers and natural scientists attacked technological challenges. More tacitly, social technology was an excuse for preserving social stratification, that is, an excuse for ignoring large-scale redistributive public policy, especially since the social technologies of the time largely focused on characteristics of the poor themselves rather than imperfections of the culture. The moon landing was as much a technological triumph as sustenance for the legitimacy of the emerging social sciences. Landing on the moon and solving poverty were presumably both feats of intellectual prowess. Equality was an American myth; inequality was the accepted reality.

Mobilization for Youth

Mobilization for Youth (MFY) was a child of the new knowledge of the social sciences and its application to social problems. MFY programs and strategies presaged much of the War on Poverty—the community action program, legal aid, and notably many of the person-to-person approaches of the OEO. It also marked the height of professional social work's influence, its time on the center stage of American need as the live expression of the new knowledge. If not perfectly rational, MFY aspired to apply the most advanced rational thinking—reasonability and coherence—to social welfare problems, in this instance to the problems of delinquency (gang violence) and by extension poverty. However, its practice reprises the wisdom that society creates its new truths.

In fact, MFY came to symbolize little more than the hubris of a new generation, the plangent ache that youth will be served. Unfortunately, MFY was not an instance of poetry that pays no price other than Byronic anguish. Its self-absorption and programmatic failures, indeed its near foolishness, undermined advocacy for the poor themselves, presumably the target of MFY's beneficence and wisdom, and it continued personal strategies of resolving poverty and its attendant problems in spite of its apparent commitment to structural reform. The fact that practical problems came to dilute the fervor of the designers' vision does not exonerate that vision but rather indicts their naivete, their inattention to the dynamics of poverty and culture.

MFY was well funded by the Ford Foundation, the OEO, the City of New York, President Kennedy's Committee on Delinquency and Youth Crime, and others. Support for the planning and conduct of the experiment followed Cloward and Ohlin's (1962) theory of differential opportunity: "The disparity between what lower-class youths are led to want and what is actually available to them is the source of major adjustment problems. Adolescents who form delinquent subcultures, we suggest, have internalized an emphasis upon conventional goals. Faced with limitations on legitimate avenues of access to these goals, and unable to revise their aspirations downward, they experience intense frustration; the exploration of nonconformist alternatives may be the result" (86).

MFY set out to provide access for delinquent youths to the conventional culture through a series of personal services, including legal assistance and later community action intended to increase the receptivity of social structures to lower-class youth. Planning began in 1957 and services were initiated in 1962, with a staff of three hundred professionals and aides under the direction of a thirty-three-member project board that included eleven faculty members from Columbia University's School of Social Work together with others drawn from prominent local and national social service agencies. The target service population was primarily composed of blacks and Puerto Ricans on New York's Lower East Side, a community of about a hundred thousand residents.

MFY's individual and family services usually offered concrete types of assistance—e.g., small loans of money, babysitting, legal assistance, escort services—as opposed to psychotherapy and counseling. They were intended to relieve the immediate stresses of poverty and thus, "by changing the client's social circumstances, by reordering his environment sufficiently, a way might be cleared for altering his pattern of response away from the self-defeating repetition, the trap of despair and hopelessness, the futility which appeared to pervade his life" (Weissman 1969c, 30–31).

Individual and family services were provided initially through four neighborhood centers that housed social caseworkers, public health nurses, visiting homemakers, escorts, babysitters, and liaisons (representatives of city agencies), and provided inquiry services (practical information about housing, welfare, consumer problems, and so on), training for social work students, referral to local mental health agencies, special planning services for very troubled families, and the reintegration of juvenile offenders through trained probation officers "taking advantage of other opportunities available within the program," namely, Job Corps and Neighborhood Youth Corps (Weissman 1969c, 31).

MFY's extensive community organizing efforts, accepting the principle that its service population of poor people "should participate in local affairs and hold the reins of decision-making themselves," but even more its confrontational and suspicious style, provoked considerable controversy (Weissman 1969a, 25). The organizing had three goals, the first of which was the reduction of juvenile delinquency, which seemed to abandon opportunity theory for a quaint notion of community in the tradition that Putnam (2000) made much of forty years later. By increasing the residents' sense of community, MFY expected to enable local adults "to serve as more adequate models of interpreters of community life for the young." Second, community organization sought to bring about changes in housing, sanitation, education, welfare, and other areas "by raising public issues and articulating their needs." Third, participation in community organization would provide "emotional and psychological gains," helping the poor to overcome a sense of powerlessness (Weissman 1969a, 23–24). MFY organized block associations, housing programs, voter registration activities, consumer affairs groups, and welfare clients. The principal organizers were drawn from the Columbia University School of Social Work.

MFY's employment and educational programs were immediate expressions of opportunity theory. A variety of projects were developed to provide youths with skills for employment: screening, work crews and dispersed work, advanced and posttraining programs, a demonstration prevocational program, vocational counseling, and a program for remedial education during work training. MFY's educational services were designed to improve the capacity of the school system as well as to assist students directly through a parent education program, efforts to improve school-community relations, reading programs, guidance and attendance programs, a program to improve the quality of teaching, a homework helper program, and a higher education program.

Comprehensive legal assistance was provided to individuals and their families rather than restricting representation to a single problem and a single individual in the manner of the traditional Legal Aid Society. MFY offered legal counsel in criminal and housing cases, family law and issues of poverty, including complaints against the welfare department, and consumer matters. Legal assistance was perhaps MFY's most successful program, with a case success rate of about 90 percent. But, as MFY's own evaluation of its achievements concedes, legal representation was neither a solution to poverty nor a successful strategy for social change (Weissman 1969d, 144). MFY's few lawyers were able to represent only a small fraction of the residents in legal matters. Even then, case-by-case litigation seemed more of a gesture than a plausible strategy to provide justice or money for the multitudes of the poor and marginal from resistant public agencies, notably including the New York state legislature.

The record of MFY's progress toward its goals was compiled almost entirely by the MFY staff. Indeed, Cloward was MFY's director of research and was thus in a position to influence the assessment of the products of his own imagination. The evaluation of MFY was funded from 1966 to 1968 by a grant from the federal government that established a special program reporting staff at MFY headed by Weissman, the editor of its four-volume report, published in 1969. That report, including an appendix of publications, pretty much exhausted the critical literature of the experiment.[3] Little of its research was submitted to peer-reviewed journals. None was conducted by independent evaluators. "The four volumes are meant to constitute an intellectual history of a project which in all likelihood represents a watershed in the development of social welfare in America," according to its author (Weissman 1969c, 10).

However, the research suffers the same basic flaws of credibility that

3. The appendix at the end of volume 4 contains a six-page bibliography of scholarly publications, largely by Cloward, that emerged from MFY. Almost all of them are anecdotal, drawing broad theoretical conclusions from little evidence and with little regard for the reliability of their observations. They fail as both memoir and journalism, but they succeed as ideological publicity. Still, the list contains a few gems, notably Cloward and Epstein (1965).

undermine the psychoanalyst's evidence from the couch—response falsification by way of weak, self-serving, unreliable data and porous research methods. In the same way that professionals are routinely
permitted to evaluate their own services (e.g., psychotherapists evaluating psychotherapy), the high-minded social scientific pretensions of
MFY were sustained by ignoring objective and neutral assessments of
its outcomes. The fact that its funding sources did not insist on credible
accountability only underscores the broader social and political stakes in
its success.

In 1964, while considering a five-year extension of the Ford Foundation's support, the foundation's consultants consistently agreed on
MFY's problems. While generally supportive, the consultants observed
that the staff, rather than the board or the community, made the
agency's decisions, and that MFY seemed to be largely responsible for
creating hostile relations with New York City agencies: "The fact that a
few [of the organizing] programs are not spontaneous but emanate directly from MFY also makes them suspect, especially when they fly in
the face of and challenge existing institutional structures" (Moss 1964).
The consultants were also concerned that MFY had made no progress
in "institutionalizing" its programs. That is, the service programs were
not being picked up by existing public agencies, and, of even greater
concern, organizing skills were not being transferred to the community.
The consultants found it quite troubling that MFY seemed to be pursuing conflict prematurely, before developing a sufficient base of support,
before making "the target area populace a more cohesive agency of protest." One consultant noted that "the reluctance of staff members to
discuss the program with ease . . . raised doubts as to whether something was being withheld, or perhaps the questions posed were being
fielded with an air of guarded caution." If anything, these problems were
exacerbated in subsequent years. Moreover, the evaluative material that
MFY finally published reflects one consultant's concerns with the quality of its plans for research and the reluctance of Cloward, the research
director, to put his plans "in black and white." In fact, the meaning of
MFY lies more in its symbolic value than in any actual programmatic
achievement.

Yet, such as they are, the evaluations portray an uneven picture of
MFY's effects. Scrutiny of the best papers in the four-volume report—
those whose methods transcend professional memoir—suggests an
even bleaker series of outcomes. There is an obvious gulf between the

large number of programs for individuals and families listed in the introduction to Weissman's report and the five programs discussed in separate chapters. Of these five, only "Reform School to Society" approximates a coherent research design in its evaluation of a one-year diversion program for delinquent youth. The design compares a small group of thirty-four delinquents who were diverted to the experimental reintegration unit with twenty-four delinquents in a control group that received customary services; the assignment of these youths to one group or the other does not appear to have been random, and the conditions for inclusion in the program are not mentioned. The reintegration unit serviced the delinquents and their families, an additional 169 adults and children.

The goal of the reintegration unit was to reduce criminal recidivism among the youths who left detention ("training schools") by eliminating "barriers to conformity so that the young people in the program would no longer have to repeat the same round of illegal activities" (Weissman 1969c, 75). While the report details the obligations of caseworkers to develop reintegration plans, it does not enumerate the actual services that were provided to implement the plan. Indeed, it is unclear whether any substantial services were in fact provided, since, "as in other areas of the Services to Individuals and Families program having to do with multi-problem families, MFY had not anticipated how far any family service would have to go in order to take real care of the needs of the clients. . . . The small staff of the [reintegration unit] . . . was simply overloaded" (80). The lack of job preparation was notable, while the "employment provided had too little meaning or personal involvement for" the youths (82).

The report concedes that the reintegration project did not lower the rate of recidivism. Almost 60 percent of the youths in both the experimental group and the control group committed crimes during the year evaluated. As with other programs that measure recidivism, the reported figures are usually unreliable and frequently undercount actual recidivism. Still, the chapter mentions that the recidivism rate was almost twenty percentage points lower for those who stayed with the program than for those who dropped out or were dropped. But the evaluation design does not allow this small difference to be attributed to the services themselves and may be a consequence of the initial differences between the samples and the fact that some youths were dropped because of their continued criminal activity. Terminating those who relapse into criminal activity obviously improves the performance of those who stick with the program.

The inadequate staffing of the reintegration project created a large disparity between the advertised program and the actual program. As a result, the project ended up performing as a traditional family casework program. Thus Weissman claims that it did not fairly test opportunity theory. Yet, paradoxically, the report insists that the youths "had access to legitimate opportunity structures" (Weissman 1969c, 89). Still, the whole point of the MFY experiment and its components was to realize opportunity theory in practice. If it failed to conform to the experimental conditions that justified its funding, then why wasn't the program terminated? The problem of treatment integrity—whether the intended services are actually provided—persists throughout MFY's self-evaluation; in fact, it is a constant threat to the value of program evaluations throughout the human services.

The evaluation of the reintegration unit, flawed and deeply compromised though it was, is the most credible evaluation of the individual and family services. The other four evaluations are chatty professional memos full of grand insights and important lessons. The most crucial of the four evaluates the neighborhood service centers, reporting that in almost five years, 1963–67, they provided services to more than 43,000 individuals in about 10,500 families. However, the chapter does not assess whether the services—most notably, interactions with the welfare department to handle client complaints and needs—were successful; instead, it relies on anecdotes of dubious representativeness to make its points. It concludes that the service centers "discovered a vast pool of need which society's welfare institutions had been ignoring," but it does not find that the service centers, or MFY generally, did anything about it (Weissman 1969c, 53). In fact, the chapter suggests that the neighborhood service centers were largely unsuccessful. Anecdotal evidence, rather than systematic information, is likewise used in other chapters that also fail to reliably describe or assess the value of indigenous workers, psychological services (asserting that patient participation in reform movements is therapeutic), or information dissemination.

The first volume of Weissman's report also includes five similarly flawed evaluations of group work programs. The best of them describes the effects of programs for adolescent addicts: work programs, coffee shops, a group abstinence program, a community development storefront program, and a narcotics information center. All reportedly failed, although no data are provided. Nonetheless, the report draws conclusions about successful treatment for addiction, citing Synanon in Day Top Lodge, but again offering few data and failing to indicate how success was measured. In fact, no intervention for addicts of any age has ever credibly demonstrated an ability to achieve abstinence. MFY board member Irving Lukoff's observation that the few cases of abstinence are more accurately attributed to maturation than to treatment has been consistently relevant since MFY's efforts.

The other chapters in the four-volume report largely underscore the failure of group work to deter delinquency or to resolve adolescent problems generally. Nevertheless, one chapter reports that fifty youths who would not have had the opportunity without MFY were participating in a variety of arts programs. Weissman concludes that while the group programs did not appear to be successful, "society needs links to slum youths, and slum youths, conversely, need to know adults in an informal and personal manner who can help them develop a sense of competency to function in the adult world" (1969c, 187). None of the chapters (or any other study) credibly demonstrates the importance of this very traditional settlement house role. In any event, the group work programs seemed to be a very expensive way to keep in touch.

Apart from extensive coverage in the media and a series of tendentious case studies, the staff evaluations, which rely on professional judgment rather than objective analysis, provide little evidence of successful community organization. A notable disingenuousness runs through all of the reports. The project advertises its commitment to citizen control, but the write-ups refer to the staff's dominant influence. For example, in reference to a change in strategy, the report notes, "the *staff* had become convinced that only through political pressure could low-income minority groups become powerful enough to bring about change in existing institutions, either local or city-wide" (1969a, 27, emphasis added). On the very next page, the author touts the strategy "of involving local people in planning for and influencing their own communities" (28). Local control was one of the program's overarching goals from the beginning, but one that was apparently subsumed under professional control. The ambiguous role of professional staff has forever hampered the theory and practice of community development; essential skills almost inevitably depart with the worker. Yet the justification for community decision making rests on the transfer of those skills to local residents, largely because they bear the risks of organizational missteps.

The reports on the organizing campaigns are sincere but not credible. They evaluate block organization on the basis of a case history that offers hardly any measurable outcomes. MFY conducted a voter registration drive, but there is no information on the number of people registered or the turnout for elections. The program started a food co-op, but there is no indication of its size or duration. It seems that very few people participated, and the report concludes that "mobilization's efforts to organize block associations were slow" (Weissman 1969a, 43). Throughout, it is apparent that the staff initiated projects and controlled the organization; the transfer of skills did not take place.

If nothing else, a slum is defined by its shambles. MFY attempted to upgrade housing in its target area through the organization of tenants' associations, housing clinics, public campaigns, and by employing a group of technical advisors on housing issues. The 1964 Lower East Side rent strike seems to have been the dramatic peak of the housing protests. A few simple questions seem pertinent in evaluating these activities. Did housing improve? Did the local capacity to address problems increase through the organizing programs? While the report provides little evidence of either outcome, the conclusion seems warranted, especially after the author moans about the complexity of the issues, that nothing of lasting or even transitory value occurred. Moreover, the rent strike failed after four months, apparently as a result of conflicts among a variety of supportive organizations (largely outside the area). Nothing discourages participation in community organizations more than the early failures of important campaigns and projects. In this regard, the mobilization staff—the organizers—appear incompetent, especially since they seem to have been in control of organizational strategy. A final question unanswered in the chapter on housing also needs attention: how many local residents suffered loss of housing, loss of benefits, loss of educational and employment opportunities, because of the confrontational organizational strategies encouraged by staff?

MFY's experience in organizing residents for consumer affairs, voter registration, and welfare was similarly ineffective. The buying club petered out; consumer education had little effect; and the staff learned after years of consumer organizing that to make use of markets, "the poor man needs money" (Weissman 1969a, 82). The voter registration drives may have increased registration, but turnout was customarily low, the common experience during decades of such activities. MFY laments the misapplication of the laws to poor people, concluding that "social agencies should be at the forefront of agitation and social action to see that the laws are fairly administered" (101). Indeed. But this role was presumably the charge to MFY.

MFY earned national press coverage in large part for its sizeable efforts to organize welfare recipients. At different times in the 1960s, six different local resident groups were organized to reform the activities of the New York City Welfare Department. Their main task was to pressure welfare department suboffices to improve their procedures and to correct underpayments. Welfare organizing may have been MFY's biggest success.

> In less than a year, these six groups have recovered well over $100,000 in entitlements for their members. This fantastic figure is a mirror of the extent to which the welfare system is not operating according to law. The right to have telephones has been won for certain categories of clients. Automated school-clothing allowances have been obtained, and clients now have a right to burial money. Clients can now have a bank account, and there has been increased acknowledgment of communications by caseworkers and better treatment from them. The benefits of the organizations can be described in terms of better living conditions, more respect from the caseworker, more hope for the future, more understanding of the system, and more knowledge about how to master the situation in terms of material benefits and human dignity. (Weissman 1969a, 134–35)

Unfortunately, the success was transitory. Resident groups fell apart over the bickering of the organizers. Moreover, welfare clients who had their grievances addressed by the Welfare Department stopped participating in the welfare rights organizations and were not replaced by a second wave of leadership. Most important, "clients on the Lower East side were able to get more from the welfare system [for a short while], but this probably meant that clients in other neighborhoods got less. The rules, procedures, and methods of operation, formal and informal, of the Welfare Department had not been altered. By the end of 1966 the welfare organizations had reached a crisis in their development" (130–31).

As the project itself concluded, Weissman wrote, "It seems clear that a neighborhood-based organization of welfare clients acting alone can do very little to change the welfare system" (135). Thus the local experience led to the development of the National Welfare Rights Organization, another MFY dead end and perhaps even counterproductive in so far as it may have exacerbated the conservative backlash of subsequent decades. The right to organize was important for the organizers, but the risks and outcomes were more germane for the poor themselves. They had little direct influence over the direction of the organizations except to decide not to participate. In fact, after a very short while, the local organizations and even the national organization were emptied of many welfare clients. For all MFY's clamor for client and resident participation in the substance of organizational decision making, no residents of the Lower East Side sat on the MFY board itself.

The reactive assault by public agencies on MFY seemed predictable, although neither necessary nor warranted by any threat that MFY posed. Community organization as an activity, in Cloward's words, to "help local groups participate . . . in the social issues—encouraging residents to choose issues, frame them in their own terms, and act within their legal rights to deal with the problems they encounter daily," was not successful (Weissman 1969a, 138). As MFY recognized, its community organization program in 1964, about seven years after planning began and a few years into operations, "had achieved only modest results. It had reached only a small fraction of the people who might have benefited from it. But it had antagonized some of the strongest vested interests in New York City, including the Board of Education, the police, and the city Welfare and Housing departments, as well as local landlords and politicians. To many of those in power, Mobilization seemed a dangerously disruptive force on the Lower East Side" (139).

Mobilization barely survived the counterattacks it provoked, although with some loss of control over its autonomy. Yet, however incompetent, cruel, insensitive, and corrupt the established agencies may have been, a community organization strategy to take them on without first developing sufficient power seems itself to be self-defeating and perhaps even harmful to local residents who had to live with the consequences of provoking the powerful. It was also startlingly naive, if not irresponsible, of MFY to antagonize the very agencies that provided its funding. Indeed, tension between the demands of the funding agencies and the requirements for their organizational reform, customarily resolved in favor of the funder, also proved to be the undoing of the War on Poverty's Community Action Program.

"If controversial action, or even the appearance of it, could bring a serious attack down on Mobilization's head, was Mobilization then to become nothing more than a token force on the Lower East Side, unable to deal profoundly with major problems because of fear of attack?" (Weissman 1969a, 161). But where did the organizers expect their mandate for reform to come from? If their base of power was to come from the poor themselves, then the staff decision to provoke conflict with more powerful opposition seems foolish and perhaps arrogant, cutting against basic rules of engagement.

Throughout the Weissman report, staff members are constantly described as deciding programmatic direction or stymieing the organizing because they are in conflict with one another (e.g., 1969a, chapter 9 and passim). There is considerable hypocrisy in the project's insistence that it was pursuing citizen control at the same time that its executive director, Bertram Beck, published a paper extolling "professionalism" and pointedly arguing that community control was "a distraction, not an answer" (Beck 1969). Professional social work and MFY are equally barren of empirical evidence for the effectiveness of any of their interventions, notably their pretensions to organizing success. Professional social work in the following decades has not improved on either the quality of its services or its modesty (Epstein 1993). The only notable change in the field is that its patronage has changed from providing jobs for middle-class liberals to providing jobs for racial, ethnic, and gender minorities (Stoesz and Karger forthcoming).

At the same time that Beck was touting professionalism, his director of research, Richard Cloward, was apparently pursuing substantial citizen participation, if not control. The conflicts between staff contributed to the confusion of the program itself, raising questions about its administrative coherence. In the spirit of the 1960s, staffers were apparently tolerated for "doing their own thing." Indeed, it is clear from congressional testimony during the reauthorization hearings of the OEO that its Community Action agencies and service programs typically employed clairvoyance, the inspirational style, and the narcissism of life experience as weapons against poverty.[4]

Protected intellectuals with little accountability for their actions initiated strategic conflicts that doomed MFY. The failures of organizing and of the project itself attest to the romance of community organizing

---

4. See, for example, U.S. Congress, Senate (1965).

rather than to the compelling force of the social problems that the organizing tried to address. Acknowledging that in the end, only "a small percentage of the neighborhood residents were ever involved . . . and only a small dent was made in the social problems within the neighborhood," Weissman can justify MFY's organizing only on the grounds that it made "the public at large aware of social issues and potential solutions" (1969a, 186). However, it is not clear whether public awareness increased or eroded sympathy for MFY-type programs.

Very unlike labor union organizers, civil rights organizers, and others whose future depends on their success in the field, the principal MFY staffers were secure in their university affiliations. They were free to engage in the pursuit of a Nietzschean will: the heroic organizer who through imagination and desire transforms the social and political system. But little evidence existed before MFY, and certainly less afterward—with pointed reference to the radical, or at least stentorian, efforts of Saul Alinsky—that the small projects of neighborhood resident organizing grew into system reform, or that heroic intentions match social reality. Indeed, the twentieth century's totalitarian bloodbaths of the Right and the Left are rebukes to the postmodern fervor for revolutions in human consciousness and the social order, the conceits of the visionary made real. MFY was not terrible in the grand tradition but only weak, oracular, and ineffective, joining the typical American sideshow of self-invention, social salvation, personal responsibility, and missions to the poor. MFY was doing little more than running on the vapors of American nostalgia for small-town governance, proselytizing about a citizenship of self-determination, if not quite yet degenerating into the employment patronage of the OEO's Community Action Program and of late twentieth-century social work.

Again and again throughout the description of MFY's community organization efforts, it seems that the organizers' preferences, strategies, and tactics displaced their avowed goal of developing local organizational strength. Without powerful local support (and indeed citywide support), the premature decisions to take on dominant city departments and industries (e.g., health, welfare, and the housing industry) were inconsiderate of the long-term interests of residents. MFY's evaluation of its own organizing activities conveyed a sense of its beleaguerment and a near-paranoid, secretive style that recalled the comments of the Ford Foundation's consultants.

Even the best results of MFY's efforts quickly evaporated. Much was sacrificed for a display of protest, indignation, and rebelliousness. The most notable outcome of MFY's organizing was a degree of controversy and vituperative confrontation that resulted in the termination of its organizing activities. The grand drama of liberating the oppressed seemed to satisfy the staff's theatrical demonization of public officials more than it did residents' need for service. Community organization neither improved services nor opened opportunities for the residents. However, the staff's pleasure in premature conflict seemed to have activated a counterforce that successfully drew on popular displeasure with MFY's tactics and goals.

The fights that staff members picked were more ceremonial than strategic, in the end failing to intensify residents' participation and commitment to local needs. It is also far-fetched to claim that the confrontational style of the organizing expressed the residents' preferences and resulted from their control of the organizing. The staff, notably Cloward, gained a short-lived prominence for its "radical chic" and a celebrity within the protected environment of the academy. But the residents of the Lower East Side remained poor and probably a bit disillusioned, if not actually alienated by endless participation in meetings, conflicts, consultations, and protests.[5]

Even worse than the failure to anticipate the difficulty of organizing the poor, MFY failed to appreciate the relative popularity of their targets of attack—city government, its agencies, and the existing political system—and the widespread reaction that MFY's tactics and goals engendered. In contrast to MFY, city government and the political system had earned a popular mandate for their policies through elections.

It would be wonderful if citizens became politically active after a short course of professional organizing. But this has not been the case in MFY, the subsequent Community Action Program of the War on Pov-

5. Under the direction of Cloward, who provided some liner notes, the Columbia University School of Social Work's Research Center pulled together a six-volume album of MFY press clippings, titled *Mobilization for Youth: A Documentary Record*. More than any butchered and self-serving evaluation, the thousands of news stories about the extended MFY "crisis" display the imprudence of the staff in precipitating a premature conflict. Yet, at the same time, MFY staffers come across as grandly humanitarian liberals bragging about their heroic efforts to secure First Amendment rights, perhaps even hinting that they were aspiring to the moral stature of the recent McCarthy era refuseniks, though of course without any of the risk. If anything, the thousands of pages in this six-volume album document the sacrifice of neighborhood organizing to the ambitions of the MFY staff. The MFY's efforts consisted of actions taken in the name of the poor but without their consent, and notably without their participation in more than a token manner.

erty, or later systematic attempts to mobilize the poor. The poor have never represented a large or consistently self-defined class in America, and pushing a political agenda on their behalf frequently precipitates a broad hostile reaction rather than Piven and Cloward's (1971) assurance of negotiation. The public agencies that reacted harshly to MFY's organizing were not simply irrationally defensive bullies, but in a profound way expressed popular antagonism to the goals and activities of MFY.

MFY's employment and educational services fared no better than its incompetent attempts at organizing. They neither prepared many people for employment through training and education nor secured many job placements. Opportunity theory produced a series of assumptions about the motivation of youths seeking employment that were not realized in practice: "Many trainees were reluctant to accept a job if they could be fired easily, if the work was dirty or highly competitive, or if the boss was always 'on their back.' They placed value on jobs in the neighborhood, or high-paying jobs with no future, and often left jobs or training after they had accumulated some pocket money. They tended to attribute unsuccessful employment experiences to external forces or other people" (Weissman 1969b, 28).

Only 25 percent of enrollees in the training and educational programs—who by seeking out services were probably among the more motivated needy youths in the area—were "ready for skill training" or "prepared for advanced training or job placement." Many of the delinquents and the youths generally had emotional and attitudinal problems (contradicting the assumptions of opportunity theory) that undercut the provision of training, education, or employment.

The kindest conclusion about MFY's training and placement services is that their effects were ambiguous and probably unknown. Yet the reports suggest a high rate of failure. An enormous percentage of applicants never enrolled, and many of those who did dropped out. Of more than eleven thousand who applied, Weissman's evaluation is based on 431 enrollees in work crews over eleven months. While 49 percent had positive outcomes—"employed, returned to school, placed in training"—those outcomes were tested at only one point in time. Weissman concedes that the success rate greatly exaggerates the real outcomes (1969b, 111). Moreover, there was no control group against which to compare the work crew members; thus the few positive outcomes may well be the result of outside factors. The employment and training programs were simply too unattractive to maintain participation.

MFY's failure with job preparation and placement was repeated many times in subsequent decades by similar public programs for youths, delinquents, adult criminals, addicts, welfare mothers, poor people, the untrained, the displaced, the unmotivated, and the troubled. These programs all shared common traits—too few resources to handle recipients' problems, ignorance of those problems, and, most important, the absence of decent jobs at the other end of the training process. With near unanimity, the evaluations of the training programs exaggerated their value.

The parent-aides program was terminated by the schools because of organizational conflicts with MFY. The program was never evaluated. MFY attempted to organize parents to challenge the schools' authority ("changing the schools"), but again without making plans to handle the school board's counterattack. Relative to school-community relations, Weissman's evaluation concludes that "home visiting, neighborhood history and culture courses, and parent-education programs should be part of every school serving low-income areas," without offering even a shred of evidence beyond short, incomplete anecdotes (1969a, 147). And so it went with programs to improve reading, guidance, attendance, teaching, and higher education.

A pattern emerges in the evaluations of MFY's education programs. The authors describe the interventions, complain about unanticipated complexities and problems, and then conclude that the program had value, citing the satisfaction of some participants. However, the evaluations fail to report in any systematic way measurable signs of progress, e.g., improved reading scores, better teaching, higher attendance rates, improved student discipline, and so forth.

To the extent that MFY provided a true test, opportunity theory did not work out. It says much about the contemporary role of the social sciences that Cloward and Ohlin's *Delinquency and Opportunity* enjoyed such pervasive influence over the design of the War on Poverty without a critical reading of its tenets and propositions. At best, opportunity theory was an immature supposition, at worst a jumble of hopeful maxims thrown together in imitation of geometry's logic—a series of propositions derived from intuition and an analysis of text, the hermeneutic style applied to the existing literature of social problems. The propositions read like axioms—e.g., "the pressures that lead to deviant patterns do not necessarily determine the particular pattern of deviance that results" (Cloward and Ohlin 1962, 49)—with the unfortunate style of deducing conclusions rather than testing insights.

It was clear even in the 1960s that the usefulness of opportunity theory lacked empirical support. Indeed, *Delinquency and Opportunity* contains little quantitative evidence and no formal test at all of whether opportunity theory adequately describes the motives, progress, or points of effective intervention for group delinquency—youth gangs—or that it is related to economic deprivation rather than to issues of character and freely chosen subcultural mores. Indeed, despite its fierce ideological commitment to structural explanations of deviance, Cloward and Ohlin frequently slip into the language of personal pathology. They recognize that there are subcultural impediments to social success, such as lower-class antagonism to formal education and "other features of lower-class socialization that impede mobility" (99). Still, they assume but clearly do not prove that these choices are the near-forced adaptations to "realistic barriers" that have been imposed on the poor by the dominant culture (103).

The grounds for their structural interpretations are consistently subjective. That is, they characteristically reconcile contending positions by reference to their own internal processes ("our view," what "we believe," "we are inclined to think") rather than to objective procedures to weigh and adjudicate disparate contentions. The studies they cite—uniformly weak, frequently simplistic case studies—at best raise questions rather than answer them.

In this sense, pathology refers as much to the poor as to the dominant society. In fact, the attachment to pathology has always been characteristic of social work, even in its most structural forms. The social work revolutionaries of MFY wanted to preserve their small program successes, their attachment to social transformation, their denunciations of structural imperfections, and, significantly, their distinguished positions at Columbia University. However, both *Delinquency and Opportunity* and Weissman's four-volume report are tributes only to partisan research for partisan ends.

The Weissman study is memoir and journalism, not science, not even nascent science, for it lacks the first crucial commitment of science to objectivity, to a reality outside its internal assumptions. Indeed, the little success stories and confessions of failure do not lead to the major structural conclusion that "only the redistribution of wealth can make a dent in the social pathology which is gripping America" (Weissman 1969d, 148). The return to pathology is a lament.

Weissman's self-evaluation, frequently styled as confession, bends the truth in the same way that the grandest political romances—communism, fascism, and theocracy—take permission from the nobility of their visions to enforce a revolutionary perception of the present, the triumph of aspiration over objective conditions. If in fact MFY had been committed to establishing the objective facts of its programmatic effects, then the evaluation would have been turned over to truly neutral researchers immune to the demands of the program staff. Self-service and even the paranoid style have very often hidden behind a convenient mistrust of others.

If the MFY experience was to be taken seriously as a failure of theory and practice, then the government, through the OEO and its other agencies, would have looked for other models in short order. Instead, the American government, with the substantial sanction of the American people, largely restricted "opportunity" to the characteristics of the delinquent and poor while turning away from political mobilization (the dream of community organizing programs) as a strategy to improve the responsiveness of American institutions. The reasons for MFY's turn to quiescence were compelling: the poor were resistant to organizing, both in their neighborhoods and nationally through the welfare rights movement; they may also have objected to being characterized as pathological and marginal or to being placed in organizations that provided constant reminders of their failures; the customary political system objected to competition with community action programs (customary political structures were also more successful political entities with a mandate from local populations); and, most notably, the poor gained a stake in the jobs that the social services provided and saw little reason to take risks with their security, such as it was. Not coincidentally, efforts to mobilize national support for broad social reform—the War on Poverty's Community Action Program and the more extensive Model Cities program—failed to inspire a sizeable constituency. The American people, including many of the poor themselves, were not up for grand change.

MFY failed, and not simply because of the cruelty, indifference, and social efficiency of the society. The failure also attested to the insufficiency of superficial concrete services, the naivete and dogmatism of its staff, and, not least, the nostalgia of community organizers. Rather than a means of delivering power, reform, and protest, community organizing proselytized the heroic American credo—self-invention, self-determination, and in the end personal responsibility—the very values that may have created the slums and the incapacities of their residents.

Almost all of MFY's efforts sought to substitute its own programs for those of existing agencies. That is, they provided desultory, second-rate, ineffective services—poverty care for the poor—outside the mainstream. This by itself tends to undercut the goal of reforming the system. Yet all would be forgiven and forgotten if MFY's services had created an organizational capacity to confront the political problems of reform. This MFY failed to do, a failure that echoes down through the decades: community organizations that provide shoddy services outside the mainstream without building the capacity for reform are tragedies that sacrifice political potential for patronage.

Yet even in spite of its isolating political radicalism, MFY itself was a consensual expression of a society uncertain how to handle the challenges of the post–World War II era. MFY was a tentative program, one among a variety of social welfare experiments. Popular policy decided that MFY was not acceptable but that a tame War on Poverty was, and both in the end simply adopted the American devotion to social efficiency: programs for the poor are to be inexpensive and compatible with conventional services. MFY continued the fantasy of the settlement houses and religious missionary work that a few intrepid good hearts and enlightened minds armed with truth and virtue could mobilize the underlying goodness, generosity, and sense of shared peril of the masses for reform. It did not work out that way, but the parable of the virtuous reformer was the point, a ceremony of social concern, but without the substance of concrete services.

In the end, MFY may not have provided a true test of opportunity theory because it may not have provided opportunities through its services or access to the wider society. But Cloward and Ohlin never specified opportunity theory or suggested how its elements might be measured. The core contention of opportunity theory is that delinquency results from frustrated aspirations; but it often seems that the authors equate frustration and delinquency itself. In a circular logic defying empirical testing, deviancy becomes the expression and not just the result of frustration.

Operating out of the Henry Street Settlement House, MFY took on the patrician style of the settlement house movement. The settlement houses embodied opportunity theory for the rich, providing face-to-face,

person-to-person opportunities for the well-heeled and socially concerned to bathe in the misfortunes of the poor, and again in search of
inexpensive remedies for social problems. A slew of similar quasi-volun-
teer and volunteer programs have followed obediently along: VISTA, the
Peace Corps, Big Brothers/Big Sisters, Volunteer Grandparents, and so
on. There are even many recent programs that charge volunteers for
international poverty tourism.

The slippery shifting back and forth between the objective and the
perceived goes far to undermine any potential clarity in opportunity theory. Are opportunities real, or are they simply negotiated perceptions?
Is the problem one of feelings, public relations, and social sincerity, or
the harder coin of apprenticeships, salary, advancement, and educational attainment? Put another way, are perceptions the anticipated consequences of social reality, or is social reality the product of received
values and embedded subcultural norms? The confusion over inner
states and objective reality is a central problem of both opportunity theory and the postmodern programs, like MFY, that it engendered. The
convictions of the staff—an absorption in their own untested insights—
created social theater rather than attention to the needs of the poor and
delinquent. In broader perspective, American social welfare has characteristically been a political expression of mass attitudes rather than any
sort of acultural or extracultural pursuit of the decent, the humane, or
the egalitarian. MFY is just one small instance of a program eventually
designed by dominant social preferences rather than by change agents
taking a mandate from God or a World Spirit that guides social progress
to predetermined ends.

But even if opportunity theory escapes the circular trap, its propositions rest on selective, simplistic arguments that became irrelevant even
during the years of its operation. To a great extent, MFY's programmatic
modesty hinged on the assumption that delinquents embraced dominant American values and wished to conform to prevailing norms. Thus
the motivation of delinquents was not the core problem, and modest
opportunities to pursue customary avenues to success would be largely
sufficient to produce conforming behavior. MFY obviously ignored the
growing use of illicit drugs in urban ghettoes and the broader society,
the huge profits drugs produced, and the alternative subcultures they
engendered. Youth gangs became married to adult gangs, with little diversion likely, through the relatively superficial MFY services. Indeed,

incapacitating drug use is itself a rejection of common norms and even a behavioral choice that rejects the dominant culture itself.

Saturating the community with opportunities for an impoverished work life at low-paying, insecure jobs is like promising people on welfare a few extra dollars; it does not change things much or trigger the imagination and loyalty of the poor. MFY exaggerated the receptivity and minimized the resistance of the primary labor market to absorbing marginal workers, whatever their claims on social justice. The expectation that free markets would accept welfare responsibilities rubs against their nature and seems to contradict MFY's basic mandate to improve the welfare functions of government.

In one form or another, opportunity theory has enjoyed a lasting popularity, notably in continuing programs such as Upward Bound, Head Start, and Job Corps, along with a multitude of diversion and community-based programs to address youth crime. All have been largely excused from rigorous scrutiny, surviving even in the face of evidence of their ineffectiveness. In a rebuke to opportunity theory, black crime increased as opportunity increased with the elimination of de jure segregation, the passage of civil rights legislation and affirmative action, neighborhood and school integration, and an apparent increase in social acceptance of minorities. Not coincidentally, every single program since MFY similarly based on opportunity theory and other socially efficient remedies has failed. Without a true production function in achieving explicit social welfare goals, it is startling that opportunity theory in one guise or another enjoys continuing popularity as a dominant strategy for handling the marginal, the dispossessed, the poor, and the deviant.

Yet the misidentification of opportunity theory as science—as rational and scientifically credible—is probably beside the point. Opportunity theory may have never existed in social dialectics as a serious approach to social problems but rather as an important ritual and ceremony of the American ethos and an outlet for the charitable heart. Opportunity theory was intellectually immature, a series of untested and tenuous suppositions, but, characteristically, it promised relatively inexpensive remedies for threatening social problems—youth gangs and by extension poverty—that were largely compatible with contemporary social service systems and expectations: interventions focused on youths, acceptance of existing job market procedures, and even the coordination of services through a single provider. It proposed to alleviate great deprivation without massive redistribution of resources, largely accepting, despite Cloward's pampered radicalism, the economic and social stratification of American society. MFY was as naive, ignorant, and ultimately unsuccessful as the customary agency-based antipoverty strategy of American social welfare history. Neither renegade nor heretic, it provided a convenient template for the War on Poverty rather than a realistic assessment of the nature of delinquency or poverty. It substituted political theater for social science, conforming generally with broad American expectations for citizenship and public support.

The insufficiencies of social efficiency mark out the terrain between conservative neglect and universal provision that is occupied by modern American liberalism and the social sciences. As long as programs like MFY seem to take even small steps toward socially desirable goals, the enormous costs of addressing inequality through genuine redistribution can be avoided. Thus efforts by Cloward and the MFY staff, as well as the rest of the social service industry, to balance putative successes on methodological stilts actually undercuts their professed commitment to achieve egalitarian goals. The obvious disparity between programmatic goals and actual outcomes is often explained away by acknowledging the complicity of the poor in their own problems, their own pathologies, rather than by confronting the hypocrisy of services.

The new social sciences were not good enough to address the actual problems of delinquents and poor people. The programs were infinitely inventive along the theme of social efficiency but not even marginally successful on their own terms. In fact, American social welfare programs are commonly not judged for achieving measurable goals but rather for their social acceptability. MFY made the mistake of challenging popular social and political institutions without popular support. Its programmatic failings were secondary to its demise.

Ford Foundation Projects and the Committee on Delinquency and Youth Crime

By 1964 the Ford Foundation had allocated $20 million in grants to MFY and to six experiments in blighted urban communities—"gray areas" (Marris and Rein 1982, 28). At the same time, President Kennedy's Committee on Delinquency and Youth Crime was getting down to the business of awarding grants for program demonstrations. The committee, greatly influenced by MFY and Ohlin and Cloward's opportunity theory, had a major hand in designing the War on Poverty, notably the OEO programs. The committee was charged with coordinating existing federal agencies in attending to the problems of delinquency and youth, with stimulating program innovation, and with involving state and charitable organizations. Stimulation, coordination, innovation, and involvement have long been the catchphrases of American approaches to social problems, in the hope that management efficiencies would obviate the need for subsidies. By 1965 the committee, in tandem with the U.S. Department of Labor and the OEO, had spent about $30 million on sixteen projects (30).

The Ford Foundation and the Committee on Delinquency and Youth Crime had shifted from a strategy of program demonstration to one of community action. Nevertheless, the goal remained to promote the adoption of innovative programs by public organizations, largely city administrations, and private charitable service agencies. Citizen involvement as the pump primer of social efficiency was intended to stimulate agency coordination, the goal initially adopted by the OEO's Community Action Program. Illustrating the new strategy, the moneys from both Ford and the federal government, impressive at the time as charitable grants, were insufficient for even small direct service programs yet expressed the expectation of great strategic profit from small investments in reform.

The policymaking boards of the six Gray Areas programs—in Oakland, California, Washington, D.C., New Haven, Connecticut, Boston, Massachusetts, Philadelphia, Pennsylvania, and another covering the state of North Carolina—were dominated by traditional American blue bloods, businesspeople and other professionals, mayors, and other elected officials, but had little if any representation from the service populations themselves. The different sites adopted a variety of approaches to program development and community action, but all largely worked within the established social welfare and political systems (Marris and Rein 1982).

The Ford Foundation boasted that the Gray Areas and community development programs promoted its public image as an "up-front" social welfare institution, characterized by

- An action-oriented rather than a research-oriented style, with emphasis on local demonstration projects;
- A willingness to test the outer edges of advocacy and citizen participation; and

- A conviction that effective philanthropy requires direct and continuing interaction between staff and grantee. (Magat 1979, 119)

The administrator at the Ford Foundation largely responsible for its community action initiatives, Paul Ylvisaker, expressed a series of program assumptions that also underpin Jonathan Edwards's sermons, Robert Putnam's books, Ronald Reagan's administration, and Newt Gingrich's Contract with America, and that justified welfare retrenchment and the unforgiving treatment of social failure as the result of moral impairment. Ylvisaker made the transcendentalist assumption of American virtue and the romantic presupposition that moral change precedes material or social reward.

> The toughest problem is that of generating indigenous leadership and the spirit of self-help . . . *the awakening of self-respect* is the most powerful agent for renewing our cities socially, and for that matter physically. . . . The element of spirit is critical. . . . Certain parts of the urban social system can be perfected by rational means and specific devices. . . . Mayors, governors and presidents have concentrated their urban programs on physical renewal of the city's urban plant, usually beginning with the central business district. . . . This is not necessarily the place to start and certainly not the place to stop. (Ylvisaker 1963, 3–4, emphasis in original)

Ylvisaker goes on to list the Ford Foundation's small-scale programs to improve education, employment, the criminal justice system, and so on. He at no time suggests that the fundamental problem is one of massive investment in education, employment, income, and health, among other things. Ylvisaker and indeed the entire tribe of poverty romantics refused to acknowledge the disjunction between the enduring nature of American need and the Ford Foundation's puny initiatives. Rather, they cast the problem as one of technological cleverness and character: "innovations and improvements which suggest themselves are matters of spirit" (5).

New Haven is consistently cited as the leading Gray Areas success and the model of coordination that was intended for the OEO's Community Action Program. Sundquist, however, points out that its success, or at least its reputation for success, "was dominated by a singularly energetic and resourceful mayor, Richard Lee, and master-minded by [an] . . .

executive director, Mitchell Sviridoff, who was as extraordinary in his role as the mayor was in his" (Sundquist 1969a, 45). Yet it is not clear exactly what was achieved—that is, whether poverty was reduced or agencies became more effective. The ability to coordinate agencies in New Haven was apparently vested in a consensus of major political actors. Coordination was not stimulated through the Ford Foundation's grants. At best, the foundation recognized a promising situation and assisted the city's leaders in consolidating their objectives. In short, the success of New Haven depended on what already existed rather than what was created by planned community interventions.

The Ford Foundation's reformist fervor, coupled with the liturgy of rationality, constitutes an update on the social gospel in American welfare. It was more than simply a cultural style. The Ford Foundation continued to appeal to traditional American institutions with the expected result of very traditional outcomes—programmatic failure but the proselytizing of popular values, ceremony triumphing over substance in denial of the influence of structural factors in social failure.

The determination of the success or failure of the Ford Foundation's Gray Areas Projects is constrained once again by the absence of independent evaluations. Almost everything written about these projects depends on sources in the Ford Foundation archives. Indeed, it says much about the logic of philanthropic social reform that it is rarely if ever open to public scrutiny but rather floats on assumptions of patrician good will, consultant evaluations, and staff satisfaction. Both the Ford Foundation and Kennedy's committee were staffed by very traditional upper-crust types whose "almost obsessive bias toward rationality" yielded, in the absence of rational information, to a reliance on class lore concerning poverty and character. These elites, very much Halberstam's best and brightest, arrogated to themselves virtuous motives along with leadership and high-minded character and thus an entitlement to handle the public trust. Indeed, many of the Kennedy administration's appointees to War on Poverty agencies had little experience in public affairs, let alone poverty issues, but they had many ties to their social set and perhaps even a reputation for lofty ideals and good character. The early programs of the War on Poverty, the Gray Areas Projects, MFY, and many of the projects of the Committee on Delinquency and Youth Crime, were gifts from the Olympians of civic concern, quite in the manner of the charities of the ownership classes. Their programs continued the spirit of the settlement houses—patrician condescension, social efficiency, and program failure.

The Ford Foundation summed up its experience as mixed. Against its principal goal ("quality of leadership was paramount"), "most was achieved in those localities where both the chief elected official and the head of the Gray Areas corporations were honest in commitment and competent in management." Some individual programs succeeded and others failed, while the foundation acknowledged that its supervision of grantees was sometimes counterproductive (Magat 1979, 122).

A few additional conclusions, less respectful of the foundation's own assessments, seem reasonable. Strong, competent leadership was an overriding goal of the foundation, but there is little evidence that it either developed, found, or protected such leadership. Most important, the projects did not succeed in developing new constituencies for reform. In its successes, such as New Haven, Gray Areas took advantage of a preexisting consensus, but even then its success seems more procedural than substantive; strong coordination from the top may be a very inadequate strategy for addressing the substantive deficits of poverty. Moreover, the priority given leadership suggests the usual faith in character rather than the allocation of hard resources as the solution to the problem of poverty.

In other sites, community action may have solidified opposition to the Ford Foundation's intended reforms. Most significantly, Ford's funding may not have played much of a role in any of the changes, such as they were. Rather, the foundation's small grants were coincidental with situations that were already developing. The true causes of any benefits that occurred in the target cities and communities probably lay in more structural factors—migration, economic growth, political realignment, and so forth—rather than in the foundation's beaky pursuit of good leadership and high-minded character, perhaps projections of the Ford officers' own insular self-regard.

The Ford Foundation's rhapsodic illusion was to assume that a latent constituency existed for the genuine reform of American priorities. The foundation assumed its "capacity to involve and to affect critical centers of community power, including the intellectual, in order to break the bottlenecks in education, employment, law, health and other fields" (Ylvisaker 1963, 7). Thus it developed strategies to coordinate disparate agencies. But coordination implies a constituency for new goals. Unfortunately, the foundation and its grantees were never able "to convince the people involved—on one level, the industrial, labor, governmental, and civic leadership, and on another level, the man in the Gray Area Street—that these programs were 'for real'—not window dressing for the status quo" (7). Yet the problem was not bottlenecks, although many agencies were certainly inefficient, but rather resources and goals. The foundation and the reformers—"professional pathologists" (Mills 1943), do-gooders, and Great Liberals—never confronted the deep popularity of the status quo but treated embedded social preferences as wayward, mistaken, unintended, and uninformed. In fact, the stability of the society—its enduring priorities—had been achieved through the massive social interactions of largely unorchestrated but immensely consensual role choices of individuals. The Ford Foundation programs were not addressing miscreant and corrupt agencies that were out of touch with American desires but rather institutions that expressed the popular will. Americans have rarely taken kindly to poorer and lower-status groups.

It does not say much for the Kennedy administration that it modeled its social reform efforts on programs that were neither obviously successful nor well evaluated. Yet that administration, just like the Ford Foundation, had a weakness for Theodore Roosevelt character analysis, jolly good fellows, and P. J. Wodehouse types as reform leaders.

Charities and philanthropic foundations reflect the intentions of their charters, the social biases of their patrons, and indeed the individualistic assumptions of the American people. Their humanitarian effusions in the manner of the Ford Foundation are deeply conservative expressions of an ingrained commitment to private-sector organizations as seedbeds of leadership, hothouses of innovation, incubators of brilliance, in short, as meritocratic institutions. In this sense American philanthropists are classic European liberals and express the conceit of the wealthy and successful that they have earned their position and the right to be custodians of the national interest.

But charities, philanthropic foundations, and the wealthy in general are not accountable in the same way that public agencies are; they never face elections; their programs never face market tests; their livelihoods are secure; and they need not consult the public will. They can afford recreational good works without accountability.[6]

---

6. Still, their freedoms are constrained by the law and thus by popular sentiment. The Ford Foundation and others who experimented with communities came under congressional review for the mischief they caused. Their IRS exemptions were questioned, with the result that they became far more cautious in underwriting unpopular social causes.

In the end, the Ford Foundation was no more innovative than any other sector of the society, although it probably was less attentive to social problems than even the public sector. Its great freedom to experiment, presumably in the area of public expenditures, was misspent. The foundations and charities, in the manner of other embedded social institutions, simply ratified institutionalized values, notably heroic individualism, while clamoring about their good hearts, worldliness, and clever insights. Indeed, the Ford Foundation's projects, then and since, pursued a conservative narrative: how the dedication to betterment and new knowledge can with very few resources transform dysfunctional members of society into good citizens. With few exceptions, the foundations and charities, and indeed the American people, are forever tolerant of budgetary constraints on social welfare goals.

The programmatic precursors, just like the War on Poverty programs themselves, were committed to small-scale, quasi-voluntary programs that operated in the spirit of Putnam's social capital through the guardianship of patrician social institutions and the commercially successful in general. Indeed, it might be worth arguing that if the Ford Foundation had given its grant money to the federal government, it would have been better spent—better focused, better administered, better evaluated, and in the end more accountable to public auditing standards—even while it is unlikely that this would have had a more appreciable effect on American poverty. No matter how it is spent, $80 per head—the amount that the foundation spent per targeted Gray Areas resident in New Haven—is a laughable amount against the vastness of social need.[7] Nevertheless, these few precursor programs, costing a few tens of millions, became the template for the hundreds of local agencies and the billions spent on direct service programs and community organizing by the OEO.

Why didn't the intellectual community scrutinize MFY and its decrepit, self-serving evaluations? As ever, the reformers were enthralled by their own ideas, while the social sciences replaced the rigorous self-scrutiny of true science with the convenience of advocacy. Social welfare histories that naively equate the intellectual life of a period with its

7. Marris and Rein's (1982) estimate for the per capita amount spent in New Haven, "for every, man, woman and child in the neighborhood its programs served" (26) in 1963–64, seems higher than that spent at other sites. MFY spent roughly that amount per capita over all the years of its operation. The per capita amounts spent through the president's committee grants were much lower, and probably lower still through the OEO grants.

meaning—the social welfare histories of this period routinely commit this error—are appreciated for their ideological commitments and perhaps for their autobiographical value as evocative statements of their authors' social preferences, rather than as valuable descriptions of what happened and why.

The More Likely Precursors

The immediate programmatic precursors to the War on Poverty were the progeny of a consistent tradition of romantic self-sufficiency and a widely shared political preference for social efficiency—the belief that problems could be adequately addressed through rational, inexpensive, and socially compatible interventions. Notwithstanding a plangent rhetoric of deep concern, the stupefying satisfaction of the nation with things as they are—its very incidental and weak tradition of dissent—even in the face of the deprivations of the 1930s, goes far to explain the superficiality of the precursors and the War on Poverty programs themselves. Out of gratitude to World War II veterans, the United States enacted a GI benefit package, unique in American history for its broad coverage and generosity. But the War on Poverty took inspiration from the longer tradition of neglect, of abiding inequality and poverty.

The civil rights movement, certainly benefiting from the stalwart determination of its leadership, flourished politically because of broader changes in social tolerance that were shaped powerfully by the Great Depression, the war, and the consistently broadening electoral franchise. The Civil Rights and Voting Rights acts, important as they are, were still only procedural, with little ability to address substantive deprivations. The War on Poverty presumably was to be the equalizing material expression of the impetus to greater equality, but it quickly adopted services that focused on character and soon became a spoils system for minorities. In near mockery of W. E. B. Du Bois, the relatively few program jobs were given to the few apparently credentialed semiprofessionals within the large minority community, but the services themselves were incapable of achieving their goals. There was no substantive response to poverty despite the capacity of the nation to access the enormous economic bounty of the 1960s.

In the face of democratizing opportunities accelerated by both demographic and economic changes, the War on Poverty was a tepid, tight-fisted, and unimaginative response to a legacy of racial injustice, inequality, and material deprivation. Relying on volition rather than economic redistribution, the War on Poverty pointedly chose a different path from the generosity of the GI Bill. Despite the din of speeches about opportunity, the good citizen remained very much a private actor responsible for his or her own destiny. Indeed, the antipoverty efforts of the 1960s and 1970s provided little relief, little educational assistance, even less manpower training, and only a halfhearted attempt to develop a constituency for broader change. Ever respectful of prevailing social institutions, the ethos of social efficiency converted Poor Richard's thrift into miserliness in determining the content of the War on Poverty.

Initiatives in other federal departments addressing the delivery of health services, housing and urban development, education, and other needs paralleled the weaknesses of the programs in the OEO. The progress against discrimination in housing and employment was more procedural than substantive. While the entitlement programs became more substantial and federalized, universalistic elements were added to the American welfare state—notably Medicare, Medicaid, and food stamps. However, they still remained inadequate, and notably so when poverty is looked at relative to the nation's wealth rather than as a matter of absolute subsistence.

Measurable progress against poverty and need, when it occurred, was not easily attributed to the programs that were specifically designed as antipoverty measures. Large portions of the gains were the result of economic growth, unplanned social adjustments, and even political changes unassociated with the planned strategies of the War on Poverty. Commentators stretch themselves to find broader meaning in the War on Poverty programs and their precursors.

The debate over whether the public or the private sector should take the lead in addressing social need swallows the actual history of the Great Society programs and subsequent efforts. During the 1960s and 1970s, but continuing for decades thereafter, the debate remained baldly ideological principally because so few studies estimated the outcomes of the initiatives, and because those that did exist were largely peripheral to the political consideration of the programs themselves. The prominent social welfare historians of the period drew principally on secondary sources that were hard pressed to find any credible primary data. Case histories were often infused with the hopes of their authors. Even simple descriptions of the programs—number, race, income of recipients, staff characteristics—were often incomplete and misleading.

Popular will determines social policy, but customarily with a rationalistic style expressed as an evangelist of social efficiency and a rule book of good citizenship. The national ethos imbued all of the War on Poverty programs with a belabored insistence on personal responsibility for individual change. The reformers were instruments of national parsimony; the period's elevated sensibilities toward systemic and structural imperfections came down to programs that targeted the poor themselves or engaged in strategies of social change in which the community participants were expendable foot soldiers. The ideas that soared in the mind hit the ground dead, not least because of professional arrogance buoyed by embedded American social preferences, the Adam and Eve of all precursors.

Without even a nod to informed consent, the Ford Foundation and public agencies experimented with the poor. Of course, one always has the freedom to take it or leave it, the ability to walk out. But the experimenters arrogated righteousness and technique in service to their own ideas and ambitions. The precursor programs were all mounted by public and private agencies that refused to extend basic American institutional benefits to the marginal but rather instituted strategies of social treatment—cheap self-help of one sort or another—obviously assuming the pathology of those in need. The programs' failure to achieve either broad participation or the sanction of those in need is an ironic tribute to poor people's ability to determine their own self-interest. The contrast between the humanitarian pretensions of the welfare state and welfare programs' actual denial of the substantive rights of citizenship to their intended recipients reveals the hypocrisy of the national will.

2

THE WAR ON POVERTY:
PROGRAMS OF THE OFFICE OF ECONOMIC
OPPORTUNITY

If all of the appropriations for programs established under the Economic Opportunity Act of 1964 had been distributed in cash to the poor, they would not have made a ding in even a hubcap of poverty. "For the nation as a whole, CAP grants over the first four years [1964–68] averaged roughly $97 per poor person. The comparable figure in the ten cities that received the largest grants was almost three times the national average, ranging from a low of $93 for New York City to three times as much for Pittsburgh. . . . Costs of the Head Start program and neighborhood centers [which by and large housed the locally developed services] accounted for two of every three dollars allotted by CAP" (Levitan 1969, 70).

Even a tiny cash distribution might have conferred a more profound benefit than the Office of Economic Opportunity programs ever did. While the beggar's mite would have failed to solve the problem of poverty as thoroughly as the OEO programs have done, a cash distribution would at least have gone a step toward addressing concrete needs. In contrast, the OEO programs reinforced the myth of heroic individualism, the citizen's overarching reliance on self-invention instead of social support. Rather than redistribute wealth, it is obvious that OEO programs were intended to serve as a catalyst; that is, they were intended to be socially efficient, reflecting optimism that strategic small investments would yield very big gains. From the start, the OEO programs were symbolic statements of personal responsibility that also operated as political patronage of the Democratic Party, reserved largely for blacks as one of the payoffs for civil rights agitation (Friedman 1977).

Some of the direct service programs of the Economic Opportunity Act were administered by the OEO: Job Corps, VISTA, and the Community Action Program whose local chapters ran Upward Bound, Legal Services, Foster Grandparents, Migrants, Head Start, and Health Service Centers. The remainder of the act's programs—Neighborhood Youth Corps, Special Impact, Operation Mainstream, New Careers, Work Study, Adult Basic Education, Work Experience, Rural Loans, Small Business Loans—were delegated to other federal agencies.

The Community Action Program (CAP) was the OEO's lead warrior; its initial task was to develop a constituency of the poor themselves and perhaps also minority group members, whether poor or not, to pursue systemic changes in states and localities. The combined constituencies would presumably be powerful enough to open the floodgates of federal spending. The initial "maximum feasible participation" phase of the program assumed that a constituency of the disaffected and their allies would, though unorganized, be motivated to seek change and be large enough to achieve its goals. Unfortunately, these assumptions were wildly inaccurate, and the pursuit of reform by the poor themselves was a romantic quest. The strategy of reaching outside the system to reform it came up against both the apathy of the poor and their identification with core American values. Even the most persistently raucous community organizing of the period, conducted by Saul Alinsky's Industrial Areas Foundation, routinely failed on the streets, even while attracting an appreciative audience for its bellicose melodramas of virtue (Alinsky 1969, 1971).

Apart from the early Community Action Program, and to a lesser extent Legal Services, all of the other OEO initiatives targeted the deficiencies of the poor—in education, health, attitude, experience, literacy, and so forth—that presumably accounted for their poverty. An ancient bit of folk wisdom stated the strategy succinctly: give a man a fish and he eats for a day; teach him to fish and he eats for a lifetime. Unfortunately, the vastly underfunded OEO programs lacked the resources, and often the will, to address the skill deficits of the poor and, notably, the conditions, including the structural imperfections of the society itself (bigotry, deficient communities and housing, weak schools, secondary job markets, and so forth) that kept them poor. Indeed, OEO and subsequent programs that focused on job preparation tried to teach people to fish at a time when fishing had become an obsolete occupation.

In a manner reminiscent of earlier public works projects in poor communities, the local Community Action Programs were often run as spoils systems. Since so much of the War on Poverty emerged along with the civil rights movement, the patronage went largely to blacks. The local Community Action Programs quickly decided that their future lay in direct services rather than direct action. Indeed, once ethnic political clubhouses had entrenched themselves in poor communities, at times as a result of early organizing by the Community Action Programs, jobs in the program were handed out to cement political loyalties. It is difficult to argue that the pacification of protest was imposed on "the people." Rather, the pervasiveness of the preference for services over social action suggests a broad consensus even among the poor.

These programs preferred dead-end efforts to increase opportunity over a broader sense of opportunity that also included, at a minimum, income supports, adequate schooling, job preparation, jobs, adequate income, and health services. Opportunity came to be restricted to socially efficient programs in the spirit of the precursor programs, as well as procedural reforms such as voting rights, equal accommodations, fair hiring and housing practices, and some others. The OEO programs and related activities were often disjointed, underfunded, badly administered, inefficient, and mistargeted. At worst, they were a hypocritical show of concern for the poor, more symbol than substance, but still consistent with American priorities. America spoke to its less fortunate citizens through the inadequacies of the Economic Opportunity Act. The biggest winners of the War on Poverty were the beneficiaries of the social insurances, and within this group, the poor rarely achieved entitlements to even basic income.

Rather than serve as leaders in formulating strategy and policy, the intellectuals provided the symbols of political necessity and compromise. Cloward's opportunity theory, for example, was not a brilliant insight into the mechanics of society and social change but a convenient excuse for the culture to mount a campaign against poverty without putting up the resources for the necessary ammunition. In subsequent decades the nation, with the encouragement of the conservatives and neoconservatives, did even less. Still, none of the "professors" did credible research. Indeed, they made a hash of even the best-funded evaluation projects.

The most careful of the evaluations, despite their methodological imperfections, demonstrated the ineffectiveness of even the most successful OEO programs. The typical evaluation lacked replicable forms of measurement, equivalent or even relevant comparison groups, measurement over time, descriptions of program participants, and even detailed statements of what the programs provided. OEO programs often aggregated happy little success stories that testified to their value.

Less than a solution to poverty, the OEO programs were accommodations to poverty—symbolic affirmations of self-help, not social help—that continued beyond the dramatic economic gains of the period. The OEO programs slid easily from focusing on the deficits of the poor into blaming the poor for their problems, especially when the recipients failed to rise out of poverty. They did, however, provide jobs to minorities, although the people who got these jobs were often untrained or otherwise unqualified for them.

The intellectuals who later broke with the self-help orientation of the Economic Opportunity Act became marooned in American politics. The nation refused to follow them into a national program that set a floor under income for all Americans as a right of citizenship. Yet even here, these structuralists, these authentic American liberals, could not sustain their position with their research. The negative income tax studies were deeply flawed, endorsing no credible direction for policymaking and assuming that it always respects rational information (see, for example, Aaron 1978; Davies 1996; Brown 1999). The move to structural reform, rather than a tribute to the rationality of social science, is still profoundly ideological, an ethical issue rather than a technical one.

The OEO's Action Component—The Community Action Program

The Economic Opportunity Act of 1964—the basic legislation of the Great Society's War on Poverty—authorized the Community Action Program to fund community action agencies (CAAs) to run social service and local organizing programs. Those programs included a series of nationally mandated direct social welfare services such as Upward Bound, Job Corps, and Head Start, as well as locally designed programs to ameliorate poverty. Specifically intending the CAAs to coordinate existing public and private agencies in their areas, the act also gave them preference as grantees of other federal social service programs.

The mandated goal of the CAAs was so broad that almost any service or program qualified as a legitimate activity. The Economic Opportunity Act defined a community action agency as one "which provides services, assistance, and other activities of sufficient scope and size to give promise of progress toward elimination of poverty or a cause or causes of poverty." The legislation gave the CAAs vaguely defined responsibility to develop, conduct, and administer these programs with the "maximum feasible participation of residents of the areas and members of the groups served." This directive to involve the poor themselves as their own advocates was the most controversial portion of the act. Paired with an administrative structure that largely bypassed state and local elected officials, the directive to involve the poor led to organizing activities that challenged existing political leadership, often the mayors of large cities. Like its precursors, the CAP pursued two types of antipoverty strategy, one to provide direct social services and the other, justified by its service role, to reform the broader service system itself.

The Ford Foundation's formal relationship with MFY and the Gray Areas Projects—a line of accountability that ran directly from the grantor to the grantee, bypassing state and local government—as well as their community organization and service projects, served as the model for CAAs. The federal government assumed that state and local governments were largely unresponsive to citizen needs and inattentive to the issues of poverty. This distrust of local government reflected the civil rights experience in the South as well as northern urban experience with bosses and their political machines.

Between 1965 and 1969, the CAP spent approximately $3.5 billion through about a thousand CAAs, although most of the funds were concentrated in a few of the larger cities. More than 50 percent of these funds was spent on nationally mandated programs and about 40 percent on locally developed services. Little was actually retained for administrative support, including community organizing (Levitan 1969, 71).

The CAP's strategic decisions were made without systematic evaluations of the programs or even much clarity about goals. Indeed, MFY and the other Ford Foundation programs, as well as the CAP experience itself, were subjected to intense political scrutiny that was largely uninformed about specific programmatic outcomes. The fight was essentially over power and purpose, and in the end, symbol. Commentaries on the War on Poverty and the CAAs as well as the histories of the period are similarly unanchored by outcome data but are uninhibited in reaching evaluative conclusions.

For example, Mitchell I. Ginsberg (the commissioner of the New York City Human Resources Administration), speaking for Mayor Lindsey, testified before the Senate that "the results [of OEO's programs] are, of course, hard to measure in any objective quantitative fashion, but in my judgment, they have been positive and indeed incalculable." But he then went on to boast that the CAAs in New York had developed effective "new kinds of social welfare agencies that are run and staffed by the residents of poor communities themselves," that these agencies were used by those in need, that more self-help programs had been initiated, and so on (Ginsberg 1969, 82–83). The only data he provided were notoriously unreliable counts of service use offered by the agencies themselves.

To take another example, Levitan acknowledged that "not only is there a paucity of data about [the CAAs'] operations, particularly their 'versatile' activities, but there is no accepted index by which to measure the success or failure of this social experiment" (1969, 74). Still, he concluded that "an objective evaluation of the CAAs" (which he has just acknowledged has not been made), "and particularly of the role of the poor in these programs, should compare the CAP-funded agencies with traditional welfare organizations, rather than with some ideal model. On that score, CAP must certainly be judged to be an innovative agency which gave the poor their first social and political role. Few would disagree with the basic CAP premise concerning the need for a new federal approach to welfare" (74). Senator Jesse Helms, representing the people of North Carolina and perhaps even a very large portion of the country, disagreed: "My contention here today is that the most responsible thing which the Federal Government can do to help the poor, to assist them in leading more productive lives, and to make them self-sufficient, not only financially, but also in terms of self-respect and accomplishment, is for the Federal Government to get out of the poverty action field, period" (Helms 1974, 320).

The CAAs had a free run for about three years, until local political officials prevailed on the White House to rein them in. The 1967 amendments to the 1964 Economic Opportunity Act (title II, part A, section 211, as amended) essentially gave local elected officials, in particular the mayors of large cities, control of the CAAs. Attributed to Edith Green, a congresswoman from Oregon, the amendments required that no more than one-third of CAA boards be composed of the poor, one-third of public officials, and one-third of representatives of "major groups and interests in the community" (section 211 [b]). The 1967 amendments also greatly emphasized the CAAs' role in coordinating services with existing public and private agencies rather than as advocates for the poor. They relegated maximum feasible participation to a tactic intended "to best stimulate and take full advantage of capabilities for self-advancement and assure that those programs and projects are otherwise meaningful to and widely utilized by their intended beneficiaries" (section 201 [a][4]). The amended law also threw into stark relief the War on Poverty's goal to promote self-sufficiency as the way to reduce poverty, again emphasizing the importance of self-help. The Nixon administration curtailed and reorganized the OEO, moving it out of the office of the president. The Reagan administration succeeded in repealing the basic legislation in 1981. Only remnants of the OEO remain today—Head Start and a few other small programs.

The CAP record both before and after the 1967 amendments recapitulates the problems of MFY and the Gray Areas Projects. In its turn, Model Cities, taking a route through elected officials rather than directly through the poor, was also unable to organize a constituency in support of deep reform, i.e., massive expenditures for social welfare and poverty reduction. The fundamental impediments remained the same but reflected again and again the deep preferences of the American people rather than the technical problems of building effective political organizations of the poor themselves.

An interpretation of American social welfare policymaking as a product of detached role organization suggests that the War on Poverty was elaborated with the broad consent of the American people. This possibility stands in opposition to theories that place determinative power in the hands of a conspiratorial and predatory elite, autonomous actors, or a series of competing interest groups. Indeed, the exercise of a national will also explains the apparent indecisiveness in clarifying goals and means at the beginning of the War on Poverty that Moynihan made so much of in *Maximum Feasible Misunderstanding*. Rather than lamentable and preventable confusion leading to lessons for social scientists, the nation went through a short period of uncertainty but obviously made its preferences quite clear in the limitations imposed on the CAP and then its repeal. The failure of both the CAP and Model Cities suggested citizens' contentment with the existing political and social system. The observation that society at the time was neither fair nor just does not refute democratic decision making but rather comments on the quality of its agreements.

On contract to the OEO, Jacobs (1981) produced one of the few systematic evaluations of the CAP, measuring its influence over the policies of local organizations that served poor people as employers, private social welfare agencies, or public schools. The evaluation was based on interviews with the executives of eight hundred organizations in one hundred communities during 1968 and 1969.

Jacobs's principal finding was that "in each sector, institutions exhibited a pattern of broad, but shallow change" (153). Between 1964 and 1968, the percentage of minority recipients served by private social welfare agencies in these cities increased from 43 percent to 50 percent, although the percentage of poor recipients declined slightly from 52 percent to 51 percent (85). However, the service profiles of the agencies hardly changed at all (86). Seventy-one percent of the agencies claimed that they had taken steps to involve the poor in the delivery and planning of agency services (90). Minimal as these changes were, if indeed they occurred at all, Jacobs's analysis of CAA grant processes led him to conclude that "it seems clear that government policies helped stimulate some of the redirection of private social service agencies" (97).

Public school policies changed even less than those in the private social welfare agencies. There was little change between 1964 and 1968 in teacher-student ratios, percentage of black teachers, special school personnel, new teaching methods, and so forth. Employers also changed very little; minority employees increased by 2.5 percent, minority foremen increased by 3.1 percent, and community involvement increased by 3 percent. Demographic changes might by themselves account for some of these gains.

Yet, modest as the findings are, they are not sustained by the methodology, and they probably inflate the effectiveness of community organization by CAAs and by other federal grants intended to change local organizations' policies. Interviews, notably those of agency executives, are uncertain estimates of the actual reasons for the responses of the agencies. Small biases in reporting accommodation to the spirit of the times rather than actual agency change might account for all of the reported gains. The interviews did not follow up with independent estimates of the executives' accuracy, nor was there any attempt to actually document agency changes over the period of the CAA activities. But even if Jacobs had audited the responses, it would have been impossible to attribute any agency changes to community organization rather than to broader social influences, such as the prominence of poverty as a social issue during that period. The actual reasons for change and the perceptions of those who change are often very different.

Jacobs concluded that the issues symbolized by the CAAs appear to have been socialized within the responding agencies. The agencies accepted the apparent priority of handling poverty. However, there is absolutely no evidence that they did anything substantive about it. To the contrary, the findings suggest that they did not. Typically, politically sensitive agencies acknowledge need but respond to it within the tolerances of their constituency. In other words, poverty was of concern to these agencies, but not enough to substantially affect their policies.

The study is clear on only one point: the community organization activities of CAAs were inadequate to mount a sufficient political force to force local change. Indeed, changes that did take place during the period are more easily attributed to changing social appetites, perceptions, and demographics—notably the de jure procedural adaptations to civil rights pressures—than to the conscious organizational strategies of decentralized, understaffed, and poorly trained community organization programs.

Still, in spite of his questionable data, a methodology incapable of identifying causal factors, and beholden informants, Jacobs stated, "I believe that the political response to community organization was certainly significant and perhaps paramount" (1981, 157). This belief is predicated on an interpretation of the motives of the very few agencies that did respond to community pressure. That community organization may be effective with weak, vulnerable, or amenable adversaries is hardly a tribute to its prowess.

Jacobs conceded that poverty reduction is best handled through the tax system and transfer payments. In contrast, the CAAs were attempting to reduce dependency on public support. "Implicit were the assumptions that one could specify the needs of the poor and that institutions in the areas of education, manpower, and social services could serve them" (155). Indeed, the preference for lower dependency on public money rather than poverty reduction itself is a pillar of American social welfare policy. The same notions of self-help and personal responsibility have justified the retrenchment of the few policy gains of the 1930s and 1960s in the 1996 welfare reforms and their reauthorization in 2006.

The CAAs were committed self-help strategies both in their assumption that the poor could be organized as effective advocates of their own interests and also in the service programs that were locally designed. But, as Jacobs observed, seemingly in contradiction of his regard for community organization, these efforts have uniformly failed: "there is no evidence that the organizational changes sought and effected had a systematic impact on the level of poverty in the nation" (156). Yet the failure of the CAP has not loosened the nation's mythic attachment to the redemptive virtues of self-help, at least for lower-income and lower-status groups.

Associated with the Jacobs study and also on contract to the OEO, Vanecko (1970a) interviewed approximately eleven hundred informants in fifty cities drawn from the National Opinion Research Center's Permanent Community Sample by way of assessing the effects of different styles of community organization in CAAs. The study suffers from all of the problems of Jacobs's, notably the lack of any independent assessment of the accuracy of the survey responses and the proclivity to draw causal inferences from nonexperimental data. Vanecko generally corroborates Jacobs but adds a fillip for active community organization.

> The conclusion of this analysis is clear. . . . The effective [CAA] is one which has central office support for community organization, which has neighborhood centers actively involved in community organizing, which has neighborhood centers uninvolved in militant activities, and which does not spend time pressing specific demands on other institutions. Since such agencies exist primarily in cities with relatively high levels of political activity in poor neighborhoods, their effectiveness is in extending or complementing the activity and involvement of the residents of poor neighborhoods. (1969, 629)

However, Vanecko's data can easily be reinterpreted for a less supportive conclusion: community organization by CAAs associated with institutional change is largely redundant with preexisting political intents. The greatest amount of institutional change took place in cities that were already concerned with poverty and in which the CAA avoided militant organizing and thus community backlash. Indeed, Vanecko sustains this reinterpretation with his observation that "the absence of a relatively high level of general political activity in the target neighborhood does not provide much opportunity for community organization" (1969, 630). In other words, CAAs that were associated with positive changes existed in communities that were already pursuing change. Yet nothing in the design of the research allows Vanecko to reach his causal conclusions. The ethos of a population—a structural condition far beyond the ambitions and capacity of community organization to effect or modify— rather than any technique of mobilization seems a more likely reason for agency change than the power of the poor, the romantic hope for the insurrection of the oppressed notwithstanding. Then again, it is worth recalling that neither Vanecko nor Jacobs ever measured independently the actual amount of change—its quality and depth.

At about the same time, the General Accounting Office (GAO) (1969) conducted a comprehensive review of the OEO that was mandated by the 1967 amendments to the Economic Opportunity Act. Congress asked for "a comprehensive and impartial investigation of the antipoverty programs" that would evaluate their administrative efficiency and the extent to which they were achieving their objectives (U.S. GAO 1969, 1). The GAO relied on financial audits by a national accounting firm, agency data, and interviews with a variety of program participants in eleven communities throughout the nation.

Perhaps because they were truly independent of at least the OEO's displeasure, the GAO's findings are more direct than Jacobs's, judging the OEO largely ineffective and the local CAAs both inefficient and financially troubled. The OEO had failed to coordinate federal programs, one of its basic mandates. The CAP had some "varying success" in developing greater resident participation, advocating for the poor, and initiating a number of new services for the poor. However, "CAP has achieved these ends in lesser measure than was reasonable to expect in relation to the magnitude of funds expended" (8).

The GAO was unable to evaluate the effectiveness of a number of later CAP programs, notably the heath centers and the manpower services. However, it concluded that while Head Start, Upward Bound, and legal services had achieved some modest gains, those programs were beset by numerous difficulties. The GAO's evaluations of these direct service programs were superseded in later years by more comprehensive and systematic evaluations.

Most important, the GAO report faults the administration of the CAP for the many program failures. "Although progress has been made in

the past 4 years the administrative machinery is still in need of substantial improvement" (10). The CAP had failed at its basic tasks:

> (1) the process by which program participants are selected, (2) the
> counseling of program participants, (3) the supervision of staff,
> (4) job development and placement, (5) the ways in which former
> program participants are followed up on and provided with further
> assistance, and (6) the record keeping and reporting necessary to
> permit more effective evaluations of accomplishments and more
> adequate accountability for expenditures. Some of these shortcom-
> ings can be attributed to insufficient and inexperienced staff, par-
> ticularly at the local level. (U.S. GAO 1969, 10)

The other shortcomings were apparently attributed to incompetence and
worse. In fact, the fundamental failures of MFY at its basic organizing
tasks are recalled in three of the GAO's observations about the CAP
generally, although softened in its general comments. First, the CAAs
had not identified the "most acute needs of the poor and the causes of
poverty in their communities" (10). While the latter task has not been
generally achieved either before or after in any but a superficial way
(Epstein 1997), the failure to identify local need was very troubling.

Second, the CAAs had failed to coordinate local agencies just as the
OEO had failed to coordinate federal agencies. "The CAAs are not likely
to achieve their potential effectiveness unless cooperative arrangements
can be worked out between these CAAs (generally through the neighborhood centers which have this responsibility within their designated
boundaries) and the local agencies to bring about such coordination"
(U.S. GAO 1969, 31). Indeed, the GAO report did not go past this observation, although the Ford Foundation consultants did indeed attribute a
large portion of the problem to the organizing tactics of MFY. Like MFY,
many of the CAAs had identified local public and private agencies as the
targets of their organizing and were pursuing strategies of conflict and
confrontation.

Third, the CAAs had not fulfilled their most fundamental mandate to
provide the poor with appropriate representation or to involve them in
the substantive operations of the agencies. "In many of the CAAs we
reviewed, representatives of the poor, particularly those on the CAA
boards of directors, had been elected by a very small percentage of the
eligible voters and attendance at meetings of some advisory councils

and neighborhood area councils by representatives of the poor on these councils and by residents of the areas was infrequent. Appropriate representation of, and active participation by, the poor are logical follow throughs of the theses of self-help which is the underpinning of the CAP."

The observation of low participation—the turnout for board elections was often less than 1 percent of eligible residents—raises questions about the legitimacy of the local organizing efforts. It seems impossible to argue that the poor were unaware of the antipoverty efforts in their neighborhoods in light of the immense and constant news coverage attending the War on Poverty and local efforts to publicize the new agencies and their programs. The very low participation was probably not the result of staff failure or pathological incapacities of the indigent but rather a free choice by the poor themselves. It is worth considering that the CAP's self-help strategy was neither appropriate to eradicate poverty nor what the poor themselves desired. They stayed away.

In light of the consent withheld by the poor, by many in the social welfare community, and perhaps by the American public generally for large changes in American social welfare policy, the insurrectionist style of MFY and many CAAs seems politically inappropriate, indeed self-defeating, and very premature. Messianic rebelliousness begins to capture the romance of the CAP and the quaintness of the "reformatarian" impulse. It seems self-centered rather than politically involved, let alone politically astute, for community organizers to give in to their confrontational mood with the expectation that the very targets of their anger would respond by continuing to fund their rebellions. Indeed, they did not, and the Green amendment ended the political independence of the CAP.

The numerous specific recommendations that followed the GAO report's findings imply the even harsher assessment that the CAA service programs were mistargeted, inefficient, poorly administered, and perhaps even corrupt. The report stresses a concern with eligibility, implying that many who were not poor or needy were receiving services. It also details the deficiencies of the CAAs in training, communication, standards, and appropriate financial procedures for basic programmatic and administrative accountability.

Although independent of the OEO, the GAO report was still a political rather than a truly neutral document. It was mandated by a liberal Democratic Congress with a liberal Democrat in the White House.

Moreover, the staff of the agency was in all likelihood quite sympathetic to the OEO's mission. TransCentury, Inc., the Washington, D.C., consulting firm the GAO hired to conduct the interviews, was headed up by a former Kennedy appointee and filled with the same fervent staff that worked for the CAAs (except that the consulting firm and its staff had great respect for corporate profit). However, the report goes far beyond the "audit work normally performed by the General Accounting Office" to make judgments for which it had very little data (U.S. GAO 1969, 1).

The GAO's distinguished history and well-earned prestige encourage some confidence in its conclusions. However, the report provides no detailed description of its methods or standards; it does not present much of the data on which its judgments are based or the process by which it selected its sample of eleven sites; the material gathered from interviews is not described, nor are there any statistical reports on the surveys. The report itself acknowledges many additional problems: "limited usefulness of past evaluations . . . difficulty of separating administrative and program effectiveness . . . lack of reliable data . . . lack of agreed upon criteria for judging results," among others (appendix 3). Yet the GAO's judgments were probably a bit of hopeful whitewash, even though the OEO's response, contained within the report itself, was predictably protective and unhappy.

Despite their many serious flaws, Jacobs (1981) and the 1969 GAO report are apparently the most systematic assessments of the CAP available. Chertow's (1974) review of research on the participation of the poor in the CAP is valuable not so much for her analysis—a superficial summary of the material—but rather for cataloging what was known, a comprehensive description of the most prominent evaluations. For all the heat of partisan assurances and hope, almost all of the evidence of outcomes consisted of anecdotes, case studies (usually of poor quality), and uncorroborated interviews with participants. The suspicion remains that the researchers found in the CAAs what they started out looking for. There was not even a large volume of material; Chertow lists only fifty items, most of which were secondary-source commentaries on the primary research. Yet the commentaries, including broader social histories, access little of this material in drawing their conclusions about the outcomes of War on Poverty programs. In fact, many evaluations of the OEO are only rudimentary attempts to develop theory and are largely devoid of data, the essential component of any reliable outcome assessment.

An exhaustive earlier review covering citizen participation and other issues in the CAP and Model Cities (Strange 1972a) better organizes a much larger volume of scholarship than Chertow (1974) but faces the same problem of a weak base of primary research. Still, it substantiates the common conclusion that the participation of poor people in poverty programs was marginal at best and perhaps even pointless. Strange also credibly documents the growing disenchantment with the participation of the poor—"emphasis on participation has declined precipitously since May 1969" (Strange 1972a, 658).[1]

One of the best of the case studies, Gilbert (1970) documents the failure of the Pittsburgh CAA to build a reform organization that placed service recipients and their representatives in positions of power in the agency. The structural reform goals were displaced by the direct service role of the CAA. The CAA never developed the poor as a coherent, self-defined interest group. Gilbert's data reflect personal experiences and two surveys, one of CAA neighborhood board members and the other of principal professionals in the agency. In commenting on the impediments to organizing the poor, Gilbert notes that "apathy and parochialism . . . are embedded in the participants themselves" (169) although perhaps more as consent and satisfaction than as anomie or fatalism.

Gilbert fails to consider that the tame CAA role was consistent with the preferences of both residents of Pittsburgh and even the poor them-

---

1. In addition to those discussed in the text, the primary studies include Brager (1969), Clark and Hopkins (1968), Haggstrom (1965), Kramer (1969), Lamb et al. (1970), Salamon and Evern (1973), Strange (1972b), and Zurcher (1969). The congressional evaluations of the CAP relied on similar research, often by hired consulting firms. Typically, the evaluations consisted of a consultant or two visiting a site for a few days, gathering information from staff, board members, and others, then writing an interpretive report. For a prime example, see the reports prepared by Community Action Associates, Inc. for the Senate Committee on Labor and Public Welfare's Subcommittee on Employment, Manpower, and Poverty (U.S. Congress, Senate 1967). This is not credible literature. It is journalism, but its conclusions are repeated in the commentaries and histories as though they were testimonial truths. The secondary literature usually develops its arguments without concern for empirical evidence. Some of the best of the secondary literature is discussed in the text, but other works of note include Beck (1969), Bould (1970), Curtis and Zurcher (1971), Davidson (1969), Dubey (1970), Peterson (1970), Rubin (1969), Seidler (1969), and Weiss (1970). The list goes on and on—Strange's (1972a) extensive references contain an accounting of contemporary material: how is it possible to write so much with such certainty about a subject that has not been measured, identified, or predicted? The answer may lie less in the writings and more in the authors.

selves—their sense of priorities and their summary judgment of appropriate civil expectation. Local public and private social welfare agencies,
perhaps targets of a few critics, were largely popular, conforming with
Pittsburgh's notion of how to handle need. The CAA's urge toward acti-
vating citizen grievances was already handled adequately enough for
local tastes by a responsive, representative Democratic Party and powerful local labor unions. Gilbert notes that the CAA, rather than being
broadly involved with the needy, was largely devoted to black poverty
and social issues. It may even be fair to conclude that the grievances of
the poor in Pittsburgh during the 1960s were neither widespread nor
intense.

Gilbert's observation that community organizing failed in Pittsburgh's CAA seems to be repeated nationally, although in similarly weak
studies. It is also disputed, but again by uniformly compromised research. Indeed, the research is more like an opinion poll of researchers,
or even a measure of their allegiances in tribute to a bit of political
cynicism that one stands where one sits.

With the exception of a few prominent critics, the literature expressed
an American consensus that was apparently quite antagonistic to large
resource-redistribution programs for the poor. By itself, the passion for
improving the conditions of the poor does not excuse distortion of the
evidence and blindness to the failure of the programs. The question
arises whether the commitment to rationality, especially when cheap-
ened as social efficiency, actually compromised antipoverty advocacy.
There is a quality of the Old Left in the quickness to protect failures that
recalls some of the worst *Darkness at Noon* episodes in the pursuit of
social welfare, no matter the altruistic motives.

An unusually incisive and comprehensive paper by English (1972)
seems to explain the CAAs' failures, but without any documentation at
all; it is written without a single reference or any primary evidence to
sustain its conclusions or recommendations. English acknowledges
three main obstacles to successfully organizing the poor: attitudes of the
dominant culture, the history of past efforts, and the poor's own problems, notably a "depreciated self-image" but also a lack of organizational
skills (225). Society stereotypes the poor as unworthy and subsequently
has more faith in minimal private charity than in public provision: "The
rendering of charity warms the heart; acceding to demands steams the
collar" (225). The history of poverty relief has made the poor "skeptical
and distrustful . . . ; there is haunting the poor a spirit of Christmas Past

which has given them mostly unfulfilled promises while academics, bu-
reaucrats, and opportunists have enjoyed a windfall" (225). Although
English does not discuss MFY specifically, it fits well into the tradition
of exhausting a community's good faith.

The obstacles English enumerated were largely responsible for the
problems of the CAAs: mismanagement, poor participation of the poor,
weak staff, dysfunctional conflict, and, notably, a lack of public support
for community action. Indeed, the frequent attack on cherished social
institutions by people whom the American public tends to view as unworthy encouraged the demise of CAAs and their loss of federal protection. While his own arguments begin with the rigid structural conditions
of American society, English's recommendations assume that the society is malleable. English the idealist, who enumerates remedies for addressing the problems of community action—greater funding, better
staff, more training, and more public support—is oblivious of English
the realist, who recognizes that those remedies lie outside the American
consensus. Lacking evidence, English's paper may stand as a political
summary of the American mood more than as a true analysis of the
obstacles to organizing poor people.

Brager (1963), the principal MFY organizer, by contrast, minimizes
those obstacles. He attributes successful organization of the "lower-class
community" to the will of middle-class organizations such as MFY.
Brager and a host of other consultant-revolutionaries, including Piven
and Cloward (1971), stolidly maintain the existence of a large constituency for reform in America. The starting blocs of that constituency are
the poor and near poor who are assumed to recognize their natural
stakes in the visions of the reformers. The obstacles that Brager
names—residential mobility, "the opposition of already entrenched organizations," intergroup tensions, the preoccupation with making a
living, and insensitive community organization strategies—largely conceive of the poor as inactive pawns of greater forces to be mobilized by
the will of informed and noble community organizers.

The reformers as well as the fatalists refuse to consider that by and
large the poor have already made choices of allegiance and organization,
although perhaps not in the preferred manner of joining formal organizations and attending their meetings. Both camps interpret the failures
of MFY, the CAP, and poverty organizing generally in ways that sustain
their own preferences. Yet, although the poor are certainly a weak group
politically, they are not passive, even while they may avoid the voluntary

associations and town-hall gatherings of participatory sentimentalists. Still, their preferences are recorded through detached role organization. In this respect, and certainly in their extraordinarily low turnout for any community organization effort, they have expressed their attitudes— first by staying away, but second by the choices they make in daily life. The symmetry between the poor and the middle class suggests that to a great degree they share common American values and wish to partici- pate in the mainstream of American life.

As sensible as it may seem to ascribe a particular kind of economic self-interest to the poor, the poor themselves may not see it quite that way, objecting to being characterized as failures and treated as limp objects pitifully in need of assistance. It is difficult to organize *de novo* any group, notably the poor, perhaps because they are already organized in ways of their own devising, if not in a form that satisfies the senti- mental reformer. In the absence of overt signs of discontent, it may be fair to conclude that the poor have in some sense made peace with their condition and social priorities. Except in times of unusual turmoil, the society has already embedded its preferences in functioning social insti- tutions through a huge number of interactions among detached role organizations.

The organizing programs of the War on Poverty failed to mobilize the poor. Those programs did not offer much beyond a doomed confronta- tion with the dominant society and a series of superficial services that uniformly lacked the resources to achieve their goals of employment and income sufficiency. But the programs did isolate the poor from common American institutions, subtly touching up the participants' scarlet "U," for unworthy.

Yet the discussion of the CAP and similar programs can be and usu- ally is reduced to partisan speculation. It is nearly impossible to come up with a credible assessment of the CAAs' community organizing ef- forts, since there is literally no independent evaluation, or even any valu- able systematic national description of what took place and what resulted. Almost all of the material, apart from the GAO report, was generated by the OEO and its consultants or by state and city agencies with an interest in the outcome. Worse, the scholarly material, when it even bothers to present a quantitative dimension, relies on this material uncritically.

Still, a few general conclusions seem reasonable, if not obvious. First and most important, the CAAs never succeeded in building much of a local or national constituency. Second, CAA staff members were frequently inept both as administrators and as organizers. Third, few poor people themselves participated in the CAAs, and even fewer in decision-making roles.

The CAP may have been too much the legatee of MFY and not enough the child of John Lewis and Eugene Debs: they did not "organize, organize, organize," and largely because their initial message—system reform—they did not capture the imagination, will, or needs of their targeted constituents. The intellectuals were more excited than the poor.

Trying to organize the poor without listening to them repeats the common patrician failure of assuming that universalistic values are universally adored. The wisdom of "starting where the people are" is itself patronizing, for it assumes that the intellectual or organizer knows where that is, and is acting on a rational understanding of the situation rather than simply on a political or partisan preference.

Whatever the nonrational sources of inspiration—prayer, study, political passion, raw ego, or desire—there would seem to be an obligation for a progressive democracy to evaluate its usefulness. The value of inspiration lies in its results, not in its style. To deny this simple proposition is to retreat into the reverie that personal epiphany forces its material truth. But the romantic fallacy is precisely what undermined the CAP: the formulation of community action without evidence of its viability; the premature use of conflict before developing an adequate constituency; the conversion of agency functions into a spoils system; and the refusal or incapacity to come to grips with the preferences of the culture and the poor themselves. In fact, studies of the CAAs and community action rarely addressed the fact of consent but rather assumed widespread dissatisfaction without actually testing it.

However, the fundamental reason for the demise of the CAP and then Model Cities lies in their failure to develop political and social support, not because of the predatory dominance of elite groups but rather because the antipoverty programs, for the short while they lasted, were widely unpopular. The plight of the poor was not then and has never been a celebrated reason for structural adaptation in American history. Yet the refusal to acknowledge embedded social resistance to structural change reflects the romanticism of the early program, its assumption that the insurrectionists' will was sufficient to mount a constituency. That it did not and could not do so was obvious even at the time. The effort of the CAAs as coordinating bodies was tolerated as an expression of social efficiency that stamped out the insurrectionist mood when it provided jobs to the poor. Indeed, community action and community development, far from rebellious expressions of the quest for justice, are cheap alternatives to the deep investment that would actually be required for transforming the poor into productive members of society or providing them with avenues to socialization. The romantic mindset is not novel but is an instance of self-absorption that thrives only when it is politically convenient.

The sources of inspiration for the CAP and much of the War on Poverty were not as estimable as the goal of eradicating poverty but rather perpetuated the self-help tradition in America. The popularity of self-invention is all the more curious in a nation that obviously rejects it whenever parents have the means to provide a quality education and comfortable life for their children and themselves. If heroic individualism were the actual reason for American success rather than its myth, the children of the wealthy would be brought up in conditions of strict abstinence and economic and social austerity—hard beds, cold showers, and regimented boarding schools—in order to develop self-discipline, character, modesty, a sense of mastery, motivation, and insight. Yet by social fiat rather than by reason, the unsuccessful are judged to be morally deficient and thus denied the opportunities, investments, and comforts of more fortunate citizens. It is a biting irony that the poor themselves frequently make the same assumptions about the justice of poverty.

The acceptance of diversity reflected in an ever-increasing franchise was not intended as tolerance for the diversity of means but rather as an expectation that diverse groups would find common ground in national citizenship. Unfortunately for the poor, the mandated conditions of citizenship stressed extreme individual responsibility rather than enforceable claims to substantial relief. The ceremonial role of the direct service programs in promoting a heroic ideal and the opportunity for an epiphany of personal change was all that sustained them.

The CAP's failure to develop a constituency for change, the central reason for its demise, was repeated by Model Cities, a parallel effort that was more professional, more focused, and more invested in a mainline approach. Model Cities was administered apart from the OEO but given a similar mandate to develop national support.

A Digression on Model Cities

In light of the CAP's administrative and program failures, Model Cities was created to extend the hope of coordinating services and agencies as a remedy to poverty.[2] As distinct from the CAP, however, this attempt at coordination was designed to be compatible with existing political structures. Community action and citizen participation were incorporated as vehicles of consensus rather than as tactics intended to provide autonomous representation of the poor. The core of Model Cities was contained in the sanction given to metropolitan regional planning agencies, which were directly accountable to local elected officials, to approve plans for federal funding.

> After June 30, 1967, all applications for Federal assistance for projects for which supplemental grants can be provided must be submitted to a metropolitan or regional planning agency for review. The application shall be accompanied by comments of the planning agency concerning the extent to which the project is consistent with the comprehensive planning developed or in process for the area and the extent to which the project contributes to fulfillment of the planning.
>
> Applications from special-purpose public bodies must similarly be submitted for review by the unit of general local government.
>
> The Secretary is authorized to call upon other Federal agencies to cooperate in insuring that all the Federal programs related to metropolitan development are carried out in a coordinated manner. (U.S. Congress, House 1966, 3)

The Model Cities program succeeded in developing a ton of plans but failed to follow through with funding, a political failure. The planning agencies could not develop broad support for their programs. At a minimum, the plans were meagerly funded, but it would take blind faith in conspiracy theory to attribute that decision to an elite acting against the expressed wishes of the American people. In the end, Model Cities was

---

2. Model Cities, which was administered by the U.S. Department of Housing and Urban Development, could logically be addressed in the next chapter, which discusses a number of War on Poverty programs outside the OEO. But Model Cities largely had the same programmatic and political goals as the CAP, and the symmetrical failures of the two programs are worth considering together.

neutered as a federal prod to local reform and its budget apportioned out to local governments as revenue enhancement through the Community Development Block Grant Program.

Model Cities outcomes are even more poorly informed and more weakly established than those of the OEO.[3] As with the CAP program, the typical evaluation of Model Cities was conducted by a partisan of the program or a beholden contractor, ignored issues of representativeness and sampling, relied on casual observations and interviews (most frequently unstructured), and rarely if ever assessed outcomes objectively and neutrally. All of the research was inferior to Vanecko (1969, 1970a) and Jacobs (1981), which were among the best of the CAP evaluations but still grossly inadequate.

Frieden and Kaplan (1975) do an estimable job of pulling the separate anecdotes together to make sense of Model Cities. They conclude that the program failed because of insensitive administration—"deeply ingrained ways of managing programs in Washington" (187)—and for lack of a national commitment to the program's goals. They make only passing reference to "the elusive public at large," as though the machinery of American democracy operated without mass participation or consent. However, their analysis is predicated on their own views of administration; their transitory comments about the quality of Model Cities programs offer little information about actual outcomes in the cities and the causes of those outcomes. At best, Frieden and Kaplan describe the adjustment of national political entities to their constituents' perceptions of priorities, a process that proceeded without much rational concern for programmatic success but with great attention to constituency preferences. Indeed, Vanecko extended this theme to local decision making and the obvious influence of mayors:

> The most important, clearest, and most confident conclusion we can draw is that mayors play a critical role in the initiation and expansion of urban renewal and public housing. . . . Constituency support, organizational strength, especially from political parties,

3. Cities, let alone larger entities such as metropolitan areas and states, cannot be randomized easily into control situations. The task of generating reliable comparison groups is treacherous. Even worse, HUD evaluation grants went to obedient consultant firms and dependent academics. At least in the OEO service programs, randomization was possible and longitudinal studies were conducted. The fact that those studies were butchered is another matter.

centralized influence, a controllable decision-making procedure, and support plus activity from the business leaders and other political actors all contribute to and provide conditions for the influence which is exerted by mayors in increasing the level of urban renewal output and the provision of low-cost public housing. (1970b, 255–56)

Yet this conclusion needs to be pushed back at least one step, to the legitimizing consent that local voters, and indeed local citizens, give to mayors and their immediate political partners. Both the national and the local decisions that determined the characteristics of the Model Cities program were probably driven by consistent citizen priorities represented by legitimately elected officials. That these decisions thwarted the progressive agenda in the implementation of Model Cities as well as the OEO programs does not change the perception of social decision making working through broad consent. It only emphasizes the deficiencies of American social welfare provisions.[4]

During the eight years of Model Cities' existence, Congress appropriated $23 million for planning activities, about $2.3 billion for operating expenses (including program funds), and about $400 million more for urban renewal projects—about 7 percent less than the amount authorized (Frieden and Kaplan 1975, 271). The total funds—about $2.75 billion of title II, part A, section 211 programs—have been insufficient to restore the sewer system in a single large American city. Still, the funding for planning and program start-up costs was certainly sufficient to stimulate a national appetite for far greater public expenditures, if in fact such an appetite existed. Apparently it did not, and local priorities remained inert and consistent throughout the nation's regional subcultures.

Coordination of services and agencies makes sense as more than a routine management task when large efficiencies of scale are possible, when competitive agencies are wasting funds or duplicating services for

---

4. Among the more extensive treatments of Model Cities, Kaitz and Hyman (1970), Gale (1995), and Haar (1975) go over the same territory as Frieden and Kaplan (1975) but with less depth, thoroughness, and knowledge of the available literature and far more partisan commitment. Unlike Frieden and Kaplan, and in the common pattern of the evaluations of the CAP and Model Cities, they generally have little concern for evidence beyond what they themselves provide, which is as scant and impressionistic as it is rare. Few if any of the huge number of publications that address the individual initiatives of local Model Cities programs are more than individual testimonials.

the same individuals, or when coordination can actually achieve important goals. None of these conditions pertained to poverty reduction during the War on Poverty. Poverty probably remains a structural problem requiring a substantial investment of money. Yet even if poverty were largely the result of deficient character, no intervention of welfare behaviorism has ever been demonstrated successfully, including the conservative's beloved idea of stern necessity and decades of experience with initiatives designed to coordinate existing services (Epstein 1997). Thus, even if poverty were the result of impaired character, coordination could not address it. Typically, grossly underfunded agencies provide piecemeal services to an overflowing pool of need. Coordination in this situation would assure comprehensive care to the few rather than desultory care to the many. The elegant possibilities of tipping points and thresholds for change have never been demonstrated.

During the Model Cities period, municipalities already had in place a variety of traditional coordinating functions and organizations, notably zoning agencies and planning boards. Some of these arrangements worked well; others did not. Model Cities added very little, never realizing Representative Wright Patman's tactful hopes for the legislation: "Programs to eradicate slums and to aid underprivileged citizens have achieved notable success in the past, but experience has shown that greater coordination is needed to obtain the maximum value for every dollar spent. Urban renewal cannot attain its full goal if we rehabilitate and improve the housing but the people who live in them still suffer the problems of poverty" (U.S. Congress, House 1966, 1). Similarly, Sundquist argued that "as early as 1966, it was apparent that the co-ordinating concept of community action had misfired, but the need was, if anything, even more compelling" (1969a, 46).

What evidence of success did Patman have? What was *apparent* after only two years, since Sundquist provides neither data nor references in his paper? In fact, Patman and Sundquist lacked the information to sustain their claims; rather, they reflected a political consensus, not a systematic and objective evaluation of strategies of coordination. The only thing apparent was a political agreement to perpetuate the illusion of coordination and thus accept standing social preferences rather than press the claims of unpopular American minorities.

Both the OEO and Model Cities advocated coordination, as though management technique, targeting efficiency, and an easy realignment of service priorities would be enough to address poverty. Their optimism recalls the fantasy of organizations like United Way and community planning councils that enduring social problems could be addressed by efficiency experts. However, the problem is not one of duplicated fund-raising staffs or even serious administrative redundancy but rather of inadequate resources that is perpetuated by the attachment of the American people to existing priorities. Except for the hope of developing a supportive constituency around the planning activities of both the CAP and Model Cities, the notion of coordination was probably disingenuous except as ceremony.

Coordination was not seen as a specific way to address need but was used as a totem for social efficiency—witness the insistence on inexpensive and socially compatible welfare interventions. Coordination has come to mean the desire to handle need through ceremonial services rather than with substantive attacks on inequality. The pantomimes of coordination animated both the OEO and Model Cities, even more so after they failed to develop support for expanded social welfare and urban renewal. The obstacle the programs faced was not one of coordination or even of involving the excluded but rather the satisfaction of the American people with things as they were.

The early split between the OEO and Model Cities over methods of reform strongly suggests a differentiation of role—an early warning of diversity's mischief—that Friedman (1977) has made much of. Blacks were allotted the diminished and increasingly marginal OEO service programs as patronage. The more serious attempt to develop support for urban renewal and poverty reduction came with Model Cities. The patronage of the OEO has lived on, but without any sweeping changes in American social welfare. Neither the CAP nor Model Cities could move the underlying American consensus to embrace greater equality.

From Cradle to Grave: The Service Component of the OEO

The principal goal of the OEO was to provide opportunities through social welfare services for the poor to rise out of poverty. Thus the effectiveness of those services stands as a direct evaluation of community action, the OEO, the War on Poverty generally, and perhaps too the rationality of social decision making. The OEO services, especially together with the War on Poverty programs in the other executive departments, appeared to cover the poor from cradle to grave with programs for preschoolers, young students, dropouts and prospective dropouts, workers, the elderly, and so on. If anything at all, the OEO's service programs constitute an encyclopedia of dead ends in social welfare and an American anthology of fables, myths, rituals, and common prayers.

The Job Corps

The Job Corps was reputedly the OEO's most successful program and probably the most expensive of the publicly funded manpower training programs. Yet even on its own terms, Job Corps outcomes were hit or miss at best. However, a more skeptical review of the best of the evaluative studies diminishes the program's modest achievements while greatly increasing its reported costs. An insistence on its positive effects, even its positive cost-benefit ratios, excuses the insufficiency of weak programs and obscures the reality of persistent and deep American social deprivation.

Reminiscent of the Civilian Conservation Corps and seemingly written into the legacy of the President's Commission on Juvenile Delinquency, the Job Corps was established to improve the labor market and social outcomes—notably higher wages, lower delinquency rates, and improved educational attainment—for "socially and economically disadvantaged out-of-school youth" between fourteen and twenty-one years of age and, with few exceptions, through residential training programs. Enrollees were typically poor, minority high school dropouts with deficient academic and vocational skills who were living in troubled communities and often troubled homes. The programs customarily provided remedial education, high school equivalency classes, vocational training, and health and counseling services. The typical six-month residential stay was assumed to be necessary in order to isolate the youth in a supportive environment away from the temptations of the streets. Costly environmental change for supposedly normal people, however brief, as a prerequisite of positive outcomes, defied the American insistence on socially efficient programs. It may have been the program's undoing.

With variations from year to year reflecting its changing budgets and popularity, the Job Corps typically served more than forty thousand youths per year in somewhat more than sixty centers. The majority of the centers were run by contract agencies, but many were run directly by federal agencies. In addition to the residential and service costs, the federal agencies also wrote contracts for recruitment, evaluation, and a variety of other administrative tasks. The cost estimates rarely included any of these associated costs and never included the costs of federal administration.

The Job Corps design came from the grand assurances of the social sciences and helping professions that their special knowledge—opportunity theory—and practical wisdom regarding youth failure and delinquency justified specific short-term interventions. The package of services promised to produce positive outcomes. While costly, the program was far less expensive than the alternatives of either eradicating the youths' deprivations or attempting to prevent their problems by providing every American a decent life through the massive redistribution of resources. That is, the Job Corps promised to create acceptable benefits relative to program costs, denying the desirability of realigning contemporary class relations or restructuring social institutions, notably the marketplace, schools, housing, families, and the rest. The Job Corps was designed as a social adjunct for a presumably limited number of youths who had been unfortunately, if not unwittingly, neglected by their families, schools, and communities. The youths were seen as a small, special group that the society could easily afford to indulge, especially if their reformed attitudes and work habits would actually produce a net social gain. The Job Corps looked like an investment with a nearly assured payoff; it would pay for itself in the coin of egalitarian social harmony. However, the actual outcomes raised questions about the expertise of the program experts and about the intentions, although not the sophistication, of even the best of the program evaluations.

The only rigorous evaluation of the Job Corps (Maller et al. 1986), a $2 million effort, compared outcomes, over a four-year period, of a large 1977 sample of Job Corps members with a carefully matched comparison group. Its cost-benefit analysis apparently convinced a skeptical U.S. Congress to continue the program (Wholey 1986, 235). Maller et al. reported "noteworthy effects" in a number of areas.

> In terms of statistical significance and size, some of the most important impacts of Job Corps on the behavior of former participants (on a per-Corpsmember basis and including military jobs) are (1) an increase in employment of nearly four weeks per year, (2) an increase in earning of over $600 per year, (3) a very substantial increase in the probability of obtaining a high school diploma or its equivalent, (4) higher college attendance, (5) a decrease in high

school attendance associated with more high school degrees, (6) better health care with a reduction in serious health problems of over one week per year on average, (7) a reduction in the receipt of financial welfare assistance amounting to over two weeks per year on average, and (8) a reduction in the receipt of Unemployment Insurance of nearly one week per year. (273)

The cost-benefit analysis concluded that every dollar spent on Job Corps members produced a benefit of $1.46.

Yet many methodological ambiguities cloud the findings, raising questions about their meaning and value. To begin with, all of the positive findings seem rather smaller and less noteworthy than Maller et al. claim. Moreover, the increased employment of four weeks per year occurred during the second year after leaving the Job Corps; by the fourth year this had declined to only 1.35 weeks, about seven days of work. Yet Job Corps graduates were still not working much more than six months per year, and only about twenty-one hours per week, nor were they making much money. The advantage of $600 over the comparison group, even in 1977 dollars, was not substantial. In any event, the $600 difference, too, was a second-year finding that tailed off considerably in subsequent years. However, the tabulations of Maller et al. failed to indicate overall significant differences (and very few subgroup differences) in earnings after four years, at which time members of both groups were reportedly earning $4,106 per year (in 1977 dollars), about 25 percent over the poverty line for a single individual at the time. Not surprisingly, outcomes improved—noticeably so for program completers—when early Job Corps dropouts were excluded from the analysis.

The 27.5 percent increase in high school diplomas (but still only 70 percent of all registrants) four years after graduating from Job Corps was probably attributable to high school equivalency degrees, even then a weak factor for improving employment outcomes. At that time there were no other significant differences between controls and Job Corps graduates in any type of additional training; fewer than 2 percent of both groups were pursuing additional education or training. All the other touted differences were small and were given weight only by the cost-benefit analysis.

However, even these modest achievements are undercut by problems with Maller et al.'s methodologies. The evaluation did not employ a randomized design but rather a quasi-experimental matched-comparison procedure that was adjusted for measured and unmeasured differences by a series of intricate statistical controls. The appropriateness of those controls depends on an enormous number of a priori assumptions. The greatest concern was that the Job Corps enrollees were more motivated than the comparison group members. Even a slight bias for motivation could have created all of the positive findings, small though they were.[5]

More seriously, their crucial outcome data were usually drawn from the uncorroborated self-reports of the enrollees. The loss of data due to lost respondents and responses does not appear to have been a problem. However, the veracity of respondents may well have been a problem, with the relatively positive reports of Job Corps members reflecting a desire to compliment the program out of gratitude or exaggerate their progress out of pride. In contrast, the comparison group had less of an emotional stake, if any at all, in distorting their reports. A very small amount of response falsification would have created the positive findings.

The cost-benefit analysis reveals the greatest distortion of the Job Corps benefits. The total size of the Job Corps advantage was accounted for by extrapolating benefits for *forty-three years,* "the expected worklife of the average Corpsmember." This grandiose wishful thinking in itself defines the authors as biased rather than neutral evaluators, especially given that many of the positive effects faded over the four years of follow-up. The knowledge sufficient to project weak effects, or any effects for that matter, over a lifetime of work, especially for teenagers, simply does not exist. The authors might have taken the next step and extrapolated the benefits for the children and grandchildren of Job Corps graduates, making the program the most cost-beneficial program in the history of good works. Without the extrapolation, the cost-benefit advantage of the Job Corps program is reduced by 65 percent to a negligible 15 percent, and then presumably only in the first year after graduation. Moreover, if the benefits are exaggerated by a series of biases—response falsification on the surveys and differential motivation—then the program's costs were not offset by its benefits.

Worse yet, the costs that Maller et al. attribute to the program may be greatly understated for the years of their study as well as the years of the

5. The sensitivity analyses of Maller et al. (1986) demonstrated that the authors' corrections for measured and unmeasured differences, as well as other elements of their specifications, greatly increased positive effects, such as they were.

Job Corps program. The reported program cost per member of $5,070 in 1977 ($16,365 in 2005 dollars) included only direct expenditures on residential centers, failing to reflect contracts for supportive services such as evaluation (for Maller et al.'s study, for example) and recruitment. They also do not include the immense indirect costs of federal administration. The Job Corps' own earlier estimates of the direct residential center costs in 1974 were much higher, averaging about $6,790 ($26,898 in 2005 dollars) per Job Corps member, but, again, they did not reflect other program costs (Levitan 1969, 53). The cost of a Job Corps slot, the operative measure for a residential program, is about twice the cost per member, since the customary stay per member is about six months. In 2005 dollars, the true costs of a Job Corps slot easily exceeded the costs of bed and board in an intensive nursing care facility. In any event, including any of the higher cost estimates for direct care along with estimates of the indirect costs, while disregarding the extrapolations and perhaps even extrapolated harm, reduces Maller et al.'s cost-benefit ratio to the level of a programmatic fiasco.[6]

Curiously, the very weak earlier program evaluations, notably by Levitan and Johnston (1975), lacked comparison groups, independent measures, neutral evaluators, representative samples, and other basic elements of good research, but largely corroborated the small gains found by Maller et al. Levitan's endorsement of the Job Corps referenced services that the residential centers provided, e.g., immunizations, outpatient visits, job placement, and remedial reading. Levitan ignores his own evidence, however, concluding that the Job Corps, having grown "from fledgling black sheep to established manpower program," is worth the effort and cost: "While the achievements may be less than originally were envisioned, they are far more substantial than critics have charged. The effort has weathered its growing pains, cost overruns, congressional scrutiny, and administration opposition to become an ap-

---

6. Maller et al. also failed to consider the possible harm of the program itself. For example, in arguing for mainstream approaches (although still not pushing for basic institutional reform), Anderson concludes that "any program that identifies its clients as disadvantaged, poor achievers, vocationally oriented, 'low-track,' etc., may create additional problems for them. So long as the private attitudes of 'mainstream' citizens reinforce public behaviors in welfare-related training programs . . . it will be impossible to wage effective war on poverty. Disadvantaged youth should be integrated with general youth population[s]" (Anderson 1973, 15). In this regard, Job Corps centers may have been "punitive and discriminatory," at least insofar as participation branded a member as deficient or deviant in some respect. Perhaps some of the program's weak labor force effects were related to this kind of stigma.

parently permanent and surprisingly effective program seeking to help deficiently educated or unemployed and poor youths who are not served by any other program (103).

The eight-part National Job Corps Study (Schochet, Burghardt, and Glazerman 2001; Glazerman, Schochet, and Burghardt 2000; McConnell and Glazerman 2001; Johnson, Gritz, and Dugan 2000) represented an improvement over Maller et al. in one important respect. It employed a randomized design that controlled for selection bias by drawing its control and experimental groups from eligible Job Corps applicants. If not impeded by other methodological problems, its results would have credibly estimated the benefits of the Job Corps for enrollees and graduates. Unfortunately, it replicated all of Maller et al.'s other pitfalls and may have added an additional one or two of its own.

The eight-part study also found that the Job Corps program conferred palpable benefits on its members in the short run: increased income, more job placements, more subsequent education and training, less involvement with the law enforcement, corrections, and welfare systems, improvements in educational attainment and health, reduction in illicit drug use, and other gains (in particular, Schochet, Burghardt, and Glazerman 2001). During the fourth follow-up year, participants earned about 12 percent ($1,150) more than controls, which works out to a difference of only about $17 per week. While statistically significant, differences in the percentage of youths employed, percentage of weeks employed, and average number of hours worked per week were tiny. The nonresidential program showed similar results, indeed often larger gains than the residential program, although the two programs served different groups (Schochet, Burghardt, and Glazerman 2001).

Compared with the control group over the full four-year study period, Job Corps participants reported $460 less received in welfare payments and small health gains. During this period, 42 percent of participants, but 27 percent of controls, obtained a high school equivalency degree. In addition,

> about 33 percent of control group members were arrested during the 48-month follow-up period, compared to 29 percent of program group members . . . which translates to a 16 percent reduction in the arrest rate. . . .
>
> More than 25 percent of control group members were ever convicted during the follow-up period compared to 22 percent of pro-

gram group members. Similarly, Job Corps reduced the percentage incarcerated for convictions by 2 percentage points (from 18 to 16 percent) and the average time spent in jail by about six days.

Job Corps had no impacts on the self-reported use of tobacco, alcohol, and illegal drugs . . . no impact on fertility or custodial responsibility.

Job Corps provided participants with the instructional equivalent of one additional year in school. (Schochet, Burghardt, and Glazerman 2001, xlvi–xlix)

This emphasis on statistically significant but still insubstantial differences hints at the authors' desperation to justify the program. Literacy is a case in point. Out of five hundred possible points that measure literacy, Job Corps enrollees had scores around 250, which placed them in the second-lowest grouping. At the end of their educational training, they had gained fewer than five points in each of three areas measuring literacy: prose, document, and quantitative. The gains in two of the areas were statistically significant but obviously of little practical value. Still, the authors judged the literacy program a success.

Flawed findings like these exaggerate Job Corps benefits and diminish its costs. The evaluation built its house of cards on the stilts of interviews. Almost all of the outcome data were drawn from the uncorroborated self-reports of the youths in the program and control groups. Indeed, the bonds that developed between participants and the often caring Job Corps staff may well have motivated participants to underreport dysfunctional and antisocial behavior and exaggerate earnings, placements, and other tributes to the effectiveness of their Job Corps experience. Especially because nearly all of the gains of the Job Corps participants were very small, prudent researchers are obligated to make a great effort to assure the accuracy of their measurements. They must also take pains to demonstrate carefully that the Job Corps itself, rather than differential response falsification, produced the outcomes. These obligations were not met by the National Job Corps Study or by any previous evaluator on contract with the government agencies that administered the Job Corps.

The small gains within the study period do not translate into a positive cost-benefit ratio for the Job Corps program; its costs far outweigh the short-term benefits. Not to be deterred, however, the National Job

Corps Study, like Maller et al., extrapolated the benefits over a lifetime of work, forty years in this case. Of course they came up with a very high cost-benefit ratio—2.02—meaning that the Job Corps conferred more than $2 of benefits for every dollar of expenditure (McConnell and Glazerman 2001). While the cost-benefit gains over time only result from amortized costs, there are no credible data to suggest that the small programmatic benefits will endure over a lifetime of work. To the contrary, there is considerable evidence—Head Start, for example—that gains deteriorate after a very few years.

The very sophisticated evaluative research, employing a variety of complicated statistical controls and cost-benefit analyses, turned the program into an almost magical success. In addition to satisfying the demands of the U.S. Department of Labor for budget justifications— more gently referred to as "the latent conservative function of evaluation studies" (Carter 1971)—the research also protected the rational enterprise, such as it was. The Job Corps was presumably a rational expression of the new social science learning, and its evaluation boasted advanced rational techniques. Yet the evaluative commitments were fulfilled without consideration of just advocacy for the children at risk, that is, the Job Corps service population. A successful program ends the search for solutions; a failed program forces attention to alternative remedies.

Probably reflecting shifting public preferences—the decades-long backlash against the social commitments of the War on Poverty—more than any concern with the actual effectiveness of the program, the GAO and others picked up on many of the problems with the Job Corps. In fact, the GAO audits, detailing the consistent and willful exaggerations of both the Job Corps and the Department of Labor, describe the program outcomes more accurately than the interviews on which the evaluations relied.

> Two performance indicators that [the U.S. Department of] Labor uses to evaluate Job Corps' success are misleading, overstating the extent to which vocational training is completed and job placements are training-related. Labor reports that nationwide about 48 percent of all program participants complete their vocational training and that about 62 percent of the jobs obtained by program participants are related to the training they received. However, we found that nationally only about 14 percent of the program partici-

pants satisfied all their vocational training requirements and that about 41 percent of the reported training-related job placements at the five centers we visited were questionable. (U.S. GAO 1998, 11)

The same report also criticized the Department of Labor's sole-source contracting procedures, which funneled millions of noncompetitive training dollars to favored unions and large businesses, the very organizations that perpetrated the placement problems. It also detailed low post–Job Corps earnings, recruiting practices that benefit the Job Corps program rather than its enrollees, and enormous amounts of missing data and unverifiable claims, and it added the nugget that, "historically, about 70 percent of all youths who enter Job Corps do not graduate." Still, the Job Corps does not seem to confer much of an advantage even on its graduates: in 1976, four years after termination, 70 percent of graduates and 86 percent of nongraduates earned $5,000 or less in 1976 ($17,160 in 2005 dollars); 47 percent and 66 percent, respectively, earned $2,000 ($6,865 in 2005 dollars) or less (U.S. GAO 1998, 2).

"Do no harm" would seem to be an appropriate starting point for any program seeking to do good. There is little as dispiriting, enraging, and profoundly discouraging as being promised a job, training for it, and then being given the very position, flipping burgers, that the training was supposed to help you avoid. The subterfuge of the Job Corps program's false claims continues, as national policy, the broken promise of post–Civil War Reconstruction, the denial of the claims of ex-slaves to forty acres and a mule. It would take a poet's skill to convey the sting of abandonment, the curdling of hope, the shriveling of ambition and respect visited on vulnerable children when they find out that they have been processed. The cost-benefit analyses failed to deduct from their rosy forty-year estimates the emotional consequences of the scam of the Job Corps program. Frustrated rats often follow one of two paths, one into psychosis and the other into rage. Both paths, in human life, are very costly.

Yet the GAO audits conveyed a sense of the political climate of the Job Corps that their contractual evaluators failed to mention. It would be a mistake, however, to attribute the subterfuge solely to the imperative of organizations to protect themselves. Continually misleading reports from public agencies are accepted as socially provident; the culture is complicit in its own deception.

Over all of its years of existence, the Job Corps has not improved on its outcomes, though its costs remain high (although certainly lower than during its early years) and notably because of its weak performance. Indeed, the failures of dysfunctional youths are intractable within current social and programmatic arrangements. The defense of indefensible social welfare programs continues to raises questions about whether the needy are being used to perpetuate ineffective but socially efficient interventions. Without demonstrable benefits that carry over into employment, education, and health, the residential services surely could have been more effectively and efficiently provided in home communities. If programs as expensive as Job Corps fail, then concern should turn back to the nature of the problem itself and the possibility that isolated human capital programs of any intensity may be inadequate without more fundamental institutional reforms. Writing about black youth, Skinner concluded, "What is clear is that the near-exclusive emphasis on overcoming a supposed skills mismatch with human capital investments is misplaced. . . . A much stronger commitment among policymakers to pursuing full employment, funding long-deferred urban housing and infrastructural development, and combating racial discrimination in housing, hiring, and job ladders is urgently needed to ease the serious job plight of young black men in American cities" (1995, 63).

Job Corps' tepid environmental approach to handling the problems of youth—placing them in a situation outside their presumably dysfunctional communities—was still not a structural approach but rather a strategy to avoid reforming mainstream social institutions. The experience of the Job Corps recalls the failures of the California Youth Authority, similar diversion programs, Supported Work (another costly manpower program), and the host of failed attempts to handle problems of delinquency, poor education, and inadequate job training for deprived and troubled youths.

The Job Corps was cut back because of its outsized costs rather than its ineffectiveness. The money was not reinvested in other strategies and was certainly not increased for more serious attempts to solve these problems. Yet the program persisted, probably as patronage and social acquiescence but also, more tellingly, as symbolism, as a beautiful gesture toward helping troubled youth. Considered against the need for intensive job preparation and remedial education, however, the Job Corps is an empty promise. Measured against the structural reforms

that might give it reasonable standing—effective antidiscrimination policy and full employment—the Job Corps is actually misleading.

The Department of Labor protected its philanthropic efforts and purchased a bit of Ivy League respectability in its contracts with Mathematica, Inc. In the typical fashion of contract evaluation firms, Mathematica
produced evidence of worth. Carter's (1971) "latent conservative function
of evaluation studies" expressed itself in this case as the provision of
budget justifications that paid tribute to a princely funding agency. The
Mathematica studies, despite their mystifying sophistication, never
achieved objective truth; but then again the point was political not rational.

Upward Bound

Upward Bound is intended for a large pool of beneficiaries: low-income
students whose parents did not complete college and who are stuck in
poor schools themselves. "At least two-thirds of the students served by
each Upward Bound project must be both low-income and potential
first-generation college students; the remainder must meet one of these
criteria" (Myers and Schirm 1999). The logic of Upward Bound is simple enough: offer educational supports that encourage eligible high
school students to stay in school, graduate, and go on to complete college. To this end, Upward Bound enrolls high school students in academic, nonacademic, and what the program terms supplemental
services, that is, programs outside Upward Bound itself. The Upward
Bound services include enriched classes and tutoring during the school
year, intensive full-day academic programs during the summer, and cultural activities such as attendance at plays and museums throughout the
year. A student who enrolls in Upward Bound in ninth grade can spend
four years in the program. In 2001, a typical fiscal year, the average cost
for the 51,600 students enrolled in 727 programs was about $4,800 per
capita (Myers et al. 2004, 3).

Upward Bound engaged Mathematica, Inc. to conduct an evaluation
of program outcomes between 1992 and 1999.[7] The unusually rigorous

7. The earlier evaluations are too weak to consider in this study, except, again, as the
commercial ventures of profit-seeking consulting firms. The review of the literature by Myers
and Schirm (1999) identifies only surveys of participants and case studies. Indeed, Upward
Bound has been operating for so long that the evaluation of its experience during the 1990s
probably applies to the rest of its history as well, that is, as a program lacking any demonstrable effect. Upward Bound was administered by the U.S. Department of Education at the time
of the Mathematica study, but it was initially housed in the OEO.

design included the randomization of 2,800 eligible students who applied for the Upward Bound program at a nationally representative sample of sixty-seven Upward Bound sites. These students were assigned to either a control group that was not allowed to enroll in Upward Bound or to an experimental group that was invited to participate. Data were obtained periodically from the students, their schools, and the Upward Bound projects. The median duration of participation in the program was nineteen months and ranged from a few months to more than three years.

Mathematica, Inc. puts the best face possible on very unimpressive Upward Bound outcomes. The big victory—progress for the least aspiring, defined as educational expectations for less than a bachelor's degree—is hardly worth celebrating: for students "who expected to complete less than a bachelor's degree (only about 20 percent of eligible applicants) . . . Upward Bound raised the average number of high school credits earned from 19 credits to 21 credits . . . , the equivalent of two more high school courses that they would not have earned in the absence of the program" (Myers et al. 2004, 25).

For the 80 percent of eligible applicants with high expectations for attending college, Upward Bound had no effect on students' grade point average or the number of credits they achieved. "However, Upward Bound increased the dropout rate for these students from 4 percent to 7 percent" (28). For higher-risk students, defined as in the bottom 20 percent of ninth-grade academic achievement, Upward Bound "slightly increased the number of credits earned in certain core subjects" (28).

Upward Bound apparently failed in its promise to increase postsecondary enrollment and academic performance. Seventy-four percent of Upward Bound students and 71 percent of students in the control group attended a postsecondary institution. There was no statistically significant difference between the groups in terms of attending four-year colleges and universities or in the total number of earned credits. This very high rate of continuation to postsecondary education in both groups suggests that Upward Bound is "creaming" students—enrolling the naturally successful—rather than targeting challenged students. Students who seek enrollment in Upward Bound—the members of both study groups—may not be very troubled but rather a motivated group of youths. Both groups absorbed a considerable amount of educational and other services (see for example Myers et al. 2004, 21–23). A greater percentage of control students than Upward Bound students consistently sought out supplemental services (23). Still, Upward Bound services appear to be more intensive than the services that control students sought out.[8]

However, Upward Bound substantially improved the enrollment of lower-expectation students in four-year institutions (from 18 to 38 percent) and the number of their earned credits (from eleven to twenty-two). Yet the program had no effect on subgroups defined by academic risk and no substantial effect on most other subgroups, except for the perverse finding that Upward Bound "reduced postsecondary enrollment from 80 percent to 73 percent" among students who met only the single eligibility criterion of being children of parents who had not graduated from college (41).[9]

The program increased postsecondary enrollment for white students from 58 percent to 69 percent and for Hispanic students from 38 percent to 50 percent. More than 75 percent of black students in both the control group and Upward Bound went on to college. The program had no effect on the number of credits earned in postsecondary education for white and black students, although the Hispanic Upward Bound students increased their earned credits in all postsecondary institutions from thirty to thirty-eight.

Upward Bound attempted to improve the engagement of students in postsecondary education, the assumption being that students who involve themselves in academic culture are more likely to complete their

8. As evidence for the greater intensity of Upward Bound, Myers et al. (2004) present only the budget of Upward Bound, which is larger than that of other programs, rather than any direct observation of the services themselves.

9. Myers et al. concede the likelihood that some study participants "reported attending postsecondary institutions that they never actually attended" (2004, 32). The misreporting may even have been biased toward Upward Bound students who felt a duty to sustain the program by reporting more favorable outcomes than actually occurred. Mathematica attempted to check the accuracy of student reports by asking the college for transcripts. There was apparently considerable misreporting and even some evidence of bias, including errors from Upward Bound students—the two-percentage-point difference for lower-expectation students who reported attendance at four-year colleges (table III.3 vs. table III.4, as one of several examples). The misreporting consistently reduced the reported benefits of Upward Bound but did not substantially affect the findings. It is noteworthy that Mathematica employs a very convenient 0.1 threshold of statistical significance—in Mathematica's terms, this is the line between strong and weak evidence. Employing more rigorous thresholds, one-tail tests of significance rather than two-tail tests, and verified data rather than self-reports, would probably wipe out most of the findings, such as they are. The Mathematica study can be read as an instance of masterly temporizing, targeted at once to the savvy reader, the credulous program administration, and, most tellingly, an open political system capable of reading what it wishes into the results.

degrees than those who do not. However, very few students reported participation in academic counseling, personal counseling, learning skills center services, tutoring, minority student services, health services, or other student support services. Similarly small percentages of students, frequently less than 2 percent, engaged in informal academic activities such as talking with faculty about academic matters or plans, participating in study groups, attending supplementary lectures, taking part in intramural sports, music, drama, and so on. Fifty-five percent of students received financial aid.[10]

Only about 40 percent of Upward Bound students completed the program, that is, graduated from high school (Myers et al. 2004, 60). Following a sophisticated analysis, Myers et al. arrive at the expected conclusion that "keeping students in Upward Bound for longer periods may substantially improve their postsecondary outcomes" (59). An additional year of participation for students who dropped out of the program before completing two years would apparently raise their postsecondary enrollment by as much as 9 percent. For those who did not complete the program, completion would raise their postsecondary enrollment by as much as 17 percent and their postsecondary credits by a full college term. However, these findings depend on two fragile assumptions: that the program could maintain dropouts until graduation and that those prevented from dropping out would perform as well as those who have already completed the program. Both assumptions were contradicted in the operation of the program itself.

The recommendation to increase the duration of Upward Bound boils down to the hope that more education will produce more educated people. However, it does not deal with the actual problems of delivering meaningful education to reluctant or unmotivated students or to those with substantial economic, medical, social, or psychological barriers to succeeding in school. The authors offer a delicate caution that their analysis "may overstate the true effects due to selection bias" (59). In light of the considerable attrition (probably of the troubled), the motivation of students, apparently unaffected by Upward Bound services, may account for all of the Upward Bound achievements, modest as they were. There is no credible way to adjust for selection bias. The study's process of

10. Apparently many students, presumably in the eligibility category of first-generation college students, were not eligible for financial assistance, further underscoring the mistargeting of the program.

statistical matching attempts to construct similar groups of students differing only in their participation in Upward Bound, in order to assess the degree to which greater participation would confer added benefits. However, statistical matching is not randomization and thus cannot assure comparability. Any conclusion derived from the statistical matching procedure is at best speculative. The study also misleads by suggesting, even after a generally thorough demonstration of the program's ineffectiveness, that Upward Bound might well be able to confer greater benefits if subtle shifts in administrative policy were made.

Students with a desire to do well in school and with families who encourage them will seek out educational assistance of all sorts. Simply comparing those who dropped out of Upward Bound with those who did not—even through matching groups statistically—says little about the nature of schooling for young people and even less about how to remedy the problem, which cannot be solved by tinkering with curricula or staff and is more probably related to low family income and other situational barriers to academic success, notably the quality of the schools themselves.

Upward Bound apparently provides little if any added value, duplicating existing services—the "service rich environment" of the authors' imagination (10)—for students who are already motivated. The bigger problem remains with the unmotivated, the beleaguered, and with school systems incapable of providing adequate education. Rather than a small enriched program for the few, the need persists to serve many millions.

The outcomes of Upward Bound are so dubious and its mistargeting so obvious that they suggest the possibility that the program is more about patronage than it is education. Indeed, the study provides virtually no description of the quality of staff or of the programs themselves: "Project staff generally hold a bachelor's or graduate degree. Many staff are from the same racial/ethnic group as the majority of their participants, which was often noted by project staff and others as important since staff members become role models for the students" (Myers and Schirm 1999). Yet there was apparently no need for mentoring, while the staff apparently failed to improve education outcomes generally.

Perhaps redirecting the $4,000 per capita annual program costs to abating the poverty of students or their families would have gone further to improve educational performance than funneling the money through Upward Bound's staff and faculty. In serving only 56,000 largely unimperiled students each year, the ritual of Upward Bound obscures the much more costly relationship between educational failure and insufficient family income. Upward Bound is a political compromise that registers a frigid point on the thermometer of the nation's concern for poorer and lower-status Americans.

Upward Bound, like many other empty displays of philanthropic concern, is only *associated* with positive outcomes rather than shown to be the cause of these outcomes. Small pots of charitable largesse are forever in pursuit of "programs that work" (the Russell Sage Foundation's encomium to the charitable imagination). Many philanthropic foundations find great comfort and protection in funding the already successful rather than taking risks to create new successes; the Ford Foundation's Gray Areas success in New Haven is typical. In fact, social welfare project grants are usually little more than an occasion for award ceremonies, Adam Smith's pageants for the masses. It speaks volumes about the nation's indifference to inequality and lack of opportunity that a program designed as an antipoverty strategy ends up so tenuously connected to the basic problem.

Head Start

Head Start reprises the experience of Job Corps and Upward Bound for another service population, disadvantaged preschoolers. It was also created to achieve a host of tangible benefits in health and nutrition as well as intangible benefits such as social skills and self-esteem. As expected, compared with all children, Head Start enrollees live in much poorer families and have mothers and grandmothers with lower educational attainment; however, the educational attainment of black Head Start mothers is greater than that of white Head Start mothers, although their family income is lower (Currie and Thomas 1995, table 2). The program was intended in the first instance to give poor children a leg up on education.

Head Start services are delivered in school-year segments that often last through the summer; the early summer-only programs were discontinued. In fiscal year 2006, Head Start served a few more than 900,000 preschoolers, largely three and four years of age, with an annual budget slightly below $7 billion, for an average expenditure of about $7,200 per child (U.S. Department of Health and Human Services 2006, passim). The program is delivered through almost twenty thousand centers.

As early as 1969 there were signs that the program was not succeeding, at least as measured by academic and affective development. That
year a Westinghouse study found that

> (1) Summer programs are ineffective in producing lasting gains
> in affective and cognitive development, (2) full-year programs are
> ineffective in aiding affective development and only marginally ef-
> fective in producing lasting cognitive gains, (3) all Head Start chil-
> dren are still considerably below national norms on tests of
> language development and scholastic achievement, while school
> readiness at grade one approaches the national norm, and (4) par-
> ents of Head Start children voiced strong approval of the program.
> Thus, while full-year Head Start is somewhat superior to summer
> Head Start, neither could be described as satisfactory. Further re-
> search aimed at the development of an effective preschool program
> is recommended. (Westinghouse Learning Corporation 1969)

The few small gains that Westinghouse attributed to Head Start apparently wore off after a few years of grade school.

The Westinghouse authors appeared uncomfortable with their own
findings. Citing their study's narrow focus and weak design—it lacked
randomized groups, among other problems—the authors offered an ir-
refutable series of alternative explanations that minimized the plausibility of their findings. These explanations have been portals onto the
terrain of political ambiguity, offering critics and partisans alike the freedom to advance their sectarian interpretations.

Nevertheless, the "fadeout phenomenon" has been broadly corroborated and widely accepted as fact. The most rigorous studies since Westinghouse have not changed the basic conclusions. In an analysis of
existing longitudinal survey data, Currie and Thomas (1995) replicated
the fadeout effect for black children, although not for white children,
whose gains seemed to be realized in the form of lower grade-repetition
rates and eventually fewer high school dropouts. The initial academic
gains measured on one test closed more than one-third of the gap between white Head Start enrollees and more privileged children. They
concluded that Head Start is worth its costs for white students.

When it came to black children, by contrast, Currie and Thomas
found that "the results for African-American children suggest that the
primary long-term benefits of Head Start are in terms of access to health

care. Hence, it is appropriate to compare Head Start's price tag . . . to the estimate for health services delivered [outside Head Start]. This comparison suggests that when viewed strictly in terms of lasting benefits provided to children, Head Start programs serving African-American children are not cost-effective" (361).

Yet the few positive findings occurred in a study that once again lacked a randomized design and that used data largely from self-reports. While sophisticated, the study also makes many assumptions that are not easily verified. The study's principal comparisons are drawn between siblings, those who attended Head Start and those who did not, a procedure designed to control for selection bias. In the end, however, the possibility of selection bias—a group of Head Start children who are not comparable to their siblings—may still account for findings in a study that lacks randomization. It is also possible that white children who attended Head Start had more motivated parents and lived in more favorable circumstances than black children who attended Head Start, even to the point that those white children were favored more than their siblings. This possibility is about as speculative as the assumptions that inform the study itself.

In a similar study of a different panel of respondents, Garces, Thomas, and Currie (2002) attempted to follow Head Start graduates into adulthood. Their findings seemed to be extensions of the earlier study: the benefits accrued largely to whites in terms of high school completion, college attendance, and earnings, and to blacks in terms of lower rates of being arrested or charged with a crime. However, the study shares the same problems that plague Currie and Thomas (1995)—the lack of a randomized design and a persistent question about selection bias, especially for whites.

Congress mandated the most recent and perhaps the largest study of Head Start to date—the *Head Start Impact Study*—which did in fact incorporate a randomized design (U.S. Department of Health and Human Services 2005). It also made more extensive measurements of outcomes than any previous Head Start evaluation. The study holds up well to scrutiny of its methods; response rates were higher than 80 percent, randomization succeeded, control and Head Start groups were comparable, and the analysis employed standard significance levels. After one year of Head Start, three-year-olds consistently gained more ground than four-year-olds, but even their progress was very modest and inconsistent. The largest gains, in parent-reported literacy skills, were perhaps the least meaningful of the study's measures. Access to dental care similarly improved. In both cases the effect size was only .34 (an advantage of only 13 percent for Head Start children). The typical effect size was well below .2 (a maximum advantage of less than 6 percent for Head Start children). About half of the measures for three-year-olds and about one-fifth of the measures for four-year-olds showed gains for Head Start children over controls. Yet the gains were so small that subtle biases in measurement, such as the apparent absence of raters who were blind to the conditions of subjects, could well account for them. It is hardly surprising that such small advantages evaporate after leaving the nurturing arms of Head Start (an observation given considerable credence by Lee et al. 1990; Lee and Loeb 1995; Currie and Thomas 2000).

The quality of Head Start programs has been criticized consistently. Yet the *Head Start Impact Study*'s small advantages for Head Start children cannot be attributed to deficient programs. The study's comparison of the quality of Head Start programs themselves with a variety of others consistently favored the Head Start program, although lead teachers in Head Start were rated about the same as their counterparts outside Head Start.[11] Achieving parity for disadvantaged children will apparently take more than one year of intensive preschool.

The general conclusion that Head Start confers only small immediate gains—a conclusion notably buttressed by the *Head Start Impact Study*—and few if any lasting advantages is generally corroborated throughout the empirical literature, although that literature is beset by methodological problems that tend to overstate the program's reported advantages (for examples of the better research see McKey et al. 1985; Oden, Schweinhart, and Weikart 2000; Bentler and Woodward 1978; Zill et al. 2001).

There would be little controversy over the value of the program if it

11. Nevertheless, the poor quality of staff and services is one of the persistent explanations for the failure of Head Start and of preschool and child daycare generally. The Head Start Bureau's own report to Congress documents an immense amount of noncompliance with federal standards. For example, of the grantees that went through performance reviews in fiscal years 2001 through 2004, 93 percent were in noncompliance with standards: 60 percent out of compliance with prevention and early-intervention programs, 42 percent with program governance, 32 percent with recordkeeping and reporting, 56 percent with fiscal management, 37 percent with monitoring, 52 percent with human resources, and so forth (U.S. Department of Health and Human Services 2004, 21). However, the reported progress in these few years seems so great—noncompliance of grantees reduced from 93 percent to 16 percent—as to raise questions about the review process rather than about the actual amount of noncompliance (13).

were not for the promise of social efficiency that justified Head Start to begin with and continues to this day. Head Start was created to provide more than enriched day care. Clearly, poor children were expected to benefit mightily from a year or two of preschool, catching up with their more privileged peers and establishing a platform for future educational and economic success, improving their nutrition and health care, and enjoying a variety of intangible benefits. All of the program's goals were expected to be achieved at a very modest price, preempting the immense costs required to replicate the physical and cultural situations of middle-class children. Thus, while the program's incapacity in education seems to be a settled issue, Head Start continues to be justified for its secondary goals. Yet, aside from some reported success in health care and nutrition (although, as above, at excessive cost), few if any of the ancillary benefits have been credibly established.

The extensive organizational constituency supporting Head Start, composed of education professionals, child development experts, program employees, schools of education, departments of psychology, interdisciplinary programs in child development and their unions, professional societies, and advocacy organizations, are loath to admit the futility of Head Start. Rather than a special interest that subverts the national will, however, educational organizations embody the national mandate for socially efficient programs. The nation accepts Head Start as it is—unsuccessful but in pursuit of remedies for poverty that entail only a narrow programmatic strategy attending to a relatively small number of children with inexpensive interventions.

Head Start has always promised unrealistic benefits, especially in light of the deprivations of its target population. The program embodies a romantic quest for a modest extension of the existing structures of schools and clinics to compensate for the serious deprivations of American inequality. Yet the fundamental strategy of Head Start—to attend only to the child[12]—may be futile at any level of intensity unless the harder and far more costly work is done of repairing families and eradicating the social environment of poverty. Still, even on its own terms, Head Start meets relatively little of the nation's need for enriched day care and preschool education; many millions of children are ineligible

12. Staff members also work with parents, but only to handle the education-related issues of the child rather than to provide assistance to the family itself. Remedying the material or cultural deprivations of the family is not part of the Head Start mandate.

for Head Start, yet their parents cannot afford comparable programs, even while Head Start provides only a bit of temporary and partial access to the social and educational advantages of more privileged children. The insights of the experts say more about political conditions than about the conditions of poorer and low-status Americans.[13]

The proponents of Head Start cannot simply be dismissed as well-meaning but uninformed partisans. Loyalty to the program rather than attention to the broader problems of inequality maroons Head Start within the careerist ambitions of the intellectual community and the divided politics of child development. The issue is shared citizenship, not rates of preschool progress. The notion of social competence as a discrete product of socially efficient interventions that sustained the advocates of Head Start is more imagined than real and is doomed by its own parsimony. Breaking social competence down to its components, and even softening the emphasis on IQ as a criterion of success, is misleading.

Health, intellectual ability, social and emotional development, family involvement, and community change cannot be delivered cheaply to people deprived of the essential social conditions that make these goods possible. Programs such as Head Start cannot and certainly do not replicate advantageous social conditions. Apart from cognitive development, the factors that are "known to be so important in determining everyday adjustment and competence" (Zigler and Valentine 1979, 503) have not been delivered by planned, discrete, and inexpensive social interventions. The pursuit of cold fusion in social welfare, that is, social efficiency, is a ritual of obeisance to cultural preferences. To insist that Head Start is making advances on any of these criteria, and, further, that its small, partial victories contribute to the broader goals of citizenship, is, at best, to capitulate to the political and social logic that limits Head Start to the few.[14]

As with Job Corps, Head Start isolates poor children from mainstream populations, an inevitable effect of tight eligibility criteria. Narrowly categorical programs like Head Start misrepresent the nature of

13. The extension of Head Start in 1995 to even younger populations seems to be more successful, at least in terms of immediate gains. But the relative success of Early Head Start may be the result of younger children's greater impressionability. The real test lies in whether the gains persist through grade school and beyond.

14. This paragraph is intended as a response to Zigler's thoughtful conclusion in Zigler and Valentine (1979).

need in the United States; they suggest that broad problems like poverty can be addressed by discrete programs. But the vital role of such programs ritualizes the underlying American value that creates an underclass of deviant and undeserving citizens. The intense attention of Head Start, and of the War on Poverty itself, to a relatively small number of poor people, as though their hardships were unique in American society, obscures the widespread difficulties of lower-income and lower-status citizens in raising their kids. More important, the isolating strategy of service realizes American priorities that are largely unconcerned with the possible harm to the individual and the society of targeted, categorical programs.

The Other Services

The other OEO programs were relatively small and starved of funds. They were even more inadequately evaluated than Job Corps, Head Start, and Upward Bound; only a rare study here and there attempted a systematic national assessment of outcomes, and these few attempts were seriously compromised by methodological flaws and interpretive enthusiasm. The typical evaluation was a case study. Attempts to arrive at national conclusions usually put together a few local case studies. Nonetheless, the central theme of ineffectiveness persists throughout. Indeed, it would be surprising if any of these ill-conceived, weakly staffed, poorly administered, desultory and underfinanced programs were able to steal a march on the serious problems that they were chartered to address. Moreover, the volunteer programs funded under the OEO—notably VISTA—seemed to replicate the charitable imperatives of the private sector and its faith that the good heart was a sufficient response to material want. The utter inadequacy of these efforts to address poverty suggests the programs' central message: the onus for financial independence and good citizenship rests on the shoulders of the individual; the society bears little responsibility for personal failure.

Denied the resources to tackle poverty, the programs performed only cultural ceremonies—little life-arc melodramas of social realism that subtly cast the poor as willful failures. With perhaps the exception of the early Legal Services program and occasional efforts by the CAAs, the OEO programs attended, with the inescapable aroma of personal blame, to the deficits of the poor themselves. In contrast, the structural weaknesses of the society that produced those deficits in the first place, and

continued to sustain them, were consistently ignored. The institutionalized preferences of the American people and their sense of citizenship,
largely shared by rich and poor alike, precede ratification by public policy, manipulation by so-called interest groups, and control by the powerful. Indeed, they determine all three.

The Neighborhood Youth Corps was established to address the problem of high school dropouts and the related problem of employment for
disadvantaged youth. An "in-school" Neighborhood Youth Corps was
created to address the dropout problem, and an "out-of-school" version
pursued youth employment. The programs were administered through
a multitude of local contractors that delivered an enormous range of
services—counseling, job training, job preparation, tutoring, and the
like. Some of the programs were intense and well run; others were decidedly not. Both the in-school and out-of-school approaches failed. The
Neighborhood Youth Corps apparently neither reduced the rate of premature high school termination nor improved youth employment. A
survey of program directors concluded that the in-school program
reached only about 9 percent of eligible youth, many of whom were
apparently creamed from the applicant pool: "Rather than looking at
NYC as a program which is to serve the most needy youth, many local
programs are viewing it as a vehicle for rewarding the disadvantaged,
but academically successful youth" (Ozgediz 1973, 19). Many of the programs ignored the most basic elements of program management: about
60 percent of program directors made only informal assessments of
enrollees; "58% of the directors responded that they did not develop
school work plans, but they were aware of the needs of each enrollee"
(19, 20).

The work placements were suspect. Most of the employers were the
schools themselves, while "approximately 80% of the job titles held by
the enrollees fell into custodial, maintenance, janitorial, clerical, library,
and museum aide categories" (Ozgediz 1973, 23). Services were spotty:
only about half of the students identified as needing remedial education
received it; only about 60 percent received health examinations, and
only about half of those who needed subsequent care received it. Follow-
up was lax; counseling was sporadic. The author concluded that "standards for judging the performance of the local programs have never
been developed . . . [and] . . . alternative methods for implementing
modular activities have never been systematically communicated to local
programs" (36). Nevertheless, the ever-cautious contract evaluator

warned that "the suggestions we have made above should not be construed as implying that In-School NYC, as a youth manpower program, has been totally ineffective. We have no empirical evidence to reach such a conclusion" (36). And yet, discounting this devastating portrait of the program even more, given the biases of the reporting program directors and the obvious attempt of the authors to soften it, "totally ineffective" seems to be just about right, a conclusion generally sustained by other studies.

The GAO found that only about 29 percent of out-of-school enrollees who left the program had met program objectives (U.S. Comptroller General 1974); but its study lacked the ability to estimate whether the program or the enrollee was the cause of the success. That is, without at least comparison groups of similar youth who did not enroll in the program, it is impossible to estimate its effectiveness. Ellard (1974) reports "good work adjustment" for only 10 percent of Neighborhood Youth Corps graduates (69).

Walther and Magnusson (1975) found no significant differences in employment outcomes among redesigned out-of-school Neighborhood Youth Corps programs, the customary programs, and a comparison group that was never enrolled in the Neighborhood Youth Corps. In a truly curious interpretation, the authors attribute the failure of the redesigned program to its being overloaded with "poorly motivated and underachieving trainees" (25)—that is, the program's primary target group.

Somers and Stromsdorfer (1970) undermine their conclusion that the program was cost-effective with their weak methodology and with data that actually demonstrated the program's ineffectiveness. It did not increase educational attainment and only increased income from work by a very small amount. This study assesses the very early program and takes advantage of demonstration effects. But, more problematic, there is no randomized comparison group, and the findings, such as they are, are quite likely the result of self-selection: the Neighborhood Youth Corps enrollees, having made the effort to seek out the program, were more motivated than the comparison group. The problem of creaming intrudes here again. Small, incidental gains that are more probably the result of imperfections in study methodology than of the programs themselves run through the history of manpower programs for the poor, reducing modest success to frank failure time and again.

The remaining programs established through the Economic Opportunity Act of 1964 account for a very small portion of War on Poverty expenditures and only a tiny fraction of the federal budget. Taken together, Legal Services, Volunteers in Service to America (VISTA), Work Study, Foster Grandparents, Operation Mainstream, programs for migrants, the seventy OEO health centers, New Careers, Adult Basic Education, rural loans, and small business loans consumed about $321 million, only a bit less than 6 percent of the War on Poverty's total budget of about $5.6 billion for the four fiscal years from 1964 to 1968. VISTA and rural loans accounted for about 54 percent of the $321 million (U.S. Census Bureau 1968, 330). The War on Poverty budget itself was typically less than 1 percent of total federal expenditures.

These programs were largely unevaluated. Occasionally a small political division, such as a city, assessed the outcomes of a particular program. Customarily these studies were poorly designed and anecdotal, relying exclusively on interviews. Many were intended simply as program advertisements. Nevertheless, within the severe limitations of their funding, Legal Services and Work Study are probably the only OEO programs that were even marginally successful. Some people who needed lawyers received legal help, apparently from a competent group of lawyers, or at least as competent as the general pool of lawyers (Erlanger 1978). Unfortunately, the program was severely underfunded. In turn, poor college students received some financial assistance, but again, very little. A few of the programs, such as Work Study and Operation Mainstream, continued past the War on Poverty but in different forms and with changed goals; their budgets remained inadequate. The tiny amounts allocated to these programs could not under the best of conditions make even a scratch on the enormity of poverty.

Interpreting the Outcomes

It might appear that the OEO's direct service programs covered the whole range of poverty needs—from preschool through retirement, including attention to employment and illness, in urban areas and in rural areas. However, narrow coverage, inadequate funding, untrained and frequently unmotivated staffs, and inappropriate strategies of service go far to explain their nearly uniform failure. In fact, the programs were so superficial as to play only a ceremonial role, belying any serious intent to address the deprivations of poor people in the United States. While

ritualizing the American demand for self-invention and personal responsibility, the programs operated as a spoils system for staff. The
function of the OEO as patronage has been suggested by such disparate
critics as the self-styled revolutionary Saul Alinsky (1968) and Stanford
University Law School professor Lawrence Friedman (1977). Yet it would
be a mistake to assume that the OEO was designed as patronage. It
seems more likely that in reaction to the antagonism of the American
public toward deeply redistributive entitlement programs, and given the
failure to mobilize a sizeable constituency for reform, a payoff to black
activists was probably expedient and resided comfortably within the
American political tradition.

As public social welfare, the OEO and the War on Poverty generally
look quite shabby alongside the provisions of the GI bill after World War
II. At a minimum, the different status of the two beneficiary groups—
the poor being objects of contempt and the veterans, heroes—predicted
different treatment. The poor were preached to; the veterans were
funded.

The precursors, the OEO programs, and the War on Poverty itself
were events in the long dispute over the determinants of public and
social decision making. The conventional histories of the period discuss
the dispute between Moynihan's *Maximum Feasible Misunderstanding*
(1969) and Piven and Cloward's *Regulating the Poor* (1971) as if their
declamations were somehow central to the policy outcomes of the period. Moynihan attributed the mess over local control—the issue of the
participation of the poor and thus the direction of the poverty program—to government confusion. The confusion was the result of unfortunate disciplinary commitments: "Just possibly one reason [for
ignoring good sense in policy was] that the key decisions in the White
House and the Executive Office of the president were made by lawyers
and economists. None was especially familiar with the social science
theory on which the various positions were based and, if an impression
may be permitted, few were temperamentally attuned to the frame of
mind of the reformers. Very possibly, a matter of professional style is
involved here" (Moynihan 1969, 169).

Moynihan's central point was that "*the government did not know what
it was doing*" because it did not heed the counsel of social science (170,
emphasis in original). There was not a whiff of doubt in the book that
that counsel was about as empty as the advice taken for convenience. In

any event, Moynihan concludes by expressing his doubt about the ability of the social sciences to invent solutions for social problems.

Moynihan's book and its arguments assume a peculiar narrative of well-meaning democracy. Concerned lawmakers look for sage advice in resolving socially disruptive issues. Therefore, the problem of the OEO programs was simply their naivete, not their intent: "The failure of the social scientists, the foundation executives, the government officials lay in not accepting—not insisting upon—the theoretical nature of their proposition. . . . To proceed as if that which only *might* be so, in fact was so, was to misuse social science" (189). Apparently, for Moynihan, at the time loyal to his professorial position in political science at Harvard and the lofty commitment of that institution to Enlightenment rectitude, democratic policy pursues rationality, a commodity enhanced by appropriately credentialed social scientists. Quite in line with the national reaction against the civil disturbances of the 1960s, Moynihan argued for the legitimacy of the existing decision-making process on grounds that went beyond electoral legitimacy. He argued that the severe limitations placed on the participation of the poor in 1967 appropriately reinforced the common consensus and that the common consensus was appropriate. Quite subtly, Moynihan was arguing for the legitimacy of existing elites, and his final comments, which limit social science to the measurement of policy outcomes, went far to justify his new allegiance.

The theme of failed administration, a variation on the autonomy of the state actor, is often picked up in the histories. Moynihan claimed that President Johnson wasted the opportunity to institute permanent welfare reform—full employment and a floor under income—on the personal service programs of the War on Poverty. For his part, Patterson (1981), in enumerating the problems of the early OEO and the War on Poverty, gives prominence to the futility of local assaults on national problems, conceptual confusion, an undue urban emphasis and bureaucratic bungling (notably Shriver's) that may partially explain the inadequacy of the program budgets.[15] The emphasis on bungling and bad information seems to suggest that if program strategy had been better informed and better handled, the War on Poverty might have succeeded better. The possibility that the War on Poverty's demise was written into the culture itself is given little attention and even less credence. The

15. Similar themes dominate Plotnick and Skidmore (1975), Haveman (1977), Katz (1986), Trattner (1994), and others.

administrative confusion, notably over the participation of the poor, is depicted simply as the ambiguity that necessarily attends the process of political clarification.

Piven and Cloward's *Regulating the Poor* was a classic example of elite conspiracy theory and journalistic scholarship and became an activist best-seller for decades. These tenured radicals argued that policymaking in America had been usurped through coercion, exclusion, and expropriation by self-serving controlling forces—classic power elites that were never specifically named. Their sense of these elites is quite subtle; they are not so crass as to name WASPs, the bourgeoisie, capitalists, or running dogs as the villains but only suggest vague, dark forces that presumably include capitalists and unnamed entrenched interests. The goal of these illegitimate elites is to manipulate welfare policies so as to regulate and control the poor and workers.

Regulating the Poor initially introduces a broad consensus of "the larger economic and political order" as determinative in social policymaking, but then goes on to detail the many ways in which workers and the poor have been unfairly excluded from social influence and the electoral franchise by a small controlling elite rather than by dint of broadly accepted cultural preferences. As a result, a great number of the excluded are in need, and they represent a large constituency for redistributive public welfare policies.

Based on the timing of civil unrest and changes in welfare policy, Piven and Cloward's historical analysis led them to argue for the tactical virtues of mass mobilization, that is, protest movements. Pointing to the association of rising welfare rolls and the turmoil of the 1960s, among many other things, they concluded that civil unrest was the likely cause of improved welfare services. Thus organized protest, especially by the dispossessed and marginal, that threatens the disruption of the intricately intermeshed institutions of the advanced capitalist state would inevitably force a favorable negotiation with the presiding powers.

> Fitted together, we think that the democratic class struggle, pluralist and state-centered perspectives offer a convincing explanation of the distinctive pattern of American welfare state underdevelopment. They point to the crippling effects of disenfranchisement, of a decentered state structure, and of limited welfare state programs in inhibiting working class electoral organization and influence in the United States. . . . The premise common to each of these theo-

ries of welfare state politics is that political institutions shape forms of political action. Or stated differently, that political structures shape political processes. (Piven and Cloward 1971, 449)

Piven and Cloward's analysis of historical civil unrest and their manifesto for protest turns on three central assumptions concerning power and motive—first, the presence of a sufficient number of the excluded to mount a successful protest; second, the motivation of the excluded to seek system change; and third, the causal tie between political structures and outcomes. The motivation of the dispossessed hinges on their self-defined preferences rather than the stakes that theorists ascribe to them in the manner of Marx. Marx assumed that workers had different political goals from the bourgeoisie, but he had to invent a very undemocratic theory of false consciousness—the notion that the proletariat frequently did not know what was good for it—to get past their own enacted social values. Similarly, Piven and Cloward are more concerned with their own ascription of true interests to the poor and workers than with the actual situation, the stated preferences, or, most important, the free choices made by needy groups.

Moynihan never had much concern for objective truth; he simply cited the work of social scientists that he found compatible, asserting the authority of their work by fiat—describing it as "meticulous field research," for example (1969, 171). By contrast, the central empirical contentions in Piven and Cloward's theory were systematically refuted by Dodenhoff (1998). Upholding Moynihan's view that the principal role of the social sciences is analytical, Dodenhoff plotted the relationship between welfare expansion and incidents of protest between 1933 and 1990. The data were conclusive: "mass disorder clearly is not a necessary condition for the authorization of new relief programs" (320). However, Dodenhoff's alternative to mass protest—calling policymakers' attention to poverty—seems too credulous of the autonomy of those in political office, ignoring the possibility that policymakers reflect the national will rather than create it. Piven and Cloward chose a narrative of selected historical events to press their claim for a causal relationship between disorder and welfare expansion; Dodenhoff *tested* that relationship.

Piven and Cloward ignored the likelihood that American political structures are themselves consensual, persisting as socializing vehicles of citizenship because of their popularity. That is, American federalism and its devolution of considerable power to the states, political parties, free economic markets, political pluralism, and the rest are expressions of American values, just as welfare policy is distinctively an institution of the nation's outsized enchantment with an ethos of extreme individualism. Moreover, *Regulating the Poor* and its irrepressible genre are attached to one of the most romantic fictions in life and literature—the capacity of powerful nefarious conspiracies to control.

Of course, if the United States is controlled by the veiled evil of secret societies, then their control is also hidden and unknowable. On the other hand, if the control of defined elites is acknowledged, then it probably operates with mass consent. In an open society such as the United States, conspiracies of elites tend to produce reactionary conspiracies that proliferate even further conspiracies, until the politics of the Masons, the Knights Templar, Trilateral Commissions, John Birch Societies, National Associations of Manufacturers, and Pinko Liberal Media Moguls becomes public farce published for serialization in Marvel Comics and the *Weekly World News*. Theories of hidden forces offer the comfort of paranoid projection but scarcely a testable explanation for social welfare outcomes in a democracy. In an authoritarian state there is no ambiguity about power, although the issue of consent remains uncertain.

Be this as it may, administrative confusion and elite control make little room for a more likely alternative explanation of established social welfare policy. It exists because it is popular, because it satisfies broad social preferences; elites by and large enjoy the consent of the masses, and they enact those preferences; they do not form them or influence them to any great degree. Power in the contemporary United States is granted and legitimate, not usurped. Thus the War on Poverty programs themselves, in all their tatters, are probably a better statement of the regnant consensus of the period than the speculations of intellectuals will ever be. The intellectuals' roles in social decision making, including their little dramas, are sideshows; they are not the determinative, heroic actors of the typical historical narrative. Populations of people allowed relative freedom in interacting with one another come up with institutions that embody their preferences. LaPiere (1965) may have scored a bull's-eye with his contention that societal change is asocial, that is, antagonistic to order and without conscience or concern. He might have added that it is largely ungovernable.

The contentment of the intellectual community with the perception of programmatic progress against poverty, complete with weak and biased research, interlocking careerist interests, and a good degree of complacency, constitutes professional introversion. Yet professional introversion may be tolerated because it is in some way functional. Much of the period's literature, and notably the historical narratives, expressed a political consensus rather than a neutral analysis of objective conditions. Indeed, the histories were more concerned with the progress of ideas and the roles of intellectuals than with the reality of social welfare provision. This is a predictable flaw: intellectuals tend to overestimate the influence of ideas. Perhaps as a consequence, data about the period, its programs, and the nature of social decision making are descriptive, partial, and frequently inaccurate. Rather than retrieve the past, the retrospectives tend to re-create it for contemporary convenience, endorsing the social welfare programs as ritual celebrations of social value. In turn, those values are not the considered choices of citizens and their representatives but free choices embedded in daily life and negotiated as priorities through the immense complexity of role organization competition. The manifest failures of the OEO programs are also matched by the similar inadequacies of social services in the other federal departments and the social insurances as well.

3

OTHER WAR ON POVERTY PROGRAMS

A variety of the War on Poverty programs were developed outside the Economic Opportunity Act of 1964 to address material deprivation, its corollary problems, and, notably with the civil rights legislation of 1964–65, some of its causes. In addition, existing programs, e.g., income transfers for workers and nonworkers, were expanded to provide greater benefits for more recipients. Yet apart from the special cases of Medicaid and Medicare, even the largest of the new programs had little effect on poverty, often offering services, notably in health, mental health, and housing, that were little better than the situations they were intended to improve; some of the programs were even less adequate, especially given the much greater capacity of the nation to address its problems. Indeed, the War on Poverty initiatives outside the Economic Opportunity Act were as flawed as the OEO programs, and in the same ways—inadequate funding, indifference to program outcomes, symbol rather than substance. Once again, these programs embodied the ethos of heroic individualism—the belief that citizens are largely responsible for themselves. As freely chosen public policies, they expressed a national meanness of both spirit and purse.

Little innocence was sacrificed in these failures. Professionals gained from increased programs and funding for specialized higher education; the public avoided higher taxes; and national values that endorsed the existing stratification of American society were reaffirmed from a variety of programmatic pulpits. What little progress was made against poverty was a tribute to the unplanned expansion of a lightly regulated economy more than to the planned programs of the Great Society.

Perhaps the gains of the black minority were the most notable exception to the general failure to ameliorate poverty. But even here the advances were more the result of opening avenues of access to an already prepared subgroup of the marginalized than of effective training or work for those most harmed by American apartheid. Procedural reforms such as the civil rights legislation of 1964–65 are customarily more socially efficient, i.e., less expensive and disruptive, than substantive measures to promote greater social and economic equality.

Neigborhood Health Centers

The neighborhood health centers are one of the many social welfare tragedies that open their little dramas with hyperinflated expectations and few resources, then linger on for five acts with few if any achievements. The original seventy OEO health centers were replicated many times over in the Department of Health, Education, and Welfare under the Comprehensive Health Planning Act of 1966 and later legislation devoted specifically to neighborhood health programs. By 1971, about 150 neighborhood health centers were operating, with a total annual budget of $419 million in federal funds (Zwick 1972). In fiscal year 2008, the number of neighborhood health centers (including "urban and rural health initiatives") had surpassed one thousand, with a combined budget exceeding $2 billion (U.S. Department of Health and Human Services 2008, 20).

The centers were initially intended to provide the poor a voice in health care services and to rationalize the health care system by providing ample ambulatory care, comprehensive care (including dental services), and a platform for organizing neighborhood residents to reform the political system. The centers were expected to provide family practice residencies, educational internships in slum life for other professionals, access to birth control for teenagers, outreach to shut-ins, care for the chronically ill, primary mental health services, on-site laboratories, and training and employment for local residents. They also promised ineffable returns in terms of reinvigorating the human spirit, as though poverty were a mood disorder: "Some of the Centers' most valuable assets and outputs do not fit easily into the ledger. They deal with the human condition and who can measure self-respect, independence, and hope?" (Bellin and Geiger 1970, 2147).

The nonmedical, i.e., "latent," functions of the health centers included "improving the image of the black male in poverty communities, . . . stimulating and maintaining solidarity among migrant Chicano farm workers, . . . [combating the] pacification of hostile communities by colonial powers [i.e., private urban hospitals], . . . discharging missionary service obligations of the medical-hospital establishment, . . . filling a political void in social and economic action, . . . politicalization or radicalization of youth" (Elinson and Herr 1970, 99). At least from this perspective, the centers fed off the same romanticism as Mobilization for Youth and ended up with similar failures.

Yet the early evaluations of the centers were as upbeat as their methods were weak and porous. Sardell (1983) relied largely on the fugitive literature of health care—speeches, interviews, doctoral dissertations, consultant reports, and reports of obvious partisans such as the National Association of Neighborhood Health Centers—to conclude that the centers improved health status and were cost-effective. Zwick (1972), an OEO official, agreed, putting forward similarly weak evidence.[1]

The centers' intended political role as advocates for the medically underserved, one of the intended outcomes of resident participation on the center boards, was justified by the enormous amount of unmet medical need: "The estimated 1 million people who were served by neighborhood health centers in fiscal year 1975 cost an average of $201. . . . About $10 billion annually would be required to reach the remaining medically underserved at the annual cost of $201 per registration" (U.S. GAO 1978, 4).

But community representation resulted not in greater advocacy but in a preference for jobs. Localism trumped need. Turnout for board elections was extremely low. Even when participation became a ritual of professional control, the centers had difficulty developing a consensus within their own ranks: "representatives of the grantee institutions,

---

1. Other apologetics for care in the centers were similarly weak and were often written by the very public officials responsible for the programs (Reynolds 1976; Seacat 1977; Sparer, Dines, and Smith 1970; Sparer and Johnson 1971; Morehead, Donaldson, and Seravalli 1971). Geomet, Inc. (1972), funded by OEO, evaluated twenty-one centers that had been in operation for at least one year; its generally positive but narrow findings relied largely on interviews with patients and nonusers, and paid scant attention to the quality and conditions of the actual services.

health center administrators and community representatives often had different perspectives on the purposes which the health center should serve" (Sardell 1983, 488). Community participation was as superficial and pointless in the centers as it was in MFY or the OEO's community action programs. The problems of authority and control undercut the centers' ability to function in every area and not just as advocates for the poor (Brandon 1977; Hessler and Beavert 1982).

The difficulty of retaining critical medical manpower, among other problems that were exacerbated by ineffective administration, plagued the centers. Typically, more than half of the centers' physicians had resigned before completing two years of service, with turnover approaching 90 percent at four years (Tilson 1973; Reynolds 1976; Torrens 1971; Pantell, Reilly, and Liang 1980). The commonly reported average annual cost per registrant for care at the centers—declining from $275 in 1968 to $141 in 1974—simply belies any claim that comprehensive health care was delivered (Reynolds 1976), even while the average cost per visit appeared to be reasonable (Sparer and Johnson 1971; Sparer and Anderson 1972). The reported data only estimated the costs to the neighborhood health centers. The estimates failed to include the total medical costs incurred by patients from other providers and consequently neglected to describe the effects of the neighborhood health centers on the health care system. Moreover, the cost data are based on a very limited number of sites—six centers for Sparer and Anderson—that are probably not characteristic of all the centers.

The GAO report (1978) was one of the very few unapologetic evaluations of the centers themselves. Unwittingly or not, the GAO report describes a spoils system of medical care—overstaffed, underutilized, and isolated from mainstream medicine. The 112 centers operating in 1976 were sustained with almost $200 million from the federal government. The study was based on a close audit of six well-established centers. Its findings largely reinforced the conclusions of earlier GAO audits of neighborhood health centers.

> Centers are overstaffed for the number of patients being treated. This underuse of physicians, dentists, support personnel, and services is costing the six centers more than $1 million annually [in a combined budget of about $16.6 million]. [Department of Health, Education, and Welfare] records indicate that many other centers have similar costly inefficiencies. Anticipated patient demand on

which staff levels were originally based has not materialized, and staffs have not been reduced to levels consistent with demand. . . . The overstaffing and resulting underuse of employees stems from several factors, including less than anticipated demand for services, a high rate of broken appointments, and health center management weaknesses. In addition, over half of the centers exceed allowable limits for general service costs which include administration, management information, and maintenance services. (U.S. GAO 1978, i, 4)

The six overstaffed centers exceeded standards by 12 percent for primary care physicians, 42 percent for consulting physicians, and 30 percent for dentists. The pattern was the same nationally among the seventy-two of the 112 neighborhood health centers that reported productivity data. Moreover, 71 percent of the sixty-eight reporting centers exceeded recommended ratios of medical support staff to physicians by almost 50 percent, a figure that would actually be much higher if adjusted for physician overstaffing. The same situation existed for supplemental support staff, general services, and administration. More troubling, all of the estimates of productivity may well have been grossly overstated, since studies validating the number of registrants at centers have shown that centers' reported statistics are overstated by about 22 percent (i, 19).

The quality of management—"numerous and continuing weaknesses in the management and operation of centers"—was a clear concern that the GAO acknowledged in existing evaluations: "organizational structure is ill-defined, inefficient, and inadequate . . . lack of communication among departments . . . duplication and overuse of services. . . . Allocation of personnel is inefficient and wasteful . . . administrative deficiencies are the result of several years of inexperienced and inept management" (i, 14).

Apparently patients had other options for medical care—notably hospital outpatient departments and emergency rooms—that they exercised in preference to the centers, suggesting perhaps a dissatisfaction with the quality or availability of care or a desire to avoid services intended for the poor. For all the excuses that the GAO report makes for underuse of the centers relating to the condition of poverty, its characterization of inadequate management and services may be the most reasonable explanation for their underuse; hospital outpatient clinics were preferable because they offered better care and perhaps even more respectful care. Indeed, the GAO report invokes the training obligation of the centers to explain underuse and overstaffing.

> [The centers] were to provide jobs as well as health care to neighborhood residents. Often the jobs provided were of the supporting service type—transportation personnel and social or family health workers—which required minimal skill or training. To some degree, this employment objective contributed to overstaffing. [The Department of Health, Education, and Welfare] has since eliminated this objective, but many centers still employ community people in supporting-activity-type jobs in excess of the number needed to serve patient workloads. (U.S. GAO 1978, i, 11)

This is a polite way of saying that many of the centers fulfilled a role in patronage and political spoils more than in health care and training. Indeed, some of the centers were clearly an arm of local political organizations, rubbing noble reformers' nose in the fact that local resident participation often contradicts romantic notions of participatory democracy.[2]

Many centers apparently attempted to increase their efficiency by seeking patients outside of their target areas rather than by improving their attractiveness to intended beneficiaries. Indeed, some centers served no medically underserved area (U.S. GAO 1978, i, 19).

In the end, the GAO report—based on only six cases and untested administrative data, and lacking a detailed description of its methods—failed to offer a definitive judgment of the centers' effectiveness. Yet the general literature on the neighborhood health centers, by contrast, is most often an apology or an advertisement for them. The research rarely rises above the questionable authority of the GAO report. The more incisive studies offer only partial, although often troubling, views of their performance. Few grapple with the inherent impossibility of curing a drought with five gallons of water, or of feeding the hungry through a food lottery.

---

2. The literature discusses the cannibalization of the centers for spoils as the result of problems of understaffing, underuse, and the like. The relatively poor quality of center physicians also seems to be avoided. Certainly some very competent and very compassionate physicians were motivated by a genuine desire to serve the poor. However, many poorly trained physicians who lacked better opportunities also ended up there. Again, it is likely that underuse reflected the inferior quality of the centers.

The centers may initially have been sold in the manner of other OEO programs, as a quasi-voluntary social welfare initiative, in the expectation that local participation would eventuate in small-town self-help—the poor taking responsibility for the poor or local jurisdictions taking over their financing. Yet it seems likely that the centers largely persisted for reasons of local patronage, accepting as tolerable their untrained and poorly motivated staffs and deficient care. They recall the settlement houses of the early twentieth century, where the corruption of tough local politics undermined the romantic impulses of oblivious optimistic reformers.

The largest problem of the centers may lie in the fundamental assumption that undergirds their development: that the poor were an anthropologically distinct group of the medically needy that required specific culturally sensitive programs. Yet universal coverage and unified systems of care are more attractive medical alternatives, especially if the goal is not only health care delivery but also the social integration of the American population.

The failure of the social system, rather than medical disease, may provide an apt metaphor for poverty. If neighborhood health services are valuable on technical grounds of efficiency, access, and coverage, then they "may be useful to a broader segment of the population rather than only for the poor" (Lemkau 1971, 2338). Programs dedicated to distinct populations of citizens tend to isolate them within the broader culture and perhaps even to stigmatize them. Indeed, the notion of treating the poor in separate facilities seems to feed the darkest American myths.

The general absence of rigorous accountability fed into the tragedy of failed service. Yet the centers never embraced program evaluation. Instead, patronage, separate care, and "latent" functions defined them. The neighborhood health centers were socially efficient symbols of charity, a poor substitute for the resources that would have been necessary for access to quality services, let alone good health, for the poor. The centers also perpetuated the nauseating sentimentality of the idea of "community," insisting on localism at a time when economic and social needs required a much broader orientation.

Community Mental Health

Enacted in 1963 and amended soon thereafter, the Mental Retardation Facilities and Community Mental Health Centers Construction Act created funding to build and staff local treatment centers in designated catchment areas throughout the nation. The act reflected the burgeoning popularity of community mental health in the United States, a movement predicated on the assumption that a community setting would enhance the effectiveness of treatment for relatively benign emotional disorders as well as for serious psychiatric impairments. Accelerated by the War on Poverty, the centers were intended to make mental health services available to poorer and lower-status groups, notably including the large number of the serious mentally ill. Psychiatry had developed a number of drug treatments that allowed seriously disturbed patients to be managed in settings that were presumably less confining, more nurturing, more socially desirable, and perhaps even less expensive than hospital care.

In the decades after passage of the act, a number of experiments in community care demonstrated the feasibility of providing for the seriously mentally ill outside conventional hospitals. The most prominent of these experiments, "training in community living," often referred to as "assertive community treatment," reappeared in similar forms abroad in the form of intensive case management and community mental health teams (Marx, Test, and Stein 1973; Stein and Test 1980; Bebbington, Johnson, and Thornicroft 2002). Training in community living offered multiple professional interventions for the seriously mentally ill in community settings. It provided a range of supports to help impaired patients adjust to living on their own, or at least without total institutionalization. The program provided food, clothing, shelter, and medical care; coping skills for navigating public transportation, cooking, budgeting, and the like; motivation for independence; support and education for community members who interacted with the patients; and

> a supportive system that *assertively* helps the patient with [these services]. . . . Chronically disabled patients are frequently passive, interpersonally anxious and prone to develop severe psychiatric symptomatology. Such characteristics often lead these patients to fail to keep appointments and to "drop out" of treatment, particularly when they are becoming more symptomatic. Hence, the program must be assertive, involve patients in their treatment, and be prepared to "get to" the patient to prevent dropout. It must also actively assure continuity of care among treatment agencies rather than assume that a patient will successfully negotiate the often

difficult pathways from one agency to another on his own. (Stein and Test 1980, 393, emphasis in original)

The experiment randomly assigned 130 residents of Dane County, Wisconsin, who sought admission to the Mendota Mental Health Institute to either customary inpatient care, followed by outpatient care when appropriate, or to the experimental training-in-community-living program. During the fourteen months of the experiment, patients in the latter group entered the hospital only rarely.

Training in community living was generally successful. Compared with control patients, patients in the experimental group spent less time in institutions, were more often employed, reported greater satisfaction with life, and, more to the point, were less symptomatic. During the final four months of the fourteen months of treatment, they spent only about 9 percent of the time in institutions (psychiatric, medical, or penal), and 82 percent lived independently, compared with 20 percent and 68 percent, respectively, for controls. Experimental patients spent about 30 percent more time employed than controls, although the difference is largely accounted for by sheltered employment. During the last four months of treatment, the average subjects in the experimental group earned $760, the average control, $420.

The benefits, measured as the differences between the experimental and control groups at the end of treatment, were small and for the most part evaporated soon after supportive care ended. The only differences between the two groups sixteen months after the termination of the experiment were found in employment and earnings. Thus, if the benefits of the experiment were to persist, the services provided by training in community living would probably also need to continue. This was no surprise, given that chronic conditions require ongoing care.

The services provided by training in community living cost about 11 percent ($797) more than control group services, while the cost-benefit ratio provided an edge of only about 5 percent. Moreover, the edge seems to be accounted for by competitive employment and other measures of work that the authors acknowledge are "derived from patient reports and as such are subject to misreporting" (Weisbrod, Test, and Stein 1980, 402). The largest benefits of the experiment, however—their social returns—depended greatly on the often amorphous benefits of independence, dignity, self-determination, and community living, which are difficult to measure and are often issues more of justice and citizen rights than of cost. The claim that the experiment provided great social benefits was sustained by the computations, data collection, and methods of observers who were obvious advocates of the program.

The interpretation of training in community living at any level—direct cost, cost benefit, and social benefit—for general community practice depends on the degree to which the experiment is generally applicable. Unfortunately, the conditions of the Wisconsin experiment differ greatly from the general situation of need. To begin with, the community was relatively tranquil, rural, and socially homogeneous. As a result, many of the patients had local relatives who cared for them—indeed, 27 percent were married. Second, the patients were relatively young, averaging thirty-one years of age, and had not endured many years of hospitalization, nor had they been isolated from community settings for long stretches of time. Although patients averaged five hospital admissions prior to the experiment, they had accumulated only a total of 14.5 months of inpatient care per person. By contrast, the urban population requiring care for serious mental illnesses, and notably the many patients who have been abandoned by family, are more seriously debilitated and enjoy far less voluntary support. Thus the application of training in community living to the typical community setting is more challenging and probably much more costly, especially where nonhospital settings cannot assure one of the primary benefits of psychiatric hospitals—the patient's physical safety.

Patient safety was not an overarching concern in tranquil Dane County, which is home to the flagship campus of the University of Wisconsin. Furthermore, the staff was highly motivated to produce positive outcomes and probably far more skilled and more rigorously supervised than the usual practitioner in community settings. In the more typical setting, staff may not be as industrious, skilled, or accountable. Indeed, the unusual motivation of the demonstration staff may itself have prevented a number of patient hospitalizations. The question always arises in experiments that test the feasibility of community placements whether patients are simply maintained out of the hospital by fiat, even when they might properly be admitted, or whether they are informally reinstitutionalized in confining placements in the community.[3]

Indeed, community care in any of its intensive forms usually failed

3. For example, see Lerman's (1975) analysis of the "alternative" community placements of the California Youth Authority.

to fulfill its promises (see also the comprehensive review by Mueser et al. 1998, which reaches the same conclusions). As in Wisconsin, reported gains were modest, usually costly, transitory, created under demonstration conditions, and thus perhaps evanescent. Lehman et al. (1997) largely corroborated the Wisconsin experience, producing better living conditions but not notably improving either medical or psychiatric care. The control group received customary community care in Baltimore, Maryland, which was probably more deficient than customary care in Madison, Wisconsin. Consequently, the deficiencies of customary care, rather than the relative high quality of experimental services, may have accounted for the reported benefits. Additionally, data problems, notably self-reporting, may have exaggerated positive findings. Generally less favorable outcomes are reported for community-based services that employ intensive case management, close monitoring, or service teams similar to those that characterize assertive community treatment: no psychiatric improvement and even fewer benefits in living conditions and quality of life. There is even some suggestion in Tyrer and Morgan (1995) that closer surveillance of a debilitated population produces more days of inpatient care (Melzer et al. 1991; Tyrer et al. 1998; Holloway and Carson 1998; Ford and Ryan 1997). "The paradigm that treats [successful models of community care, e.g., the Wisconsin program] like a drug that can be expected to have standard effects under any social conditions, if administered properly, seems implausibly asocial. It ignores social contexts: the living situations of people with severe mental illness, the problems they face, the attitudes toward mental illness in the wider community, and so on. These may well be major factors influencing what is effective" (Bebbington, Johnson, and Thornicroft 2002).

Recall that the modest benefits of the Wisconsin program may well have been generated by location and the unique conditions of the experiment more than by the program itself. Without resources for improved living conditions and day activities—the bare bones of caring for debilitated psychiatric patients—community care seems futile. The failure of community programs for chronic and disabled patients reflects the political refusal to fund community services, including the refusal to provide a decent living environment for people who cannot care for themselves. Nevertheless, the socially efficient substitutes for care, inspired by the notion of treatment itself, have been the profoundest failures.

The behavioral treatments that sustained the possibility of community care are not credible adjuncts to drug therapy, which established the initial plausibility of handling seriously ill patients outside mental hospitals. Social skills training for psychiatric patients, an important component of training in the repertoire of community living service, has produced only marginal results in optimal settings, and that is according to studies that consistently rely on uncorroborated patient self-reports for their data. Marder et al. (1996) concluded that "the effects of social skills training on social adjustment measures were relatively modest in absolute terms, averaging less than a point on a 5-point scale over a 2-year period," and were restricted to particular types of patients (1590). Lieberman et al. (1998) report similar initial outcomes, but they evaporated over time. Hayes, Halford, and Varghese (1995) reported even smaller gains for skills therapy compared with a discussion group that served as a placebo control, again relying on patient self-reporting. Both the skills therapy group and the discussion group reported similar gains, suggesting either a placebo effect or, more intriguing, the possibility of report bias generated as a reward for the kind attentions of caregivers. Pilling et al.'s (2002a) meta-analysis of nine randomized trials concluded that social skills training for schizophrenics was generally ineffective.

However, Pilling et al. (2002b) concluded on the basis of their meta-analysis that family intervention and cognitive behavior therapy were successful with schizophrenics. This is an unexpected finding in the context of research that had generally given up on the value of psychotherapy for seriously debilitated mental patients and had never sustained the value of any family therapy through scientifically credible research.[4] Yet meta-analysis is an imperfect technique for summarizing research, especially when its inclusion criteria for primary studies are stuck with the inadequate state of the art and its analysis does not or cannot adjust its findings by the actual quality of the included studies. Thus Pilling et al. selected studies that employed randomized controlled procedures, the gold standard of clinical research, but failed to consider other serious pitfalls—lack of blinding, poor reliability of measures, including diagnosis and symptomatology, biased patient self-reports, failure to introduce protections for researcher (and practitioner) expectancy biases, and others—that impair the credibility of the findings. In any event, the findings were very modest.

4. In addition to comments below, the research and its flaws are discussed at length in Epstein (1995 and 2006a).

Family therapy reduced relapse by about 13 percent, but the benefits seemed to evaporate with longer treatment. Indeed, the benefits are so small as to hint that deferred relapse may even have been a product of the research, especially since true blinding was probably impractical and since some combination of families, patients, and therapists may have been caught up in the drama of the research situation and thus motivated to suppress the report or recognition of relapse in the hope of producing positive outcomes. Family therapy reduced hospital readmissions by about 10 percent, but it is not clear whether the gain was taken in the patient's best interest or whether the patient was essentially confined in a community setting, notably through heavy medication.

Many comparisons across different studies and different conditions of family therapy failed to consistently produce significant and substantial benefits. It is provocative that family treatment seemed to increase treatment noncompliance even while greatly increasing compliance with taking medication. It is likely that the actual conditions of family therapy amounted simply to surveillance of medication compliance, which by itself may have accounted for the reported gains in relapse and rehospitalization. Nevertheless, Pilling et al. (2002a) reached the happy conclusion that "our analysis demonstrates that the early promise of family intervention in schizophrenia has been maintained" (this statement appears providentially on page 777). But the authors do not address the rapid falloff in benefits, nor do they consider alternative explanations for the modest findings, including the methodological weakness of their meta-analysis.

The meta-analysis found that "CBT [cognitive behavior therapy] offered no other advantage in the treatment of schizophrenia" (Pilling et al. 2002a, 777). The authors then attempted at considerable length to wring success from failure on the basis of desultory evidence that CBT improves mental states. However, mental states are among the most elusive qualities to measure and are surely amenable to reporting bias. Still, the popularity of family therapy and cognitive behavior therapy for schizophrenics probably has little to do with clinical efficacy. Indeed, much of the research is actually misleading, relying on the appearance of scientific credibility rather than its substance. CBT is a trope of social value—rationality, self-reliance, and personal responsibility. Family therapy complements the CBT ceremony with voluntary care and, again, personal rather than public responsibility. In the end, community alternatives to hospitalization for psychiatric patients seem to confer small gains in optimal settings and even fewer in actual practice, while adjunctive behavioral treatments seem ineffective.

To turn the twin failings of psychiatric care for the seriously impaired—the inadequacy of community programs and adjunctive treatment—into a hat trick, even the efficacy of drug therapy seems sporadic at best. Lieberman et al. (2005), published in the *New England Journal of Medicine*, is one of the rare articles that bankrupt psychiatry's prized franchise. The study randomized 1,493 schizophrenic patients at fifty-seven sites across the United States either to older or to second-generation antipsychotic medications. Following the contemporary logic of intention to treat—the inclusion of all randomized patients, not just program completers, in final evaluations of effectiveness—Lieberman et al. reported an average attrition rate of 76 percent; that is, drug treatment for schizophrenia starts off with a failure rate of 76 percent, which is then increased by the number of patients who comply with medication regimens but who do not improve. They concluded their study with a museum-quality understatement—"this outcome indicates that antipsychotic drugs, though effective, have substantial limitations in their effectiveness in patients with chronic schizophrenia" (1216). This is like describing Noah's flood as unusual weather. It is impossible for even the most blindly loyal psychiatrist to discount Lieberman et al. as "the usual anti-psychiatry, anti-Ritalin, Scientology-flavored rants."[5]

Grob, a respected historian of American mental health care, summed up the situation well on the basis of an institutional analysis of mental health programs and politics. He reached outside of his assumptions about the influence of traditional interest groups and organizational actors, however, to offer an aside on the apparent consistency between embedded national preferences and policy choices. He might more profitably have started with mass preferences and assigned dependent, peripheral, nearly inevitable roles to psychiatrists, hospitals, treatment centers, their organizations, and the ostensible politics of Congress, the administration, and the judicial system.

The consequences of the innovations that transformed the mental health systems, like those of all human activities, were at best mixed. When the emphasis on treatment in the community was

5. Personal communication from a prominent psychiatrist and editor of one of the field's leading journals, commenting on criticism of drug therapy.

combined with an expansion of services to new groups, the result was a [policy that often overlooked the need to provide supportive services for the seriously and chronically mentally ill]. . . . A policy that emphasized therapy, but left care unassigned, appealed to both the public and mental health professionals. [Americans'] view of care (often equated with welfare) has been more ambivalent and reflected the pervasive belief that dependency in part was a function of character deficiencies, which in turn resulted in social and economic failure. . . . [Thus] severely and chronically mentally ill persons were often released from public hospitals after relatively brief periods of time into communities without adequate support mechanisms . . . including housing, medical care, welfare, and social support services. (Grob 1983, 211–12)

Still and all, the limitations of the experiments in deinstitutionalization do not justify neglecting the seriously mentally ill. Rather, they challenge a compassionate and wealthy society to extend the rights of citizenship to the disabled. The notion of community care itself, as opposed to the goal of nurturing the potential of all citizens, is a romance of neighborliness, a nostalgia for voluntarism and personal responsibility. Yet modern America is decidedly not a network of caring small towns that extend themselves quickly and generously to the least well off. The vulnerable need protection and often respite from the abrasions of contemporary society; public responsibility for their care would recognize the serious shortfalls of American charity. Debilitating psychiatric conditions cannot be consistently treated as transitory diseases. They require continuing *care,* which is often expensive but rarely provided, rather than *treatment,* which is relatively inexpensive but ineffective. Cure, prevention, and rehabilitation are budgetary goals frequently at war with the need for ongoing care.

It is programmatically possible to do the decent thing and provide humane care for poor people with serious debilitating illnesses, although that care might profitably be removed from psychiatric auspices. Decent care would cost a bit more than care in total institutions. Instead, however, on the pretext of providing community service and the theoretical possibility of emptying long-term mental hospitals, the nation chose to save money. As a result, the chronically mentally ill were either reinstitutionalized in places that were often worse than state hospitals (e.g., prisons) or were simply abandoned to grossly inadequate outpatient pro-

grams. The circumstances of the obviously debilitated, a robust me-
mento of the nation's Puritan legacy, go past the excuse of heroic
individualism to suggest an indifference to need.

Community Treatment for the Less Disturbed: The Effectiveness
of Psychotherapy

The reciprocity between embedded national values and social welfare
policy is graphically illustrated in services for the less disturbed patient.
Distraught but still emotionally ambulant patients who are less impaired
than the seriously mentally ill make up the larger and preferred population for community mental health services, notably including community mental health centers originally designed during the War on Poverty
to serve poorer and underserved groups. Psychotherapy is also a core
element of an enormous range of programs that attend to poverty. Some
form of counseling was offered or mandated as a central part of nearly
all War on Poverty programs. Psychotherapy continues uninterrupted to
this day as the prime recourse for a host of social and personal problems, including poverty (e.g., case management in Temporary Assistance to Needy Families), divorce, spousal abuse, fear, depression and
sadness, shyness, belligerence, smoking, obesity and other eating disorders, violence, juvenile delinquency, addiction, drunk driving, and so
on.

However, in the manner of the other personal social services, psychotherapy has failed to accumulate any scientifically credible evidence of
its effectiveness. There has never been a scientifically credible demonstration that any form of psychotherapy has ever been effective with any
patient group in any setting.[6] Instead, psychotherapy has produced a

6. The primary research fails on several basic counts: compromised randomization if
randomization at all, high attrition and censoring, biased measurement procedures, unreliable measurement instruments, and, most devastating, unreliable patient self-reporting. The
field responds to this kind of deep criticism with denial, pleading that its studies are based
on a special sort of science (Epstein 1995, 2006a). In keeping with its core predisposition, it
tends to dissect the motives of the critic rather than address the implications of the criticism.
The tendency to psychologize objective arguments is perhaps a predictable professional
weakness—learned defensiveness—that falls back on the central tenet of cognitive behavior
therapy: that the problem lies in the distorted thoughts of patients (and critics) rather than
in objective social conditions or perhaps even in the behavior of the therapist. People who
make a living from the introjective tend to have a curious disregard for reality. That so many
postmodernists cherish psychotherapy, and notably Freud, is very revealing of the field's

distorted science of evaluation and a community of practitioners that, with the permission of the American people, block systematic, independent investigations of the live conditions of treatment. Psychological treatment—cure, prevention, and rehabilitation—is an illusion, and apparently a very useful one. Indeed, the community mental health centers, and psychological treatment in general, persist as ritual celebrations of American values, local institutions of civic virtue that constantly reemphasize the desirability of self-reliance—however perversely as dependence on therapy.

The small tradition of criticism of the field is overwhelmed by Americans' love of the ideals of self-invention and heroic individualism. National bookstore chains reflect the market of ideas, that is, the appetites of the American public and its dedicated professions of psychic healing—psychiatry, psychology, social work, counseling, and their innumerable subspecialties. These bookstores allocate hundreds of linear feet of shelf space to self-help, psychology, counseling, spirituality, and the enormous range of alternative medical treatments and self-healing—e.g., herbology, aroma therapy, deep massage, chiropractic, yoga—usually without so much as even one slim dissenting volume. In fact, there are very few dissenting volumes at all; they sell poorly, and they are met with hostility by reviewers, many of whom are protective of their therapists and cherish the time they spend talking about themselves. The therapeutic has triumphed over the caring as America's civic religion, but more as a conformist belief system than as a philosophy of release (Rieff 1966; Polsky 1991). Dineen (1996) recasts the field as a soulless business.

Yet even the small number of demurrals often try to rescue the field with their own prescriptions for new and improved treatments. They seem more like intramural skirmishes than true analyses. Dawes (1994) favors therapists with doctorates from approved schools of psychology, but he fails to offer credible evidence for his braggadocio that "psychotherapy works." Even the very best of the clinical research, such as it is, which presumably employs the best practitioners, drawn from the faculty and doctoral students of leading departments of clinical psychology, fails to demonstrate the effectiveness of psychotherapy.

---

social meaning. Ideas are judged guilty by association. But Freudian psychoanalysis is deftly denied scientific and clinical probity by Crews (1993), Macmillan (1997), and Dufresne (2000), among others.

Lilienthal, Lynn, and Lohr (2003) draw the line between presumably effective mainline treatments that require standard university training for practitioners and flakey, cultish, and idiosyncratic cures that they insist fail. But mainline research in psychotherapy is distinguished from crackpot studies only by style. Both employ pseudoscience to certify their procedures, and both types of treatments remain indeterminate at best, most probably ineffective, and perhaps even harmful. Therapy and spiritualism are drawn from the same reservoir of faith.

Zilbergeld (1983) and Gross (1978) wrote devastating critiques of psychotherapy that detailed its clinical weakness. Still, Zilbergeld held out hope that the more cognitive forms of therapy were effective with some patients, notably phobics. But even this glimmer in the dark depended on a convenient reading of the literature. In counseling patients to accept their limitations and enjoy the human condition, Zilbergeld echoes Becker's (1973) magnificent meditation on psychotherapy. And even Becker never suggested that any form of psychotherapy was effective, treating it only as disciplined self-reflection, a bit of applied moral philosophy, and the necessary obligation of good citizens to scrutinize their own behavior at various times in their lives.

Smail (2005) indicted psychotherapy as a frank extension of the capitalist industrial state. People would be more content and more productive in a more caring society. But his criticism undercuts his argument that counseling can still offer distressed patients some relief. Smail, like a few of the field's insistent boosters, may be confusing the pleasure of the therapist's company with curative prowess; the voiced appreciation of the distressed with the resolution of their problems; patient adherence with treatment regimens (including regular, prompt attendance); and sociability with behavioral change.

Practitioners in the field of psychotherapy respond to critics from within the protective arms of a society complacent about welfare minimalism. Most notably, they argue that psychotherapy should enjoy a special immunity from scientific rigor, that the study of psychotherapy requires a special adaptation of science and that randomized clinical trials are not appropriate. Smith, Glass, and Miller, whose 1980 *Benefits of Psychotherapy* is a cherished argument for psychotherapeutic effectiveness—endorse the canons of science as requisite for testing the outcomes of psychotherapy, yet in the same breath they limit the application of science to the field. They dismiss randomized controlled trials as "textbook standards," as "methodological rules, learned as dicta in graduate school and regarded as the touchstone of publishable articles in prestigious journals" (38). Horwitz (2007) concurs, writing,

> Psychotherapy is beyond conventional science; the double-blind, randomized, placebo-controlled, and standardized methods that are suitable for evaluating treatments for physical health and for medication therapies for mental health may be inappropriate for testing the effectiveness of psychotherapies. Indeed, a pure double-blind placebo group in tests of psychotherapy is conceptually impossible. . . . The sorts of factors that placebos are intended to control for . . . should not be eliminated in the standardization of treatment because they are major components of psychotherapy. (1092)

Such is the psychotherapist's special pleading, defiantly dismissive of the consequence that this pleading absolves the field from the requirements of conventional empirical evidence and reveals it for what it is: an enterprise of faith. Psychotherapy gets away with its hypocrisy only because its rituals are socially convenient. The field covets the authority of science but refuses to accept the requisite rigor of objectivity and coherence.

In fact, research methodologies for psychological treatments need to be more rigorous, sophisticated, and careful than those for many natural sciences. Quarks are presumably unconscious; human subjects have motives and react to research situations, including researchers, in ways that may threaten the integrity of tests. The various potential threats to the credibility of clinical research necessitate enhanced design considerations to address placebo effects, researcher bias, demand characteristics, demonstration effects, rater bias, spontaneous remission, and other pitfalls. Researchers can unwittingly affect a subject's response. Many emotional conditions are seasonal; sometimes they are exacerbated, sometimes quiescent. Evaluators can be influenced by knowledge of the patient's assignment to the experimental or the control group. As has been amply demonstrated, patients may benefit simply from believing that they will get better, that the therapy or the drugs are working.

Yet if the placebo effect is responsible for many psychotherapeutic benefits, as many psychotherapists acknowledge, then practitioners do not need advanced training for their allegedly special skills, but rather an easy smile, a comforting arm, and a soft lap. Wittgenstein's comment

130   DEMOCRACY WITHOUT DECENCY

hits the mark: "Psychological concepts are just everyday concepts. They are not concepts newly fashioned by science for its own purpose, as are the concepts of physics and chemistry. Psychological concepts are related to those of the exact sciences as the concepts of the science of medicine are to those of old women who spend their time nursing the sick" (1980, 12e).

Yet the biggest problem of all is psychotherapy's typical reliance on patient self-reports, which are notoriously reactive to the research situation. It is a point of scholarly incredulity that the field is permitted to conduct expensive, advanced research without having developed reliable and valid measures of the phenomena it studies, a situation akin to a physicist's studying heat without an instrument to measure it.[7]

In the end, the field of psychotherapy has failed to provide a single scientifically credible test of the efficacy of its treatment during its many decades of vaunted research. Its literature boils down to the "erroneous and scientifically unvalidated claims of psychotherapists, using subjective and unreliable methods," which undercuts all psychotherapies and not just those that Lilienthal, Lynn, and Lohr deem insubstantial, marginal, and untested (2003, xiii).

Some of the problems of psychotherapeutic research, such as patient self-reporting, may be intractable. But intractable research problems do not grant psychotherapists special permission to elevate ambiguous findings to the level of clinical truth. To the contrary, they prevent the maturation of a field of study and proportionately reduce its clinical value. In just this way the universal absence of scientifically credible evidence of the field's clinical prowess suggests that the deployment of

7. Still, some problems remain seemingly intractable, notably self-selection and self-reporting. Patients included in the test samples are almost invariably those who seek treatment. Randomization procedures assure that the control and experimental groups are comparable and thus that the findings estimate the ability of the treatment to handle the complaints of patients who seek care. However, these findings do not apply to the unmotivated. To test effectiveness among the far larger number of patients who do not seek treatment, presumably the unmotivated, an extraordinary effort needs to take place to survey populations to identify potential patients and then to recruit them. This may not solve the problem, as many of the unmotivated presumably will not agree to treatment. The findings thus need to be interpreted in the first instance as amenable only to the motivated, lending even greater urgency to the need for randomized controls, using both placebos and true nontreatment groups. Further, absent a true physical test for emotional conditions, the studies are stuck with some form of self-reporting. The situation is ripe for serious public regulation and deep disclosure rather than the current preference for private practice behind tightly closed doors. It might help if psychotherapy were listed frankly as an alternative medical procedure—alternative because of its science rather than its *outre* techniques.

psychotherapeutic interventions should be cautionary and limited, rather than the promiscuous and often mindless prescription of mental and emotional treatments that are in fact the case. Apparently the society does not wish to experiment with other, more costly forms of social welfare programs. Psychotherapy is a form of social denial in two senses—for it refuses both to come to grips with the nature of social need and to allocate more resources.

The wide popularity of the field cannot be explained by its results in the clinic but only by its social value as a form of intellectual flattery and, more trenchantly, as an affirmation of basic social beliefs. Indeed, without empirical sustenance, traditional psychotherapies—cognitive behavior therapy, psychodynamic therapy, and behavioral treatments—act as powerful social metaphors, symbols, and rituals, divorced from cure, prevention, and rehabilitation, that reinforce the boundaries between groups.

The chosen method of therapeutic intervention parallels the social and economic stratification of the nation. Each of the dominant, mainstream therapies assumes a different factor in human learning: cognitive behavior therapy emphasizes thoughtfulness, psychodynamic therapy focuses on emotion, and behavioral treatments rely on rote conditioning. It is not simply coincidental that behavioral therapy is largely reserved for recipients of public welfare, including those receiving cash assistance, miscreants, and children in care; they are presumably less thoughtful and more impulsive and require mindless learning regimens that bypass their limited intellectual capacity. In turn, the cognitive and emotional therapies are deemed appropriate for higher-class and presumably higher-functioning citizens, prized for their intellectual capacities and tastes.

The application of behavioral therapies in orphanages such as Boys Town, in the case-management process of reformed welfare, in job programs for the dependent poor, in Job Corps, and in other similar War on Poverty programs and their contemporary progeny, conveys the need for discipline, even taming. These institutions proudly display their reward and punishment schedules on bulletin boards and relish the language of conditioning in describing themselves to funding sources. Many behavioral patients are involuntary, receiving treatments that they neither sought nor particularly enjoy but endure under penalty of sanction.

By contrast, the cognitive therapies and the psychoanalyst's interminable exploration of the fascinating depths of the patient's narcissism flatter the thoughtful clients that they and their insurance companies can easily terminate at will. In the behavioral therapies, conditioning bypasses free agency; the cognitive and psychodynamic therapies assume self-determination and employ a process of "rational induction" (an arrogation of rationality that amounts to little more than sorting through one's thoughts and feelings). The public purse is grudgingly opened for behavioral treatments, but largely in the expectation that they will produce a degree of obedience if not actual regimentation. Cognitive and psychodynamic therapies are processes of romantic overcoming, endowing the patient's complaints with a seriousness that ennobles their insights and emotionality.

The poor need to learn to adjust to social demands; paying customers deserve the leisure to explore their inner lives and creative impulses. Thus the choice of therapy replicates American stratification and endorses its assumption of individual heroism, social merit, cognitive capacity, and social contribution. While therapy has not yet become a ritual of public shaming—a process of stigmatizing deviance—it reinforces socially ascribed characteristics and thus retards social mobility. Yet it fails to achieve its goals of cure, prevention, and rehabilitation. Psychotherapy, manifested in both pietistic and liturgical schisms, is no remedy for personal and social problems, after all, but part of a civic religion that reinforces popular values.

The depth of institutionalized belief in psychotherapy is measured in part by the field's resistance to rigorous evaluation and the nation's tolerance for professional discretion as a substitute for credible evidence of its worth. The social conditions of psychotherapeutic research, equally applicable to most other social service research, make neutral, objective research virtually impossible. Indeed, the intransigence of the practitioner community reflects the pious certainties of the broader culture that psychotherapy is valuable: "Data generated [by community mental health centers] are sometimes corrupted because they are used by centers to present a favorable image to potential funders and any interested members of the local community." The deception is encouraged in part because "it is not clear that there is any systematic evidence for these evaluations" (Cook and Shadish 1982, 245). Professional organizations, journals, and public funding sources, notably the National Institute of Mental Health, are content with the situation as it is, assuming effectiveness in the absence of scientific testing. Indeed, the popular ritualism of mental health—the emphasis on guided self-cure rather than caring, individual and private solutions rather than public subsidies—has become sacramental.

The most comprehensive (indeed, it is nearly interminable) review of the state of mental health services—*Mental Health: A Report of the Surgeon General* (U.S. Department of Health and Human Services 1999)—is a paean to the prowess of professional mental health services in the United States. It refuses to acknowledge any systematic evidence of ineffectiveness except occasionally to boast about how far the field has come in both treatment and evaluation. The same boosterism prevails in England, where Lord Layard's (2005) influential white paper recommended substantially expanding psychotherapy in lieu of more concrete welfare provisions. As Cook and Shadish (1982) noted, few dispute the value of mental health care as currently practiced. Policy remains congruent with popular tastes.

Sheltering the Homeless: Transitional Housing

The War on Poverty never established an extensive housing program. What it did institute, and what was added in subsequent years, was largely reversed during the Reagan administration but never restored afterward. The absence of subsidized and affordable housing for lower-paid workers and the poor has produced a growing homeless population, peopled to a great degree by the forlorn graduates of the nation's community psychiatry programs. Approximately 40 percent of the 280,000 single adults who are chronically homeless have serious psychiatric problems. The chronically homeless adult population is swelled by a large number of episodically homeless adults whose unemployment puts them on the streets, as well as by a substantial number of homeless children. Approximately 840,000 people were homeless at some time during 1996 (Culhane, Metraux, and Hadley 2002, 140n22).

Nonetheless, federal housing policy addresses only the most financially costly of the homeless rather than, in American terms, the most deserving. Apparently a "power law" of public costs, the brainchild of Philip Mangano (a federal official in charge of homeless policy), dictates government action on this issue. The homeless who generate the greatest costs in health care, crime, and mental health have received the greatest attention.

Culhane, Metraux, and Hadley tested the effects on total public costs of two types of transitional housing—community residences and supportive housing—for homeless people with serious mental illnesses, a group that accounts for an enormous amount of expensive public care. The theory was that the public would save money by placing the seriously mentally ill in apartments with readily available social supports. The costs of transitional housing would be offset by reductions in even more expensive hospital inpatient care, prison stays, and other public services. If the experiment panned out, the public would have a strong financial incentive to solve a large part of the homeless problem by offering decent housing with social supports to severely disabled people.

The experiment, referred to as NY/NY, emerged from an agreement between New York State and New York City to house homeless people with serious mental illness. The study compared the experience of the 3,365 persons placed in NY/NY supportive housing with a matched group drawn from the New York City shelter system during the two years prior to placement and the two years afterward.

Culhane, Metraux, and Hadley found that transitional housing did in fact reduce the draw on public services, but not by enough to demonstrate the cost-effectiveness of the program: "The average chronically homeless person with serious mental illness drew down approximately $40,451 in health, corrections and shelter system costs" (2002, 138). The average transitional housing placement cost an additional $1,425 per year, although the supportive housing placements, which made up two-thirds of all placements, cost only an additional $744. Both estimates increased somewhat for year-round housing costs. Approximately 30 percent of placements failed, with the tenants presumably returning to the streets. The additional costs of transitional housing generally corroborate estimates of the increased costs of community care compared with hospital care.

The authors describe the additional costs as minimal—"95 percent of the costs of the supportive housing (operating, services, and debt service costs) are compensated by reductions in collateral service attributable to the housing placement" (138)—and probably temporary, since service use appears to decline after the initial period of housing. Moreover, the authors justify the additional costs as humane and wise.

Many of the potential benefits of the housing initiative were not measured here. Residents of supported housing are more likely to secure voluntary or paid employment . . . and to experience an improved quality of life. Investments in supported housing have also been shown to be associated with improved neighborhood quality and property values. . . . Lastly, the social value of reduced homelessness and of providing greater social protection for those who are disabled, while not possible to translate into economic terms, constitutes an important if less tangible benefit to society. Were all such costs and benefits included, these unmeasured costs of homelessness and benefits of the housing intervention would have increased its already significant net benefit (and potential cost savings). (Culhane, Metraux, and Hadley 2002, 139)

This study is flawed in a number of important ways that obscure the true financial costs of the experiment. In the first place, all of the costs of public services—e.g., hospitals and prisons—are based on average daily costs rather than marginal costs. Minimally reducing the number of patients drawing on a hospital's emergency room, for example, will not have a proportionate effect on staff reduction, hospital beds, and the like. The hospital will still need to maintain its very expensive core services and probably most of its staff. Thus substituting marginal cost savings for average cost savings would show that the savings of NY/NY are lower than the authors of the study claim. They acknowledge this problem indirectly in their comments about the difficulty of shifting budgets from one public department to another.

In addition, the subjects in the NY/NY experiment were neither randomly chosen nor randomly assigned to supportive housing and control conditions. Indeed, there may well have been a good degree of self-selection, with the possibility that those who were placed were also more motivated to stay in housing than were the matched controls drawn from the shelters. Furthermore, the service staff hired for the experiment were probably very industrious and committed to the success of the transitional housing. Without their enthusiasm—that is, when similar services become routine and are delivered by less committed staff—outcomes may well change.

In the end, NY/NY is tricked out in rational garb, but the American people are not buying. The issue remains decency, not cost, and the experimental outcomes claimed by Culhane, Metraux, and Hadley are misleading. The payments of Supplemental Security Income (the welfare program dedicated to the totally and permanently disabled), combined with food stamps, still provide payments below the poverty level. Indeed, NY/NY was only possible because of additional funds provided by the state and city, even while those funds purchased housing for a small percentage of the target population. Concentrated public housing remains the federal government's primary method of providing housing for low-income people. Decentralized housing (Section 8) is a very small program.

The high visibility of homeless people makes the need for an explanation of how and why they became and remain homeless more pressing than is the case with some other social problems. Either they are the unfortunates of the American system, or they are moral degenerates, or the American people simply do not care about them. However they are viewed, they are certainly a testament to the inadequacy of public housing programs.

If even the seriously mentally ill—surely among the most deserving Americans—are neglected, then the less disabled presumably have even fewer claims on public relief. The American people have made a choice reflected in the low priority given to services for the homeless. American neglect of the homeless has persisted largely unchanged since the public mental hospitals were emptied.

The paucity of advocates for the homeless and the poor, and the resulting lack of substantial care, are not due simply to organizational neglect, although this certainly exists. The more likely explanation for homelessness—that Americans' role choices leave few resources for neglected groups—is more cruel than casual: the homeless are street theater, ever-present cautionary tales of what befalls the improvident, the indulgent, the lazy, the slothful, the morally decayed. They are the casualties of family breakdown, the result of a moral choice rather than a sociological imperative.

Manpower Programs for the Poor and Unemployed

Beginning with the Job Corps and Neighborhood Youth Corps, the strategies of public training and employment programs that target the poor and unemployed seemed reasonable enough: to provide the unskilled with marketable skills, the unmotivated with motivation, the beleaguered with solace, and the burdened with some assistance. Yet none of the manpower programs—Manpower Development and Training Act programs, Community Experience and Training Program, Supported Work, Concentrated Employment Training Act programs, Job Training Partnership Act programs, the state waiver experiments stemming from the Omnibus Budget Reconciliation Act of 1982—were successful. They mark a consistent refusal to come to grips with the failure of social interventions to address the incapacitating deprivations of many Americans. The persistence of pointless, underfunded work-training programs, encouraged by the Clinton administration's 1996 welfare reforms, are perhaps best explained by their symbolic endorsement of the basic American preference for individual responsibility and, again, their provision of patronage jobs for staff rather than material sustenance for the unemployed and impoverished.

Evaluations of manpower programs for the poor represent some of the most sophisticated applications of social science. The Manpower Demonstration Research Corporation (MDRC), a blue-ribbon group of the nation's intellectual and social elite, was established precisely to conduct bias-free credible research. The most credible evaluations, specifically including the many MDRC studies, have reached a consensus that endorses the value of these programs: manpower training typically achieves small but important income gains for welfare recipients, among others. Yet the evaluations suffer from debilitating flaws in spite of their sophistication and fashionable provenance.

A more accurate assessment of the evaluative research reaches a very different conclusion:

> Employment and training programs for the welfare population and other low income groups are routinely ineffective against basic employment goals, let alone against grander hopes for alleviating poverty through adequate wages. This is hardly surprising since the customary training programs, even the higher-cost programs, provide only a minimal and short-term compensation for longstanding economic and social deprivations. From the perspective of the unemployed and the poor, the frequent tendency of the evaluations to contrive a redeeming cost/benefit virtue for these minimal social programs serves unfortunate political motives at the expense of broader egalitarian ideals. (Epstein 1997, 145)

The Work Incentive Program

The Work Incentive Program (WIN) was specifically designed in the 1960s to move welfare recipients into paying jobs. Largely a voluntary program in all of its iterations, the version that Ketron, Inc. (1980) evaluated provided work experience, vocational training, on-the-job training, public service employment, and job placement assistance. Paid for by WIN itself, the evaluation followed for three years more than thirty-seven hundred 1974–75 program graduates, comparing them against the experience of five thousand recipients of Aid to Families with Dependent Children (AFDC). Ketron, Inc. concluded that the program was largely successful. In terms of lifetime earnings, WIN participants, depending on the program elements they participated in, earned between $15,000 and $23,500 more than the comparison group, which works out to less than $20 per week. On-the-job training produced an annual boost in income of $7,700 for men and $5,100 for women. However, Ketron's cost analysis, which they took pains to undercut, reports no net benefit; Ketron did not apply the same self-effacing scrutiny to their core evaluation.

A host of methodological problems vitiates all of their very modest findings. The comparison group was not an adequate control. Program participation was voluntary and thus captured the more motivated welfare client. Motivation, intelligence, prior experience, and other tangible and intangible factors entirely unrelated to program participation may have accounted for the gains, such as they were. As Burtless observed, "It seems likely that the choice not to participate in WIN made this comparison group quite different from the group that chose to participate, not only in measurable ways—such as age and education—but also in unmeasurable ways—such as intelligence and ambition. The two groups therefore differed from one another not just because only one of them has received WIN services but additionally because one group may have greater average levels of intelligence and ambition than the other" (1989, 101).

The attrition rate was enormous: 46 percent of the WIN participants and 55 percent of the comparison group were lost to the analysis. Thus Ketron's outcome estimates are based on only roughly half of the initial groups. If the "intention-to-treat" rule was applied, i.e., if attrition was counted as failure, then the reported outcomes would have been much smaller.

The follow-up was probably not reliable, either, being drawn from unverified retrospective interviews. Income, hours worked, and the like may have been inflated by those who went through training and sensed some obligation to the program.

Finally, and perhaps most problematic, the WIN edge, if it even existed, may be accounted for by the employer subsidy, a temporary 20 percent tax credit for WIN wages. The very sharp decline in postgraduation rates of income and hours worked may be the result of having exhausted the employer tax credit, at which point workers were replaced by new WIN graduates.

The typical WIN experience was very superficial, consisting of little training and few services, which largely explains the program's failure in spite of Ketron's gloss. Indeed, Ketron's poorly designed evaluation amounts to an indictment of the use of public funds for program justifications. WIN provided only a sham version of employment, not the real thing.

Supported Work

Operating during the mid-1970s, Supported Work targeted presumably the most intransigent groups of the unemployed: long-term welfare recipients, ex-addicts, ex-convicts, and troubled youths. It was "based on the premise that its participants can be successfully employed if they work in the company of their peers under close supervision by technically qualified people who understand the work histories and personal backgrounds of the crew members. The supervisors gradually increase standards of attendance, productivity, and performance until they resemble those of unsubsidized jobs. After 12 or 18 months, depending on the site, participants are required to leave their Supported Work jobs whether or not they have found other employment" (Masters 1981, 603).

Supported Work was possibly the most expensive of all the training projects, averaging more than $7,000 per capita in mid-1970s dollars. It was also the Manpower Demonstration Research Corporation's inaugural evaluation. The evaluators were very happy with the outcomes of the program. As a study by Hollister, Kemper, and Maynard put it, "From the viewpoint of society as a whole, Supported Work can be judged to have been successful for the [welfare] and ex-addict target groups in terms of increasing opportunities and reducing dependency and social costs. For the youth group, Supported Work did not significantly alter opportunities or behaviors from what they would have been in the absence of Supported Work experience. For the ex-offender group, no firm conclusion can be drawn; some aspects suggest positive net effects, others negative net effects" (1984, 4).

Others were even less restrained, claiming "large earnings impacts" that compelled the program's broad adoption (Manski and Garfinkel 1992, 187). Ginzberg, Nathan, and Solow declared that the program was evidence that society need not accept the existence of a permanently disadvantaged group of citizens (1984, 311).

Once again, however, the actual data fail to sustain the enthusiasm of the program's designers and its evaluators, who are often the same people. The program generally failed for two of the four targeted groups—ex-offenders and troubled youths. The income gains for the welfare participants were small, averaging $600 (25 percent) more per year than for controls, for a total annual income average still below standard poverty thresholds. In fact, the $260 average monthly wage for Supported Work trainees was below the eligibility level for welfare and food stamp benefits in many states. Increased income for ex-addicts, $100 per month more than controls, did not emerge until the three-year follow-up.

Yet even the small reported benefits of Supported Work, and especially their relevance, are diminished by a number of design problems. The project did appear to enroll its target groups, and the evaluation did randomly assign study participants to either a control group or Supported Work. But participation was voluntary, which means that the trainees were probably more motivated than, and thus unrepresentative of, the other members of the groups from which they were drawn. Indeed, participants went through three selection screenings before being accepted into the program: by their own volition, by the agencies that referred them, and by Supported Work itself. In fact, the highly motivated participants may largely have benefited from the job search that staff provided rather than from the training, supervision, or motivational sessions. In a tight labor market, jobs were found for Supported Work participants but not for controls. But few apparently benefited.

Further, the data were drawn from participant interviews of questionable veracity. Whether out of gratitude or fear, data may have been reported differently by Supported Work participants and controls. Indeed, participation in the underground economy was not checked, and the apparent but small differences between income levels of the two groups became smaller as income increased and may result in the first instance from the amount of illicit earnings. The highest-quality sites, as judged by staff, did not produce the best results, which further suggests that factors outside the program may explain the findings. Moreover, older participants did better than younger ones, another indication that the aggressive job placement efforts of staff may have been a more determining factor than the expensive core activities of the Supported Work program. Indeed, the limited success of many of the experiments in work preparedness for poor and marginal groups seems to depend more on the availability of jobs than on any other factor.

Concentrated Employment Training Act Programs

The Concentrated Employment and Training Act (CETA) of 1973 largely consolidated Work Incentive and a variety of other programs, including the Neighborhood Youth Corps and the Job Corps, but in 1978 its eligibility was restricted to the very poor. A further consolidation of training programs in 1983 under the Reagan administration's Job Training and Partnership Act further diminished services.

The most credible evaluation of CETA—Bassi et al. (1984)—replicates all of the flaws of the WIN and Supported Work evaluations and in similar fashion attempts to graduate lackluster findings into program successes. The reported wage increases for trainees were again customarily less than $20 per week. However, the matched comparison groups for the CETA trainees were often more socially impaired, thus exaggerating the benefits of training. Without appropriate controls, wage gains can as easily be ascribed to a natural increase in youths' work activity as they grow into their twenties, rather than to the program's services. Moreover, income data were taken from Social Security files and again failed to include unreported earnings and thus to reflect a true estimate of total income. Other data were drawn from longitudinal panel surveys. In addition to the problems of self-selection, uncertain data, and inappropriate comparison groups, 35 percent of participants dropped out of the study.

The evaluators insisted that CETA, particularly its on-the-job training, was largely successful for poor, unskilled women. Yet poor, unskilled women hardly benefit from empty programs. To the contrary, Bassi et al.'s advocacy passes off the ritual of work as truly gainful employment, and in doing so provides impetus for the premature removal of public support for poor people. Again, CETA paid for the evaluation.

State Workfare Experiments

In 1982 the states were provided waivers that allowed them to bypass federal welfare rules and experiment with a variety of services intended to reduce public dependency. MDRC's evaluations of experiments in eight states are the most sophisticated of the more than twenty evaluations of state experiments. The reported success of these experiments inspired the passage of the welfare reforms of the Family Support Act of 1988, which emphasized skills development as the way out of welfare dependency. The Maine experiment was one of the most successful of the MDRC sites; its activities are typical of all of the welfare-to-work and other training programs for the poor. It also illustrates the contrivances of research that create the illusion of success where none actually exists.[8]

The Maine experiment set out to train and place hard-to-employ welfare mothers in private-sector jobs. The experimental program, Training Opportunities in the Private Sector (TOPS), was distinguished from its control by a sequence of activities: prevocational training, unpaid work experience, and on-the-job training (OJT), which was subsidized by diverting a portion of the AFDC benefit to the employers. A customary low-service WIN demonstration program, WEET, was the control. In all, 444 AFDC mothers volunteered for the experiment, of whom 297 were randomly assigned to TOPS and 147 to WEET. The net cost of TOPS relative to WEET was $2,244 per participant, an amount that recalls the "intensive" casework approach to dependency.

The selection process for study participants "creamed" atypical welfare recipients out of the much larger number of long-term welfare recipients. The participants may even represent an upper limit on the percentage of prime work candidates in the welfare pool, because not all of the available slots for the experiment were filled. The voluntary nature of participation and the discretionary screening process, together with Maine's tight, recessionary labor market, produced a group of prime candidates for employment, but not the hard-to-employ candidates who would have given meaning to the experiment. These relatively few "dis-

---

8. Portions of this analysis of the Maine experiment are drawn from Epstein (1993, 27–31).

placed homemakers," who possessed appropriate skills and child care arrangements, emerged from the large pool of 3,157 WEET registrants (those on AFDC with children over six years of age) and the much larger pool of 16,556 AFDC heads of household in Maine. Since the resulting sample could not test the effectiveness of the TOPS program, why didn't the researchers select a more representative sample, or, alternatively, why wasn't the study aborted?

In the event, only sixty-nine TOPS enrollees reached the OJT stage; sixty-three of the sixty-nine continued their jobs after training. Seventy percent of these OJT positions entailed service or clerical jobs that paid an average of about $4 per hour. One-third paid more; two-thirds paid less.

Equally high proportions of both groups (81.8 percent of TOPS and 80.2 percent of WEET) worked at some point during the two-and-a-half-year follow-up period, during which time the average TOPS participant earned $1,745 more than the average WEET participant, a difference that works out to less than $13 per week. The $2,300 difference between the groups reported for the full five-year follow-up works out to an even smaller average weekly differential of $10.

Based largely on these earnings differentials and on soft responses to interview questions about the value of the work to the participants and their employers, the authors of the Maine study concluded that TOPS was modestly successful in producing a net social gain. A more reasonable summary of the Maine data, however, especially in light of the study's flaws, would conclude that TOPS made no difference for its participants. Its costs were not justified in terms of employment gains. OJT subsidies for employers were not needed. Moreover, the study is of questionable theoretical importance, given that the experimental subjects were unrepresentative of either the state caseload or the national problem of dependency.

The experiment did suggest that a jobs program, rather than a counseling program or a superficial training program, might reduce both welfare dependency and unemployment. The participants in both groups apparently took full advantage of work opportunities. TOPS had no edge on WEET in this respect. A program that provided jobs or access to jobs would probably be attractive to many welfare recipients and presumably to an even larger number of unemployed people not yet impoverished to the point of AFDC eligibility. But a jobs program, especially if it were open to anyone who was unemployed and not just the relatively small number of people on AFDC, would cost far more in terms of public transfers than a relatively underfunded TOPS program reserved for a few qualified AFDC mothers. Again, however, the minimalism of the training programs and the absence of a full employment policy may accurately reflect popular values.

GAIN

California's Greater Avenues for Independence program (GAIN) was similar in almost every respect to the earlier state waiver experiments: services, recipients, organizational arrangements, exaggerated claims for success, butchered evaluations, but wide public acceptance.[9] GAIN also added intensive case management that provided a personal counselor who supervised each welfare recipient's progress toward independence, and its services appear to be somewhat more intensive than services in many other similar training programs. The cost per registrant ranged from $3,500 to $7,000, depending on location.

The program was initiated in six California counties as a randomized controlled experiment in 1988 and persisted for three years. Thus GAIN was taken to demonstrate the feasibility of the 1996 welfare reform's principal assumption that large numbers of welfare recipients could be placed in jobs with relatively inexpensive, minimal preparation. GAIN may have also been MDRC's most sophisticated training program evaluation.

The authors of the MDRC study planted the flag of success in their evaluation: the program would create "jobs, reduce welfare costs, and save taxpayers money; . . . [there were] notable successes in all six counties; . . . GAIN increased single parents' three year earnings by 22 percent; . . . in one county . . . earnings went up 49 percent and welfare costs fell 15 percent; . . . GAIN demonstrated the potential to succeed with a wide range of groups in the welfare population, including very long-term welfare recipients and people in a major inner city" (Riccio, Friedlander, and Freedman 1994, v–vi).

The state waiver experiments and GAIN repeatedly emphasized the goal of reducing dependence on public welfare rather than reducing poverty itself. The social consequences of this preference, which is a

---

9. Portions of the description of GAIN are drawn from Epstein (1997), which presents a detailed analysis of welfare-to-work programs in chapter 5.

pillar of American culture, were never seriously considered. Indeed, subsequent welfare reforms, notably in 1996 and in the 2005 reauthorization, were consistently modeled on GAIN, again with only passing concern for the actual conditions of welfare recipients, two-thirds of whom were children.

Even given its relatively modest goals, the actual GAIN experience does not sustain the buoyant conclusions of the evaluators or the decision, reflected in subsequent legislation, to promote the GAIN service package as a solution to welfare dependency, let alone poverty. The least expensive GAIN program, in Riverside County, spent only $23 per registrant on core training and education services. GAIN registrants in Riverside County earned about $1,000 more per year than the $2,600 average annual income of controls, which amounts to about $20 per week. The largest welfare savings ranged from $275 to $600 per year. The advantage of GAIN registrants in the percentage ever employed during the third follow-up year ranged from 2.4 percent in Los Angeles County, where 16 percent of controls were employed at some time during the year, to 6.6 percent in Riverside County, where 25 percent of controls were similarly employed.

These tiny differences are probably the result of job placement, especially given the near absence of any education or training services in Riverside County. The dominance of job placement is also suggested by the relatively small percentage of GAIN registrants who participated in education and training services (40 to 60 percent) and the short duration of these services, usually only a few months. Indeed, in the recessionary conditions of these counties, MDRC might have made the effort to identify people who were displaced from work or who did not get work because of the preferences given to GAIN registrants, especially since GAIN salaries were publicly subsidized. The state may have saved a few dollars in welfare payments, but apparently at the expense of unemployed people who were not eligible for welfare.

In spite of these paltry benefits, MDRC still insists on "the fact that all six counties produced modest-to-large earnings gains or welfare savings or both" (Riccio, Friedlander, and Freedman 1994, 270). Yet this "fact" is belied by the serious methodological shortcomings of the research. Aside from job search and possible placement preference, the small benefits of GAIN may be the result of unusually dedicated staff working under the scrutiny of a demonstration program. The demonstration effects are likely to disappear in more routinized circumstances with less skilled and dedicated staff. As in other experiments (e.g., the massive negative income tax experiments of earlier years), off-the-books income was probably underreported, with the likely effect of diminishing both the relative earnings differences between the groups and the absolute differences, insofar as GAIN registrants had less opportunity to earn illegal income.

In addition, the considerable variation among the counties points to the impact of local employment conditions rather than services. Because of great differences in administration, local economic conditions, and program content, the six sites end up as independent case studies that leave open the question of the national applicability of the outcomes. GAIN certainly did not demonstrate the value of its services in reducing the welfare rolls, while the evaluation studiously ignores the inadequacy of marginal work for poor people. If anything, GAIN is a failure begging for a national employment program that pays adequate wages and provides decent benefits.

These publicly funded training programs for the poor and other low-status groups never challenged the basic American assumptions that people end up pretty much where they deserve to be, that ample opportunities for advancement already exist, that the marketplace is open, and thus that American social and economic stratification is fair. Indeed, the programs failed largely because they did not make sufficient attempts to address prior deprivations through investments in skills training. They also never tackled the problem of insufficient jobs for the unskilled but in effect promoted job sharing among the poor. The meager programs reflect once again the American people's obsession with personal responsibility, the expectation that it is up to individuals to work hard, with few protections against failure or need.

History and Public Policy in an Open Society

The institutional and intellectual histories tend to dramatize the importance of the idea and the determining influence of the intellectual, the conceit that ideas matter and that therefore thinkers matter. Typical American social welfare histories of the past fifty years, notably histories of the War on Poverty, attribute the "discovery" of poverty to a number of largely journalistic tracts. They suggest a tug-of-war over policy conducted by different factions and interests. The histories consistently lack appreciation for the determinative influence over social welfare policy of persistent mass preferences, the institutionalized values of the population. Indeed, the histories tend to reject the notion that American social welfare policies are the choice of the vast majority of Americans.

Emphasizing the obligatory themes of personal influence, pluralism, or institutional prowess, the histories fail to prove that the intellectual dicta of the times—the recorded and archived impressions of influential groups and insightful individual actors—played any decisive role in policy choice. Individual actors and the variety of groups that achieve power may well be simply reflecting the social choices of the American people; that is, the dramas of great people and great power may emanate from strong mass preferences rather than form those preferences. The histories seem trapped in a fallacy of selective proof, going forward from their assumptions of institutional importance to explain what their authors believe are institutional choices. However, the narratives of power fail to defend their fundamental assumptions about the determinants of social policy.

In contrast, wisdom may lie in first taking the policy choices themselves as the definitive statements of social value in an open society, and then going back to explore the patterns of uncoerced citizen behavior that built to those choices. The failures of the War on Poverty, and even the minimal improvements in Social Security since the 1960s, reflect the national will, its refusal to tamper with the market and its sense that by and large people get what they deserve. Thus the actual conditions of American social welfare programs belie any national enthusiasm for poverty reduction or for the claims of the poor, let alone for the claims of the large number of Americans who worked consistently throughout their lives but fell into poverty when they retired.

The American people have shown clearly and consistently that they are comfortable with allowing market forces to determine the social and economic position of citizens. By and large they see the market as just, and they perceive little need to regulate it or to compensate for the harm it causes. In the debate over whether individual character or social structure determines individual outcomes—whether poverty exists because the poor have flawed characters or because of an unfair system—the former position has clearly prevailed.

More generally, the War on Poverty and American social welfare convert structural concepts such as opportunity into issues of character by providing very limited resources for supportive and compensatory services. The War on Poverty emphasized the need to provide opportunities for disadvantaged groups, but at a low level of funding. The implicit assumption was that poor people's ability to take advantage of even limited resources was a question of moral will.

Murray's (1983) inversion of the concept of helping as a "moral hazard"—his argument that the War on Poverty programs perversely *created* the problems of welfare dependency and poverty by relieving people of personal responsibility for their own conditions—fortified a new generation of conservative intellectuals. The more structural and liberal arguments by Patterson (1981), Katz (1986), and others offer sentimental and improbable explanations for the failure of social welfare interventions, when their failure is even acknowledged.

The argument between the conservative and liberal camps cannot be resolved in rational terms, because it is practically, legally, and morally impossible to conduct experiments to test the true causes of the failure of the War on Poverty. As a consequence, the camps bicker back and forth with no prospect of resolution, both sides hampered by inadequate evidence. They often cite "evidence" that merely bears out their assumptions. And they uniformly ignore the possibility that the failure of welfare programs is, in effect, intentional, reflecting a deep and enduring national consensus.

Traditional American liberals searched mightily for villains and usually found them in the undue influence of business, special interests, the media, or preexisting economic inequality. Yet the programs of the War on Poverty were largely the contrivances of American liberals. While conservatives seem stuck on moralizing, liberals seek refuge in the ingenuity of social invention and the social sciences in the hope that meager social interventions can reverse decades of serious material deprivation and habitual personal dysfunctions. As we have seen, however, the War on Poverty programs and their progeny were too weak to achieve any significant material result.

In a manner common to almost all personal and community social welfare programs, the OEO and the War on Poverty ignored the programmatic record, in this case the experience of MFY and the Gray Areas Projects. Instead they followed the playbook of political acceptability, the imperative to satisfy the ambitions of important actors and groups, strongly implying conformity with popular notions of how to approach social problems. The cheat in the game is not the program, the disingenuous evaluators, the dueling intellectuals, some nefarious elite, or even the hidden forces of capitalism, but the American people themselves.

The catchphrase of the War on Poverty—opportunity—entailed the rejection of a more profound approach to poverty, namely, entitlement. Sufficient American wealth existed during the War on Poverty years, and has increased greatly since then, to simply close the economic gap. But the nation, including large proportions of potential beneficiaries, refuses to put a floor under income, to provide a livable wage, to enact universal health and mental health care, to assure adequate public education, and so on. A sufficient constituency does not exist for these reforms.

The more or less uniform failure of welfare services to resolve serious social problems attests to the emptiness of the liberal vision and the enduring influence of popular preference. The American will has defeated the rational enterprise in social welfare. Indeed, American liberals are closer to the so-called conservatives than to the progressive ideal of social and economic equality; the conservative faith that stern necessity is a sufficient incentive to propel people out of poverty is little more than smug cruelty. The War on Poverty was merely an episode in the serialized melodrama of American social welfare—a highly stylized morality play that elaborated the fundamental choices of the American people.

American ingenuity has yet to invent either cold fusion or inexpensive, culturally compatible programs that successfully short-circuit enduring deprivation. And if the history of technological innovation and social change is any indicator, America will enjoy cold fusion well before a public policy designed to achieve greater social and economic equality.

4

THE SOCIAL INSURANCES AND WELFARE

There is a profound parallel between American social insurance and American welfare. Core social welfare programs like TANF and food stamps are tied to the social insurances by a consistency in benefits that is evidence of a consistency in popular values. Pointedly designed for two different beneficiary groups—workers and nonworkers—both types of public program are inadequate, largely because they mirror the embedded social preferences on which the country's socioeconomic stratification rests in the first place. Rather than the pieties and vacuous hopes of its July 4th and Memorial Day speeches, the true, active values of the United States have determined the nature of the nation's public services. Workers are valued over those who cannot or do not work, and higher-paid workers are valued, *pari passu,* over lower-paid workers, with little regard for their different needs or social contributions.

Traditional welfare analyses explain the inadequacy of welfare benefits by the principle of less eligibility—people who qualify for public benefits should receive less than the lowest-paid worker earns. However, this enactment of a stern work ethic, assuming that incentives for work need to be maintained even among those who cannot work, has become somewhat distorted as wages for many working people have fallen in the United States since the 1970s. Rather than raise the minimum wage, increase wage supplements, or improve the ancillary benefits of employment, notably health care and retirement, public policy has sought to maintain the work incentive by decreasing the level of welfare. This choice is made without compelling evidence that less eligibility is an important factor in work participation rates among poorer people and welfare beneficiaries (Epstein 1997). The United States has the resources to put a culturally decent floor under all American incomes and to provide universal access to important services, pointedly health and mental health care. It chooses not to. The decision is cultural, a matter of active consent rather than economic necessity.

Despite some obvious remnants of abject want in contemporary society—homelessness, neglected children, forgotten institutionalized patients and prisoners—absolute poverty has largely vanished in the United States. People do not starve to death; indeed, the principal nutritional problem seems to be obesity. Few are homeless. Most people receive medical care, even if it is not continuous, timely, or particularly effective. However, the absence of third world deprivation does not testify to the presence of a decent society or decent standing in society. Something more than universal subsistence is required to capture the gravity of social need in contemporary American society.

That something more has much to do with citizens' relative participation in the central institutions of a society. In this sense, poverty is a condition of isolation from the core social activities and experiences that confer respectable standing on citizens. Minimally acceptable citizenship in contemporary American society requires adequate family life for children or substitutes that provide socialization, participation in community, including the community of popular culture, education, training for employment, housing, medical care, resources to rely on in the event of emergencies and catastrophes, and so on. Well beyond food, clothing, and shelter, modern life also requires sophisticated socialization and literacy, along with the capacity to negotiate the complexities of ever changing social conditions. Therefore, a more serviceable concept of poverty reaching beyond physical survival speaks to relative deprivation, the degree of separateness between common experiences in cultural institutions and the conditions of the poor.

If the minimal package of activities and experiences required for physical and social survival were to be cashed out, they could be measured as an absolute minimum. The social minimum might be justified in some objective sense as necessary points in human growth and development without much reference to the actual conditions of a society. However, the poverty threshold could also be measured relative to common social institutions. In the latter sense, taking income and schooling as two examples, as median income and years of education changed, so too would the poverty standard for these goods.

In 1966 the United States adopted an absolute economic definition of poverty for families of different sizes and residential locations that, except for cost-of-living adjustments, has not changed in more than forty years, despite enormous increases in national wealth and expectations for the citizen's social, economic, and political participation. The standard, adjusted to account for family size, was based on the observation that the typical family spent about one-third of its income on food. Thus the poverty standard was defined as three times the cost of the minimally nutritional food basket (Orshansky 1968).

While the American poverty standard sets the mark of social need and sometimes even serves as an eligibility criterion for services, it does not set the level of benefits in any public welfare program, including both Social Security and traditional welfare services (e.g., Temporary Assistance for Needy Families, Supplemental Security Income, and food stamps). No American social welfare program, including Social Security, provides enough assistance to raise the income of all recipients above the poverty line. Those who do rise out of poverty usually started off only slightly below the poverty line. Thus, in its commitment to insurance equity, the highest benefits typically accrue to those with the highest incomes. In other words, the system provides the most social security to those who need it least, and the least security to those who need it most.

In contrast to this absolute measure of poverty, a relative measure fixed at the same 1966 threshold's percentage of contemporary median family income—about 50 percent—would produce a far higher estimate of social need. Under an expansive definition of income in the Luxembourg Income Study—"disposable household income"—which in addition to market income also includes government transfers and near-cash income such as food stamps, minus tax payments, 17 percent of Americans, including 21.9 percent of children, fell below 50 percent of national median income in 2000 (Burtless 2007, table 1). The absolute poverty rate for the same year, again measured by disposable household income, was only 8.7 percent. The official poverty rate for 2000 was 11.3 percent (U.S. Census Bureau 2001).

Compared with nineteen other wealthy nations, the United States, which arguably has the greatest wealth and therefore the greatest capacity to redress income deprivation, makes the least effort. It suffers the greatest amount of economic inequality, even after accounting for government programs. Relative poverty in Denmark, for example, is only 7.2 percent, including only 5 percent of children (Burtless 2007, table 1). To the extent to which comparisons have been made, economic mobility between parents and children is lower in the United States than in other wealthy nations.

From 1979 to 2003, measured against the National Research Council's definition of income (Citro and Michael 1995), which is even more inclusive than Luxembourg's standard of disposable household income, the gap between poor and nonpoor in the United States grew. Moreover, the amount of extreme poverty, i.e., the percentage of people with income below 25 percent of the median, increased in the 1990s despite unprecedented national income growth: "The figures underscore that what happens to the economic status of the poor near the poverty line may not be the same as that far below the line, and that for a more complete picture of poverty one needs to move beyond the head count rate" (Ziliak 2005, 168).

In 2003, and measured against the National Research Council's definition of income, the American absolute poverty gap (the amount needed to bring all people up to the poverty line) was about $183 billion, about $2,942 per person, compared with $46 billion total and $1,979 per person in 1979 (all in 2004 dollars) (Ziliak 2005, table 3.1). It is a tribute to the American spoils system of welfare that the poverty gap for a white person has been greater than for a black person since 1979: $3,003 versus $2,688 in 2003, the most recent year reported by Ziliak (table 3.3). The ability to fill the absolute poverty gap—an amount less than 10 percent of the 2006 federal budget and less than 1.5 percent of the gross domestic product—is well within the means of the United States.

The natural progression of an expanding economy tends to remove a large proportion of the population from an absolute standard of poverty, even while the relative conditions of a large portion of its population may be deteriorating. Indeed, this anomaly has characterized the United States at least since the early 1970s, as wages have stagnated for lower-skilled workers and profits have been concentrated at the highest income levels. The rising economic tide has not lifted all boats.

Even against its absolute standard, America's core cash-transfer programs—old age insurance (OAI) and TANF—given considerable impetus by the War on Poverty, have failed. They are inadequate against standard absolute poverty thresholds. Yet measured against relative standards of poverty, they express the nation's lack of concern with deprivation, evidence of its complacency about growing inequality. Few are removed from poverty; even fewer are provided with access to the central institutions of the culture.

The choice of a poverty threshold and the interventions designed to address it reflect a culture's values. The American decision to maintain a series of weak antipoverty measures, and to allow an initially low absolute poverty standard to deteriorate over the years against a backdrop of generally improving economic conditions, suggests a deepening disparagement for those in need and a cruel refusal to attend to social integration.

Old Age Insurance

From its inception, OAI, the centerpiece of Social Security, has been a very inadequate program, largely because the American people refuse to share their resources compassionately or generously.[1] Even the traumatic dislocations of the Great Depression were insufficient to convince the nation to protect itself from the economic turbulence of the business cycle and the common risks of living, notably unexpected death and incapacity. Indeed, the very notion of social insurance was concocted to disguise the fundamental nature of Social Security as a social welfare program, although one without much income redistribution. While people contribute and receive benefits, there is no justiciable contract between insurer and beneficiary; the benefits and contributions are acts of legislative negotiation that reflect economic capacity as much as contributions; beneficiaries do not hold a contract that assures them benefits proportionate to their contributions. The program offers a social contract rather than a legal one.

The program is in essence an intergenerational transfer whose major function is to smooth out and replace a large portion of traditional intrafamilial transfers but with very little redistribution between wealthier

1. In this study, Social Security refers broadly to the provisions of the enacted social insurances, old age, survivors, disability, and health insurance. Uncapitalized social security refers to the general concept of reducing the risks of living. Thus OAI, a central provision of Social Security, is justified as providing social security through assured public pensions that reduce the risk of poverty for beneficiaries, most of whom are retirees.

and poorer contributors; the program exports children's voluntary transfers to their parents into an involuntary, near-universal public program
that assures those transfers, but between generations rather than individuals. On the basis of a single cohort, born between 1931 and 1941,
Gustman and Steinmeier (2001) estimate that only about 9.9 percent of
total benefits are redistributed from wealthier beneficiaries to the poorest 50 percent of beneficiaries and that a total of only 10.6 percent is
redistributed in all. Yet while this redistribution increases benefits for
poorer recipients by a substantial *percentage*—as much as 50 percent—
the *actual monetary gain* is still very small, since the unenhanced benefits
are tiny to begin with. However, when marital status is considered, the
percentage of social security benefits redistributed from the wealthier
half of beneficiaries to the poorer half shrinks to only 2.5 percent, reflecting the benefit given to wealthier recipient couples with a stay-at-
home spouse, and their longer life expectancy in comparison with
poorer recipients (Gustman and Steinmeier 2001). Indeed, the major
redistribution within OAI occurs within income classes, from married
beneficiaries who both worked substantial amounts of time to married
beneficiaries with only one earner. Redistribution would be further reduced to the extent to which the system is privatized.

Moreover, there has been little forgiveness for personal failure in either the early program or any of its revised versions; minimum payments are extremely low and even together with Supplemental Security
Income do not lift recipients out of poverty. Gustman and Steinmeier
estimate that "without redistribution, the social security benefits of
26.4% of the [OAI recipient] households would be below the poverty
line, but after redistribution only 21.8% would be below the line" (2001,
25). However, in 2000 the poverty line for those over age sixty-five was
only $8,259 for an individual and $10,419 for a couple. Those who
started off poor largely remain poor after retirement, a rather perverse
sense of the concept of security as continuity rather than as adequacy.

Because social security constrains traditional family discretion (e.g.,
over how much to provide for older relatives) and employs contemporary
tax capacity rather than investment or savings as a basis for benefits,
conservatives have attacked the program as a threat to family solidarity
and a poor return for capital. There is no way to refute the charge and
no way to support it. No control group for social security is possible; no
controlled experimental situation can be created for a national program
of this kind. The question of whether OAI has accelerated changes in

the structure of American families or has simply been ancillary is unanswerable. The desirability of the change itself—from family discretion to bureaucratic equity—is an infinitely convoluted problem that may not be amenable to any sort of empirical resolution.

Yet it is obvious that if contributions had been invested in the stock market over the years since World War II they would have grown far faster than the cost of living and the benefit increases of the program. However, the program intended security, not risk taking for maximum investment returns. Yet OAI has failed to achieve its most basic goal; it does not provide security for the largest and neediest number of recipients. The very meanness of the program's benefits represents the collective choice of the American people to perpetuate into retirement the inadequacies of economic redistribution in the United States.

The program assumed, perhaps romantically, even in its early years, that retirees would have less need for income after they had raised their children. Their homes would be paid for, and workers were expected to have put aside additional savings for their retirement during their productive years; many would also enjoy private pensions. Moreover, the high proportion of contributors to retirees—about five to one during the early years—was projected to continue, while greatly increased life expectancy was not anticipated. Medical care was envisioned as a continuing private responsibility. For these reasons, the program was assumed to be relatively inexpensive, a small tax burden with low ceilings on taxable income. Thus economic security for retirees seemed easily within reach.

Yet true security has not been achieved for either early beneficiaries or current ones, despite numerous liberalizations of benefits. Even against standard poverty thresholds, considerable poverty persists among aged Social Security beneficiaries—18.2 percent for those who rely on Social Security for all of their income and 9.3 percent for those who rely on it for between 80 and 99 percent of their income (table 1). However, against more realistic but still minimal standards, OAI is very deficient. Based on Social Security Administration tabulations of the Census Bureau's March 2004 Current Population Survey, more than 90 percent of aged individuals relying on Social Security for all of their income lived on $15,000 or less; more than 90 percent of couples relying on Social Security for all of their income lived on $25,000 or less (table 2). Overall, 52.7 percent of single aged Social Security beneficiaries live on $15,000 or less and 29.4 percent of married beneficiaries live on $25,000 or less. Almost 10 million "aged units," representing more than 14 million individuals, rely on Social Security for at least 80 percent of their income (tables 1 and 2). These levels of income—$15,000 for an individual and $25,000 for a couple—although higher than the official poverty standards, are barely sufficient for a minimally decent life. It is worth recalling that Social Security is restricted to the presumably deserving—former workers, most of whom have put in a lifetime of labor.

Granting that the precise details of OAI's inadequacy are probably not widely known—survey data generally suggest nearly universal ignorance of program details—popular awareness is probably not a necessary condition of *intentional* popular approval. OAI expresses the national priority for retired workers. The priority emerges through the competition of role organizations that do in fact carry the sanction of the American people, although split into an endless number of representative organizations. The sanction is provided through the huge number of choices that the American people make in living out their existence. In this way, the formidable AARP (formerly known as the American Association of Retired Persons), arguably the largest lobby in the United States, represents only one role preference. But even here, the complexity of AARP's membership, drawn from the full range of Americans but weighted toward the middle classes, has created a constituency of cautious centrist values—a bit more generosity, a bit more redistribution—that itself has balanced the appetite for benefits against the reluctance to tax. The AARP is clearly not the advocate of the elderly in need or the feared dragon of socialized universal services.

Representative organizations, carefully accountable to their constituencies, are extraordinarily well informed about OAI and every other public welfare program. In this way, while the deficiencies of OAI may be broadly lamented in the same spirit of life's many disappointments, the deficiencies are surely intended. The perennial and overwhelming approval voiced in polls for Social Security is an approval for the program as it is. Surveyed opinions that call for more benefits are simply the reflexive yes to being asked if the respondent would like more money.[2]

2. Huge percentages, often as high as 90 percent, of polled respondents have reported support for the extension of Social Security to a variety of uncovered groups since the program's early years (Schiltz 1970), and support for the liberalization of the program in subsequent decades (Epstein 2004). The contributory programs were gradually extended to uncovered workers. However, the failure to greatly liberalize the program's benefits can be seen as an instance of the popular will's being thwarted by a controlling elite. Nevertheless, the reported preference has not translated into an active priority of citizen organizations—labor unions, fraternal organizations, membership organizations such as the AARP, church

The real social value and true preference is shown in the choice of program conditions—eligibility, contributions, administration, benefits. OAI is a profound instance of the American value of self-reliance, the broad national refusal to share resources generously, the view of citizenship as a personal responsibility rather than a social enterprise.

There is no financial crisis facing Social Security. The problem is political, a question of competitive values rather than financial resources. It may be quite true that projected benefits will outstrip current contributions, which is only to say that the system must change to either fund current levels of benefits or to reduce benefits.

> If there is no legislation changing Social Security, trust fund assets and payroll tax revenue (and revenue from the taxation of benefits) are projected to be sufficient to pay all the benefits scheduled under current law until 2042. . . . After the trust fund assets are exhausted the payroll tax revenue would continue to be available to pay benefits, with the flow of revenues at that time sufficient to pay roughly three-quarters of the benefits scheduled in current law. The estimate for the end of the 75-year projection period shows enough revenue to pay roughly two-thirds of scheduled benefits. (Diamond 2004, 1)

The proposal to index Social Security to wages rather than prices would by itself cut in half the anticipated OAI shortfall. However, this would also entrench the inadequacy of retiree incomes, particularly for poorer beneficiaries, since prices customarily increase by about half a percentage point more than wages do (White 2001). Reducing the ability of retirees to keep up with prices or even to gain a bit as they grow into their frail years would emphasize the current system's fixation on maintaining vertical equity, that is, the stratification of American society.

Plans to increase the redistributive characteristics of OAI while

---

groups, ethnic and racial groups, and the like—that are obviously not dominated by traditional elites. Especially because of the flaws of opinion polling, an indirect method of ascertaining preference—one removed from situations of choice themselves and from the behavioral choices of Americans in allocating time, effort, and money to an overwhelming number of possible choices—seems to constitute a better estimate of true priorities (Epstein 2006b). Often hysterical projections about the demise of Social Security have met with relatively little citizen reaction. The American affection for OASDHI seems best understood as the support for the program as it is, complete with its inadequacies and affection for insurance equity rather than social equality.

achieving actual balance test the American tolerance for change. Diamond and Orszag (2004) would draw on taxes from incomes above the
current social security tax ceiling and rely on a revived estate or inheri-
tance tax to increase the adequacy of benefits. Their plan, however, includes some degree of internal redistribution of benefits, including
decreased benefits for many, among them the retiree with high average
lifetime earnings, while focusing increases on those most in need. It
improves the system's fairness by increasing the progressivity of the
Social Security tax base and thus loosens Social Security's attachment to
the principle of insurance equity. For the first time, it assures that minimum wage workers eligible for full benefits would be assured a retirement income above the standard poverty line. However, the poverty line
is antiquated, and the improved benefits would remain quite inadequate
for poor workers.

In this way, Diamond and Orszag's plan makes an important gesture
to adequacy but still fails to answer the substantial shortfalls of the system. Indeed, it accepts cuts in benefits for many with very modest lifetime incomes. Its commitment to achieve long-term actuarial soundness
without depending on general revenues as a major source of Social Security funding constrains its ability to provide a decent income for all
retirees. The Diamond-Orszag proposal seems to be among the more
liberal reforms. As such, its modest provisions mark the upper boundary
on Americans' willingness to revisit the individualistic assumptions that
bind the current system. Extensive overhauls of Social Security that actually provide security in retirement are not on the table. The international
perspective, which references extended families or tribal solidarity in
preindustrial societies, seems quaintly irrelevant to the American experience, or already rejected when it illuminates European systems (Midgley
and Sherraden 1997).

Other reforms that attempt to avoid higher allocations for retirees
and thus higher taxes (e.g., Murray 1997)—notably through greater redistribution within the system, which would reduce benefits at the top
and increase them at the bottom—would pierce the system's myth of
insurance while only minimally addressing the inadequacy of benefits,
especially if the redistribution is intended to tie the increased number
of future beneficiaries to projected resources. Internal redistribution assumes that benefits are crucial for poorer retirees but redundant for the
wealthy. Moreover, in frankly acknowledging a central welfare role, the
justification for a separate, largely regressive tax evaporates in favor of

sustaining the system with general revenues. Yet the change to general revenues would seem to imperil Social Security's powerful ceremonial role in endorsing the American credo of just deserts: you get what you work for.

Having argued for centuries that public benefits of any kind corrupt the American work ethic, family responsibility, civic participation, the vitality of the business sector, individual enterprise, and so forth, conservatives have been stalwart opponents of social insurance from its inception. Whatever its ideological and putative empirical virtues, their latest notion of privatizing all or a portion of contributions comes up against the requisite transition costs, estimated at trillions of dollars. The transition costs to a privatized system would be accrued as future contributions went into private accounts while the public paid to sustain benefits for current beneficiaries and those who would retire into the privatized system. Yet privatizing the system would eliminate security, since the welfare of privatized beneficiaries would depend on the vagaries of the market. It would also ignore the residual responsibility to those whose investments fail.

The debate seems to be fought on conservative territory, with an enormous and often technically impenetrable fuss in macroeconomics over the broader effects of Social Security benefits and taxation on labor participation, capital accumulation, profits, price stability, and the like. The fear of economic collapse stalks proposals to increase public expenditures and thus taxes. Yet the volition of the American people—what they customarily do about work, savings, and sharing—determines public policy choices. If seen as appropriate, fair, just, and an extension of family responsibility to the broader community, greater contributions to public welfare, including the resulting higher taxes and less disposable income, would be accepted in the same way that Americans accept the annual cycles of their gardens, sports, school, vacations, and the rest, including mustard on hot dogs, orotund Sunday sermons, grandma's beloved wrinkles, and the large increases in OAI during the 1970s as a patriotic reward for the aging World War II generation. In fact, the technical features of the debate—economics as science and objective truth— may be as arbitrary and ideological as religious commitment (Nelson 2002). In this sense, economic theory and public policy are as expressive as painting, music, and literature, offering aesthetic truths that often graduate into political symbols of self-interest. The controversy over Social Security may already have been settled, if the values of the American people are settled.

The policy dispute over Social Security's long-range financial viability—its actuarial soundness—will not be resolved through a better distribution of information to the masses, or even a more effective popularization of the technical material (e.g., Shaviro 2001; White 2001; Diamond and Orszag 2004). A shadowy elite is not manipulating the American people; they are not being hoodwinked by narrow interests with insider influence; they have not been betrayed by an autonomous leadership class. Their will has been done.

The situation of Social Security is known democratically but not widely. The deficiencies of the early program, enacted by an economically strained society, have persisted into the wealthiest society in human history, and notably against contemporary expectations of citizenship and the capacity to redress social deprivation.

> "Only to a very minor degree does [Social Security] modify the distribution of wealth and it does not alter at all the fundamentals of our capitalistic and individualistic economy. Nor does it relieve the individual of primary responsibility for his own support and that of his dependents." . . . Eligibility and benefits in [OAI, for example] were closely work-related, government contributions were omitted, and fiscal conservatism prevailed in the emphasis upon . . . the equity principles of private insurance. (Lubove 1968, in part quoting Witte)
>
> In many respects [the Social Security Act of 1935] was an astonishingly inept and conservative piece of legislation. In no other welfare system in the world did the state shirk all responsibility for old-age indigency and insist that funds be taken out of the current earnings of workers. By relying on regressive taxation and withdrawing vast sums to build up reserves, the act did untold economic mischief. The law denied coverage to numerous classes of workers, including those who needed security most: notably farm laborers and domestics. Sickness, in normal times the main cause of joblessness, was disregarded. The act not only failed to support a national system of unemployment compensation but did not even provide adequate national standards. (Leuchtenburg 1963, 132)

After the 1930s, coverage became nearly universal; a variety of insurance programs were added, notably disability insurance in the 1950s and health insurance (Medicare) during the War on Poverty; and bene-fits were both indexed to purchasing power and liberalized. Moreover, the initial act was expanded to include other noninsurance, charitable types of programs, notably SSI and Medicaid, while improving existing provisions. Yet considered against the financial capacity and changing conditions of American life, the Social Security Act during the first dec-ade of the twenty-first century remains "an astonishingly inept and con-servative piece of legislation" and, Leuchtenburg would probably add, cheap and mean-spirited. While it is certainly an improvement over the desperate times of the 1930s, its continuing inadequacies are profound. In tribute to the force of embedded cultural belief, the great victory of the Social Security Act of 1935 to finally acknowledge a large public role in the nation's welfare has been fulfilled in transmitting private attitudes that are decidedly antagonistic to sharing and social security itself.

The inadequacy of Social Security in the United States, exemplified by OAI, is continuously sanctioned and revitalized by a large American consensus that is expressed in the daily choices of life rather than in dubious poll responses. The American people do not want to put more aside for a decent retirement, with adequate health services for all citi-zens, because they have not put more aside. American families have tolerated current conditions for elderly relatives, refusing to politicize any deep grievance over their care. The current pattern of American expenditures reflects the nation's true priorities and the sanction of the American people. The sorting through of items in the social budget has been completed. Getting out the data on the program's deficiencies to the American people, even as an overwhelming number of them are ignorant of the facts, would be akin to confronting them with their own faulty character, an exercise in theology rather than politics. The body politic, in all of its consensual forms, is indeed informed. It has chosen with deep knowledge and broad participation, regardless of the fact that most Americans are quite unaware of the specifics of the program.

Yet, inadequate as they are, provisions for the aged who are less well off are better than benefits for younger groups who are less well off.

> Except in the lowest ranks of the income distribution, when in-
> come is measured using the Census Bureau's money income
> definition, aged households look considerably worse off than non-
> aged households in the same part of the income distribution. How-
> ever, under the broadest measure of household income, aged and

nonaged households appear to have similar incomes in the middle of the income distribution, and aged households have higher incomes than the nonaged both in the top quarter and the bottom quarter of the income distribution. (Bosworth, Burtless, and Anders n.d., 27–28)

Welfare for the Poor

The shortfalls of the Social Security Act are even deeper in provisions for the nonworking poor, which can be explained largely by the American insistence on a stringently bifurcated and gendered social welfare system.[3] The social insurances are designed for workers, presumably more deserving—that is, better—citizens than those who need assistance but cannot or do not work. Gordon (1992, 1994) argues that the difference carries powerful gender associations. The masculine social insurances are ruled by bureaucratic rationality—benefits provided by right to all who qualify—but the welfare programs allow for a large amount of "maternal" discretion. The poor apparently abdicate their "masculine" independence by relying on public assistance, opening themselves to "mother's" interpretation of their motives and needs. The gendered distinction takes on compelling force in light of the welfare reforms of 1996 and their reauthorization in 2005. The changes largely revoked the rights of welfare recipients gained during the War on Poverty, returning the program to its more "maternal" years with the introduction of administrative subjectivity in assessing the cooperativeness of recipients and applicants.

Federal cash assistance for the poor, largely restricted to single-parent

3. There are few words as ambiguous as "welfare," even in a discussion of public and social policy. In its narrow sense, welfare refers to the core cash and similar assistance programs for the presumably able-bodied poor: Temporary Assistance to Needy Families (previously Aid to Families with Dependent Children) and food stamps. In a slightly wider context, it also includes additional assistance programs for the able-bodied poor such as Medicaid, housing programs (both public housing and rent supplement provisions), and special nutrition programs. In yet a broader sense, it includes the Earned Income Tax Credit and the Supplemental Security Income program for impoverished groups apparently too incapacitated to work—the blind, the totally and permanently disabled, and the elderly. In its most inclusive sense it refers to an amorphous sense of general comfort and contentment that includes Social Security as well as all of domestic welfare and perhaps even foreign policy that affects "domestic tranquility." This section relates the narrowest concept of welfare, largely TANF and food stamps, to the broader uses of the term. I avoid ambiguous use of the term "welfare" by employing specific references.

families with children since the original legislation was passed in the 1930s, reached its most generous level in the early 1970s.[4] Between 1970 and 1996, the average monthly AFDC benefit for a family declined by almost 50 percent, from $734 to $374 (in constant 1996 dollars) (U.S. House 1998, 414). The decline in public assistance—the combination of AFDC and food stamps—was softened by increases over the period in food stamp benefits. Still, public assistance (AFDC plus food stamps) that consistently denied benefits sufficient to bring recipients above the poverty line was reduced by more than 20 percent between 1973 and 1996. The decreases were not specifically legislated but accrued as the states refused to adjust AFDC benefits to keep up with inflation. This universal tolerance for constrained public benefits prevailed at the same time that the national wealth increased greatly, suggesting a proportionate disaffection for redistributive policies and the declining priority of addressing economic deprivation.

The AFDC caseload exploded during and after the War on Poverty, rising from fewer than 4 million recipients in the early 1960s to more than 11 million by 1976 and peaking at more than 14 million by 1993. The great increase seems consequent to changing sexual practices, particularly among whites, that resulted in many more children born out of wedlock, a liberalization until 1973 of benefits and eligibility, and the declining stigma attached to public relief. Typically, blacks and Hispanics account for about two-thirds of the caseload (U.S. House 1998, 441).

The reforms of 1996 were animated by the conservative criticism of public welfare, notably Murray's (1983) argument that public assistance programs actually created the poverty and dependency they were originally designed to address. The conservative worldview sees poverty as just deserts for laziness and imprudence, even going so far as to value it as a useful spur to industriousness. The Personal Responsibility and Work Opportunity Act of 1996, which replaced AFDC with Temporary Assistance for Needy Families (TANF), reflected widespread displeasure with the enormous increases in the number of public assistance recipients. The reforms of 1996 also seem to have been part of the national

4. Single people and childless couples in need relied on local and state programs. The AFDC-UP program was severely restricted by most states, which wrote eligibility rules to exclude almost all applicants. Fewer than half the states offered the program before the 1990s. In 1996, for example, even with the participation of all states and an enormous amount of need in two-parent families, the AFDC-UP caseload of 1.2 million was only about 10.5 percent of the AFDC caseload (U.S. Congress, House 2004).

disavowal of progressive policy impulses and the imagined liberality of the War on Poverty. In keeping with American society's general tolerance for stark deprivation among its lowliest members, TANF sought to reduce public dependence on welfare and only secondarily poverty.

More broadly, TANF embodied the national rejection of redistributive policies and public responsibility for the social welfare of poorer and lower-status citizens. Reading the mood of the nation and committed to political expediency, President Clinton, by some standards a liberal in name only, signed the legislation, even though it failed to include the central pillars—national health care, day care, a jobs program, and intensive job training—that he claimed were necessary to transform "welfare as we know it."

TANF and the rest of the Personal Responsibility and Work Opportunity Act of 1996 did not simply reform AFDC. It eliminated a legislated right based on universal principles, replacing a guarantee of minimal (and inadequate) support with pointedly limited public charity. With broad national hostility to AFDC as too generous and lax, TANF attempted to retract not only the social impulses of 1960s, such as they were, but also the legislation of the New Deal, deficient as it was. With some exemptions, lifetime relief was replaced with a limit of five years, and episodes of dependency were often limited to two years. AFDC's open-ended funding was terminated through block grants to states, with the clear understanding that government had no obligation to continue assistance after the money ran out. With some exceptions, assistance was available only to recipients who worked. A series of sanctions were instituted to compel compliance with a variety of goals, notably relating to fertility, marriage, and employment. Most tellingly, TANF instituted case management: each applicant was assigned a worker who developed a plan—a "contract" in the newspeak of libertarian welfare reform—for "independence." Recipients who failed to comply with the plan—by not showing up for work or training, becoming pregnant, cursing the case manager, or any other sort of behavior deemed inappropriate to the furtherance of "independence"—could be sanctioned by the reduction or termination of their TANF support. Welfare provision was returned from the national government to the separate states as a local responsibility, with the federal government providing limited block grants that amounted to federal sharing. There was no longer any right to welfare, only an obligation to demonstrate personal responsibility. Good citizens went to work, saved their money, and relied on their own abilities, family, and friends. By decree, there were to be few allowable deviations from this pattern of social participation.

Other portions of the Personal Responsibility and Work Opportunity Act retrenched the Food Stamps Program so that it covered only five days' worth of food per week and eliminated the eligibility for public assistance of resident aliens, addicts, and children with attention deficit and hyperactivity disorder. The rationale was built on the myth of American self-sufficiency. Food stamps encouraged dependency and were abused for liquor and drugs (church-run food pantries seemed delighted with their renewed usefulness). Addicts were not medically infirm but morally deficient, and the state should not enable their sins. Children with attention deficit and hyperactivity disorder did not need psychiatrists but only parental discipline.

While AFDC and the rest of the American welfare state had never been generous to the poor and had always largely ignored lower-paid workers, the TANF reforms became actively abusive by reducing dependent Americans to true subsistence levels and subjecting them to childlike supervision. The reauthorization of the Personal Responsibility and Work Opportunity Act passed through Congress in 2005 with barely a murmur of dissent. The reauthorization, a portion of the Deficit Reduction Act of 2005, increased the stringency of the TANF provisions and added a series of individual treatment initiatives—additional iterations of "welfare behaviorism" that expressed the American contempt for people in need. The policy changes from AFDC through the TANF reauthorization marks a national march away from ameliorating social need and further into enchantment with the myth of heroic individualism.

The 2005 reauthorization appeared to increase outlays marginally for TANF, by $374 million from 2006 through 2010, and to decrease expenditures in other public assistance programs by the same amount over the full ten-year period beginning in 2006. When even modest estimates of inflation are factored in, however, the result was a substantial cut in funding. The reauthorization also greatly increased the work requirements for TANF recipients. It insisted that the previous obligation that states enroll 50 percent of recipients in work activities be applied to a more resistant base of recipients and also include recipients receiving assistance from so-called state programs. Since TANF funding is capped, a serious economic recession can occasion great unmet need, especially in poorer states, if the nation maintains its insistence on minimal public responsibility for personal hardship. The reauthorization modestly increased child care funding by $200 million per year.

In keeping with the nation's long-standing, if implicit, view of welfare as largely ceremonial, the reauthorization instituted new grant programs designed to promote marriage and responsible fatherhood, specifically including religious organizations as potential grant recipients. The legislation retreated even further from a view of public assistance as a response to structural failure, assuming instead that the poor need moral instruction and that their dependence results from improvident decisions, personal irresponsibility, and a lack of pride, dignity, and good sense. "Healthy Marriage Promotion" and "Responsible Fatherhood Initiatives" were funded at only $150 million per year but seemed designated for the faith-based community as the heavenly pork of God's spoils system. These two programs have four virtues and one incidental flaw: they cost very little; they allow the sanctimonious to buy its way into national politics; they promise sinners redemption if they marry and acknowledge their children; they ensure that sinners who fail to reform themselves confess their lack of deservingness by failing to respond to the programs' imprecations and thus endorse the exclusionary harshness of TANF itself.

The flaw is that they cannot be effective. None of the War on Poverty programs was able to manage behavior far less intimate than family formation. The goal of helping "couples improve the skills they need to form healthy, mutually respectful, non-violent relationships that lead to more stable, loving and committed marriages" has forever eluded the best efforts of the personal service semiprofessions, in particular, clinical psychology, social work, applied criminology, and counseling, including its pastoral subspecialty (U.S. Senate 2005, 5).

But the marriage and fatherhood initiatives were ceremonial rather than serious attempts to nurture families. The issue of effectiveness was incidental. Real support for families in need would cost far more, and would be obliged to address unemployment, inadequate education, insufficient job preparation, inadequate wages, a paucity of well-paying jobs for unskilled and semiskilled workers, and, finally, inadequate public welfare and human services for families outside the labor force.

TANF and its reauthorization express the antagonism of the American people rather than the will of a wayward Congress beholden to insidious special interests. The American people endorse the privatization of government functions, in this case the weakening of public assistance in favor of charity and churchly discretion. Indeed, public assistance policy for decades has been moving closer to the profile of American charitable giving. The record of voluntary donations reveals Americans' true preferences more trenchantly and reliably than opinion polls do. Only the smallest portion of charitable donations are given to organizations that address poverty and the needs of the poor (this issue is treated in greater depth in the next chapter) or to groups advocating greater equality. Similarly, the failures of both the private sector and civil society to either volunteer as foster parents or sustain private child welfare organizations are mirrored in the inadequacies of public child welfare programs. In the same way, the public sector's initially errant War on Poverty was brought back into line with standard American preferences.

Between 1995 (the year before TANF became operational) and 2002, the number of people on public assistance—the welfare rolls—fell from roughly 13.5 million to roughly 5.15 million, a decrease of about 64 percent (U.S. House 1998, 7–31). The legislation estimated that under TANF, and including ancillary benefits (Earned Income Tax credits and food stamps), the income of the typical recipient working full time at minimum wage would rise a bit above the poverty line in every state (7–49). But this estimate failed to deduct from income child care expenses, work expenses, including transportation, taxes, and medical expenses. With a more accurate estimate of true income and against a relative poverty threshold, TANF does not seem to have narrowed the poverty gap appreciably. But poverty reduction was not the point of the program; the point was to reduce the welfare rolls.

Nonetheless, conservatives claimed victory. Liberals were relieved to have signed on. Still, it is not at all clear that TANF had much to do with the decline of the welfare rolls or that the work alternatives to welfare conferred much benefit. Many former recipients, largely children, may have been considerably worse off under TANF than they were before, even in the few instances in which their parents felt compensated for their material losses by renewed pride and a sense of self-worth. When TANF money did indeed encourage "independence," as perhaps in Kentucky, it seems to have been spent often in a manner that recommended national, universal, and generous social services, quite contrary to the intended message of TANF.

The reasons for the drop in welfare recipients after 1996 are not as easily ascribed to TANF as its supporters would wish. Great improvement in the economy is a plausible alternative explanation for the reduction, especially given that the welfare rolls have traditionally risen and fallen in tandem with national employment. The welfare rolls were already falling substantially before the 1996 reforms (U.S. House 2004). The size of the welfare rolls is determined not only by the length of time that recipients receive benefits but also by the number of new enrollees. Moreover, typically half of welfare recipients leave the rolls in approximately three years (Ellwood and Bane 1994). Thus the drop in welfare recipients may be explained by the number of needy people who are discouraged from applying, as well as by the number who leave the rolls either because of administrative regulations (e.g., time limits and sanctions) or because they found jobs. The argument that the 1996 welfare reform was a critical factor in reducing welfare dependency says very little about the actual economic situations of needy populations.

The technical literature, impressive for its size and complexity more than for its authority, may not have settled the question of the effects of welfare reform, notably its contribution to reducing the welfare rolls. The most compulsively thorough and intricate analysis of the literature, conducted by the Rand Corporation, reaches ambiguous and uncertain conclusions (Grogger, Karoly, and Klerman 2002; Grogger and Karoly 2005). Financial incentives and mandatory work requirements seem quite logically to increase work participation, although the size of their impact is not clear; however, "it appears that, on average, the gain in earnings just offsets the loss in welfare payments, leaving income roughly unchanged . . . [while] incomes tend to rise among participants who are toward the top of the recipient income distribution" (Grogger, Karoly, and Klerman 2002, 235). The sixty-month maximum on TANF benefits tends to reduce welfare use, perhaps as recipients anticipate the date after which their assistance will run out, which may not be a desirable outcome for families who must rely on welfare during precarious times. No clear effect can be discerned of the 1996 reforms on marriage, childbearing, or other factors that affect children.

A related Rand study, which estimates the relative contributions of the economy and TANF rule changes to the decline in the welfare rolls, concludes, "Our simulations suggest only a moderate role for any specific reforms in explaining the large observed drop in the welfare caseload. We attribute about a fifth of the caseload decline to time limits and sanctions, about a quarter to the economy, and about a third to a residual policy bundle; the remainder of the decline is absorbed by unexplained time effects" (Lerman and Danielson 2004). A less polite summary might attribute less relevance to TANF: a quarter of the caseload disappeared because of the buoyant economy of the 1990s; a fifth left the rolls because they were thrown off or exhausted their eligibility; a third left for ambiguous reasons, including being discouraged from applying, at times because of agency hostility; and the cause of the remainder of the decline is not known. The research does not address head-on the issue of the appropriateness of the decline. More recent research has begun to suggest that the softening economy after 2000 is reducing the earlier gains associated with the TANF reforms, including gains in employment, wages, and relative economic position (Acs and Loprest 2007).

Yet all of the findings are weakened by serious flaws in the primary studies on which they are based, flaws that undercut the authority of the published conclusions, such as they are. Most important, the experimental studies on which Grogger, Karoly, and Klerman (2002) relied were seriously impaired by some combination of attrition, researcher bias, questionable and incomplete data, compromised sampling procedures, and, notably, breaches of randomization (see Epstein 1997 for examples). Moreover, their significant findings are customarily very insubstantial, e.g., tiny gains in income, wages, employment, welfare independence, educational attainment, and so forth. In addition, the nonexperimental studies, as well as Lerman and Danielson (2004), relied on procedures that arrogate the authority of randomized designs but employ comparison groups that are not equivalent.

The studies that the Rand analysts summarized, largely in box-score fashion (simple counts of positive results versus negative results), were often contradictory, while many important issues were either rarely addressed or not addressed at all. The Rand authors point out that of one hundred thirty-two areas of research relating to the effects of TANF, sixty-one were completely unaddressed, twelve contained only insignificant results, and another fifty-nine contained only a single significant finding. "Furthermore, even where a substantial research base exists, most results pertain to the short run. . . . [Yet] *limited available evidence suggests that the effects of reform tend to fade over time, largely because the control group eventually catches up to the treatment group*" (Grogger, Karoly, and Klerman 2002, 248, emphasis added). "Eventually" means only a few years and in itself raises the issue of whether TANF, apart from an apparent short-term savings in public assistance budgets, is causing more harm than good.

Quite to the point, at least some of the drop in the welfare rolls is accounted for by service provision—"the residual policy bundle." Many states enjoyed a bounty of unspent TANF block grant money as their caseloads declined in the years immediately after 1996. Some of them, like Kentucky, spent the TANF surplus to facilitate employment by providing education, child care, transportation, serious training for work, postsecondary education, extended health care, and even improved work subsidies (Barber et al. 2003; Miewald 2003). Eligibility for the services was extended beyond TANF to include other low-income groups. The TANF caseload declined further.

The reforms may have worked best when states secured decent employment conditions, a precedent that the federal government should be encouraged to follow by instituting an adequate minimum wage, national health coverage, universal day care, affordable housing, and a welcoming environment in all public agencies. This one element of the TANF experience contradicts the program's harsh assumptions about the motives of the poor. Yet in most analyses, declines in the caseload that are attributable to generosity sit uncomfortably together with those that resulted from the harsh imposition of the TANF rules.

In any case, the nation declined to adopt the experience of states like Kentucky as a model for national policy in the way that Wisconsin welfare programs prefigured some of the New Deal legislation. Indeed, most states diverted much of their TANF budgets to other recipients and other budget areas, reducing their efforts to relieve their neediest citizens (Acs and Loprest 2007). The 1996 reform of public assistance was popular for its meanness and stringency, reflecting the nation's impatience with and hostility toward the poor themselves.

Conclusion

At their most generous, public provisions, including Social Security and tax transfers, may have reduced underlying poverty rates from about 20 percent to about 10 percent (U.S. Census Bureau 1979–2002 [2000]).[5] These rates are calculated against America's absolute threshold but employ an expanded definition of income. The rate of relative poverty, espe-

---

5. Evidence of the limited role of public policy in reducing hardship has been consistent over the past few decades. See in particular section 1 of Danziger and Haveman (2001) and Ziliak (2005).

cially at 50 percent of median family income, is about twice as high—17 percent in 2000—as the absolute poverty rate, since more people are covered by higher poverty thresholds and public benefits fall off considerably as income approaches and passes the absolute poverty line. Relative poverty is higher in the United States than in eleven other rich nations (Smeeding 2006, table 1). Intergenerational economic mobility (the difference in income between parents and their children) is low and probably the lowest among wealthy nations (Mazumder 2005; Jantti et al. 2006). Moreover, both the poor and the wealthy in the United States seem to exhibit the least amount of mobility, belying both the promise of egalitarianism in America and its claims for exemption from the sorry rigidities of other nations (Mazumder 2005).

The inadequacy of public assistance in the United States cannot lean on the excuse of constrained capacity. The growth of wealth in the United States since the 1960s—from $14,420 per capita in 1960 to $39,682 per capita in 2006 (in 2002 dollars)—is as startling as the American refusal to share with its own citizens (U.S. Department of Labor 2008). It is a matter of wonder that American stratification—the country's economic and social differences—is broadly consensual, and this consensus has become even more incongruous with the increase in inequality since the early 1970s. The Gini coefficient, a measure of inequality, has been rising steadily in the United States since 1967.[6] In fact, the United States is the least egalitarian of the world's wealthiest nations (Burtless 2007, 13).

The 1996 reforms, and notably the reauthorization of TANF in 2005, were immensely popular, even while posing great threats to the security of many tens of millions of Americans—those in poverty and the even larger group of lower-paid Americans at risk of falling into poverty. Social Security seems to be popular for its affirmation of the "free market" position, and to arouse very little concern about the fact that it fails to provide a retirement cushion for lower-paid workers. The national preference for a harsh and limited public assistance policy and for public retirement based on a strict insurance principle illuminates the ascendency of heroic individualism over economic self-interest—America's preference for the illusory benefits of self-reliance, the romance of self-invention, and the rejection of greater sharing.

6. See http://www.sustainablemiddleclass.com/Gini-Coefficient.html (accessed July 2007).

It is a tribute to the American creed of extreme individualism that the character-based fatherhood and marriage initiatives of the TANF reauthorization are right in line with one of the largest citizen mobilizations of recent years. The 1995 Million Man March, a project of the Nation of Islam and an expression of Afrocentric self-help, called for a revolution in spirit as the solution to the problems of the black community. The impassioned oratory of personal responsibility featured at the Million Man March addressed the legacy of racial discrimination in the United States as if it were only a state of mind. The Nation of Islam shares the sentimental illusion that civic virtue is a product of individual will. Whether out of frustration, isolation, despair, or romanticism, the choice of a development strategy based on self-help fits well with the ideology of small government and self-reliance of American conservatives, epitomizing the culture's sleight of hand, which routinely turns radicals into Republicans.

Poverty and want persist in the United States because they are embedded in the preferences of Americans rather than imposed on an innocent populace by predatory elites and secret forces of evil. The values that created TANF and Social Security are persistently evident in the cultural choices of Americans, displayed in the way Americans choose to live their lives. The absence of dissent in an open society signals contentment with current conditions. Even more than a willingness to abide social conditions, the American consensus has created those conditions, notably a tolerance for huge divides in income and a sea of social need. The turmoil among intellectuals is not necessarily evidence of dissatisfaction among citizens, a mistake that bedevils analyses that offer intellectual history as though it were social history.

By and large, Americans are satisfied with current conditions. It is notable that the 2008 presidential campaign largely ignored the issues of inequality and persistent poverty in America. Indeed, issues relating to the economic conditions of working people have been notably absent from presidential politics for decades. Even the Democratic presidential primary, a ritual in which candidates presumably try to appeal to the most liberal of American voters, is generally quiet on issues of economic stratification. Presidential politics centers on the large middle class and its increasingly conservative inclinations.

The same can be said of American politics generally. Issues of need and inequality are rarely mentioned because the electorate, and even many of the poor, accept current American stratification as largely fair.

Electoral turnout among the poor is very low; fewer than 20 percent of eligible voters turn out in poor Hispanic congressional districts, and only slightly more than that in poor black districts. Indeed, even turnout for presidential elections rarely rises much above 50 percent among all eligible voters. As much as some hold out hope that low turnout is a sign of disaffection, it seems equally plausible as a sign of acceptance.

There has been little protest over the distribution of income, wages, and wealth, and thus little evidence that economic disparities are priority issues even for the poor. Union membership has been declining steadily since the 1950s. At present only about a tenth of the American labor force belongs to unions, with precipitous declines among industrial workers. If workers were dissatisfied with working conditions or wages, they would flock to unions, arguably the only strong organizations that represent their economic interests. Unions, for their part, have become syndicated, with their industries having largely lost any pretense to the broad social advocacy of working-class interests.

Ethnic organizations, particularly among poor minorities, have lost their earlier vigor and apparently much of their membership. They seem to have become vehicles for middle-class ascendency, with declining attention to the needs of the impoverished.

The women's movement is dominated by the aspiring more than by the needy. The National Organization for Women is far more concerned with equal pay for equal work and the limitations of the "glass ceiling" than with the needs of poor single mothers; the Nine to Five union movement, representing lower-paid women, was a stillbirth of working-class advocacy.

Even in the 1960s the civil disturbances and protests against inequality and poverty were only sufficient to mobilize a constituency strong enough to protect the self-help programs of the War on Poverty. The Civil Rights Act and the Voting Rights Act, two important procedural reforms, exerted little influence over economic stratification. Medicare and Medicaid were the two great social welfare expansions of the Great Society, opening medical care to many who would not otherwise have been served. But even Medicare is amenable to the same interpretation as OAI—it smoothed out the provision of health care rather than equalizing access across income levels. The virtues of Medicaid are ambiguous: Medicaid perpetuates the social divide between the poor and the rest of society, and it fails to provide adequate access or standard quality to many beneficiaries. Indeed, the benefits of both programs need to be discounted by the degree to which they exacerbate the inflation of medical costs. There is little popular interest in health care reforms that actively control costs by rationing care or that truly equalize access to services.

Other social movements that followed the War on Poverty have also pressed relatively unthreatening agendas. The consumer movement was more concerned with truth in packaging than with access to the market or the effects of prices on equality. The gay rights movement has sought social legitimacy and funding for AIDS research but has put little effort into broader political action even for disability.

It is notable that the generosity of the GI Bill has never been replicated in programs for the poor or lower-paid workers. But even the GI Bill has become a much less adequate program over the decades than it used to be (Humes 2006; Mettler 2007).

Both high and popular culture in the United States are entranced by wealth and success, largely ignoring poverty and need except as they present opportunities for heroic overcoming. Contemporary movies, books, and the graphic arts rarely express criticism of the society's inequities; they are much more interested in the themes of personal striving and heroic triumph. Character dominates the narratives of contemporary literature.

Popular enthusiasms and reform movements since the 1960s have consistently moved away from substantive redistribution to procedural reforms. The poverty and civil rights movements that inspired the War on Poverty were substantive, but they were abandoned as the reformist impulse subsequently moved toward procedural justice—first as opposition to the Vietnam War and then into consumer affairs, women's equality, gay rights, the environment and conservation, and Christian fundamentalism. Political pressure for greater economic equality, carried along for decades by the civil rights movement, dwindled into affirmative action and an esthetic of diversity that largely accepts current resource distribution and institutions. Affirmative action and diversity perpetuated the social welfare spoils system but failed to address inequality, substituting anthropological poetry for social and economic justice. Indeed, by encouraging ethnic, racial, and gender identity above a shared culture of mutual regard, the principles of affirmative action and diversity endorse the reactionary tribalism that fostered America's long history of ethnic conflict, racism, and prejudice.

The competition among interests—actually roles—is resolved by the daily choices of Americans rather than by a presumed rationality of agenda and analysis or by a hijacked democracy. None of the cultural and organizational expressions of contemporary American preference was coerced. All of them demonstrate the considered priorities of Americans as they divide their time, money, and affections among an enormous number of alternatives. They all express consensual and consistent choices in line with a public policy that neglects the problem of economic want. Enduring public policy is itself the most powerful expression of the national will.

Technical solutions, such as a national minimum income realized through a negative income tax, or national health insurance, are doomed without broad social support. Social support cannot be created by a planned campaign. Even if forced through government by a committed minority, an unpopular program will be undermined in practice. Restrictions on social welfare are embedded in the American ethos—the widely shared and internalized rules of behavior that define relations among citizens.

5

CHARITY AND COMMUNITY ORGANIZATION

Charity and community organization are among the enduring, prototypical American responses to social need that define the obligations of communities and their members. They are dominated by the romantic momentum of American social welfare—its belief in extreme individualism, self-help, self-invention, volunteerism—in short, personal responsibility. Charity and community organization are animated by these classic myths that reconcile aspiration with reality: their methods of addressing social need are secondary to their meaning as symbols of social values. These myths of social service express national priorities, explaining at the same time both the persistent privativism of American social welfare and its yawning inequalities.

The primarily ceremonial function of charity and community organization may explain the stunning absence of systematic evaluations of the services they provide. Yet even without credible program assessments, it is apparent that charity and community organization have failed to fulfill their promises to address social problems, notably the problem of material insufficiency. Charity and community organization emerge from the deep faith of Americans in the rightness of their own beliefs. Rather than purposive assaults on social problems or vehicles of humane consciousness, creative force, or novel imagination, they are tradition's bulwarks against change, and they enjoy the broad consent of the citizenry.

Charity and the Voluntary Sector

Encouraged by a large tax subsidy, voluntary giving sustains cherished communal institutions—churches, hospitals, schools, and other philanthropic organizations.[1] However, the common assumption that the voluntary or nonprofit sector is animated by selfless humanitarianism is false. Even an exaggerated estimate of nonprofit expenditures aimed at alleviating poverty suggests that only about 30 percent of revenue goes to helping the poor. The overwhelming portion of voluntary assistance is provided to the same groups of people that donate the funds and provide the volunteers. Moreover, the quality of services administered by the voluntary sector to those in need, usually with large grants from the public sector, has been consistently dubious.

The Center on Philanthropy's annual report on philanthropic giving (2006) lists a total of about $260 billion in charitable giving in 2005, about 2.1 percent of the U.S. gross domestic product. About 75 percent of this total came from individuals, 12 percent from foundations, 7 percent from bequests, and 5 percent from corporations, much of it in the form of in-kind contributions (e.g., pharmaceutical companies donating medicine). Religious organizations (e.g., churches and church charities) received about 36 percent of the $260 billion, educational institutions (e.g., universities) 15 percent, human services (e.g., United Way) 10 percent, and health organizations (e.g., hospitals, disease societies) 9 percent; the remaining 30 percent was split among the arts, the humanities, "environment and animals," international affairs, gifts to foundations, and others.

In a separate report, commissioned by Google, the Center on Philanthropy (2007) estimates that in 2005 households with an annual income

1. The various terms for the private charitable sector engaged in supposedly good works are ambiguous and are often employed interchangeably. The common bond among the philanthropic, charitable, and nonprofit sectors seems to be their freedom from direct, extensive government control. Still, both local and federal governments charter and license charitable institutions and contribute mightily to their budgets. Indeed, public money dominates many private social service agencies. "Charity" connotes donations to the indigent; "philanthropy" implies private contributions to good causes. "Nonprofit" still carries the sentimental notion that cutting out the profit motive will ensure attention to humanistic goals. But the nonprofit sector includes a huge number of organizations such as hospitals, universities, membership associations, trade associations, research organizations, and others with little or no pretense to charitable or philanthropic services. Moreover, many nonprofits rely almost entirely on public funds. The context of their use is more important than the attempt to purify their definition.

below $100,000 accounted for about 37 percent of total charitable dona-
tions (notably including corporation and foundation giving). It is debat-
able whether charitable donations are actually as progressive as federal
taxes; they may in fact be a regressive substitute for progressive public
taxation; the wealthy may account for a greater proportion of general tax
revenues than of philanthropic donations.[2]

The Center on Philanthropy's 2007 report also estimates that across
the different nonprofit program areas, 30.6 percent of $252.55 billion in
total philanthropic giving in a year shortly before the report was issued
was "focused on the needs of the poor."[3] If cashed out, this would have
provided about $2,500 to each poor person in 2005. But these estimates
of charitable giving are as inflated as American claims to generosity and
altruism. As the Center on Philanthropy acknowledges, "In this research, because the focus is not on how much is given, but how much
of the total is allocated to a specific purpose—a purpose which has public policy implications—we have elected to take the broadest possible
view of how much is directed to the needs of people of low income.
Thus, given an option between two values, we selected the higher value,
the one that showed a greater amount focused on the needs of the poor"
(2007, 14).

The confusion of "people of low income" with "the poor" exaggerates
the number of needy and thus the proportion of voluntary giving allocated to them. Further, the data on which the Center on Philanthropy
relied were drawn from service organization surveys that asked responding agencies to estimate the portion of their budgets spent on the poor.
The estimates were not drawn from detailed program audits, few of
which seem to exist. Thus, the data reflect what nonprofit agencies guess
are the proportions of their budgets that go to whomever it is that they

2. IRS statistics on income for 2005 indicate that the same income class (but based on
federal tax returns rather than households) produced a comparable percentage of personal
taxes. The remainder of federal taxes, however, notably luxury taxes and corporate taxes, are
probably drawn from wealthier groups. See also Clotfelter (1992). The point of regressive
contributions becomes much more profound if the marginal utility of the dollar is considered. That is, the value of the dollar *to the contributor* decreases as income increases. Poorer
contributors are making greater sacrifices than wealthier contributors when they donate similar proportions of their incomes.

3. The difficulty in being precise about the time period during which these expenditures
were made lies in the report's use of data sets from different years, one from 2003 and
another from 2006, with a variety of ancillary data drawn from other sources in other recent
years. This is probably not a serious problem, as there does not seem to have been any
dramatic change in recent years in philanthropy of one sort or another.

conceive of as "the poor," and are thus of questionable accuracy. Indeed, most agencies, except in the few cases in which they are obliged to impose strict financial eligibility criteria, have only a vague notion of who actually uses their services. One would need either a charitable concession to good intentions or a direct interest in inflated estimates to accept the accuracy of the center's numbers at face value.

Furthermore, the Center on Philanthropy does not subtract from its estimates of charitable giving the costs of fund-raising, administration, and other pass-through expenses. At the same time, agencies' perception of what constitutes service to the poor, rather than the objective conditions of the recipient, defines the services.

The 2007 report estimates that more than $12 billion in religious "benevolences" reach the poor. It cites *The Yearbook of American and Canadian Churches* (2006) as the source for the claim that benevolences among Protestant denominations accounted for "23.9 percent of total religious contributions" (Center on Philanthropy 2007, 18). In fact, however, *The Yearbook of American and Canadian Churches* reports that benevolences accounted for only 15 percent of total religious contributions (Lindner 2006). More to the point, the Center on Philanthropy attributes about 85 percent of religious benevolences to the poor. Yet the Council of Churches is quite clear that only a small portion of benevolences, at least among Protestant denominations, reach the poor; most are allocated to overseas ministries, boards, societies, commissions, and denominational churches, none of which directly benefits the poor.[4] Quite clearly, the overwhelming portion of religious donations and benevolences are spent on the customary organizational functions of churches and very little on the poor. Similarly, the report assumes that all of the money spent to "help meet basic needs" ends up assisting the poor in basic ways. Yet while the United Way may assign to the poor all of the money going to a Boys and Girls Club, many members of these clubs are not poor. Many "need-based" educational scholarships are provided to athletes, ethnic and racial minorities, women, and others who are not poor.

It is a tribute more to survey bias than to accuracy that many agencies respond to survey questions about poverty with self-congratulatory assessments of their own contributions to relieving the problem. Exagger-

4. Tenny Thomas, National Council of the Churches of Christ in the USA, personal communication.

ated pro-social biases in surveys have been well established, and it would be foolish to assume that surveys of philanthropic organizations are free of the same pattern of bias (Epstein 2006b). About 75 percent of Americans said they voted in recent presidential elections, when only a little over 50 percent actually did. In the same way, reported incomes are routinely falsified, as are drug and alcohol use, criminal acts, and sexual behavior.

The basic data on charitable giving are derived from the amounts reported on income tax forms. After comparing tax submissions with audited returns, Slemrod concludes that in 1982 deductible contributions were overstated by 7.2 percent. He points out, however, that the IRS "auditing process is an imperfect one, [and] there is no presumption that the auditor-adjusted figure for charitable contributions represents the actual value of contributions" (Slemrod 1989, 519). Indeed, it is possible that IRS audits may allow undocumented charitable contributions that appear reasonable but are not in fact real.[5]

In the end, actual charitable contributions total less than the amounts reported to the Internal Revenue Service, and far less than the Center on Philanthropy's estimated 30 percent is likely to be allocated to the poor. The American people, in contributing to charity, are stating their private priorities, which are quite symmetrical with the priorities of public policy; both pay little attention to the needs of lower-income citizens.

The companion problem to the congestive charitable heart is its faulty functioning. Philanthropic agencies customarily support activities that benefit the general public rather than the poor; they are philanthropic in the broadest sense rather than charitable per se. Aside from religious activities, philanthropy most often replicates the functions of government in education, community services, the arts and humanities, health, research, and services to the poor. America's philanthropic social services are not much different from tax-funded social services. In fact, many nonprofit and philanthropic agencies are major recipients of public money; some were established specifically as outlets for publicly

5. This possibility is supported by the disparity between the reported estimates of church contributions and the totals derived from IRS reporting. The sum of charitable giving reported by the Catholic Church, together with the National Council of the Churches of Christ in the USA report for Protestant giving, totals less that half of the $101 billion that the Center on Philanthropy takes from IRS reports. The large apparent disparity between what churches say they receive and what people claim on their tax forms as church-related contributions raises the possibility of inflated tax deductions for religious giving that far exceed Slemrod's (1989) estimate of a 7.2 percent falsification for all charitable deductions.

funded services. More than 50 percent of the budgets of charitable and philanthropic agencies that provide services to the poor are drawn from public sources (Smith and Lipsky 1995).

However inadequate, the public sector spends far more than the private sector does to relieve the material needs of poorer and lower-status groups. Still, private charitable donations, like public expenditures, sustain activities that by and large benefit the core of contributors and taxpayers. The small amount that is spent on the poor most frequently attempts to reform them—their spiritual lives, their behavior, and their motivations—usually through the demeaning relationships of personal charity rather than through impersonal material subsidies that improve the conditions of their lives.

The quality and content of charitable services for the poor are even more disappointing than their distribution. Indeed, philanthropic services for the poor have a very troubled history. Standard American social welfare histories have consistently documented the inadequacies of charitable provisions for the poor, including blacks, Hispanics, Native Americans, immigrants, the infirm, the mentally ill, dependent children, and others.[6] After reviewing charitable provisions for Native Americans and the poor, Wagner laments "how little social service, volunteering, or charity really achieves" (2000, x). Traditional community service nonprofits like the United Way and the YMCA have largely turned their backs on the poor. Wagner and similar critics view philanthropy as pernicious benevolence, serving the vanity and interests of the wealthy rather than benefiting the poor.

Yet Wagner's pervasive regard, following Piven and Cloward (1971), for theories of elite dominance does not stem from his observations about the quality of philanthropy, nor are other historians able to pinpoint the determinants of social policymaking through their observations about social welfare provisions. The symmetry between public and private social welfare policy suggests a far less innocent view of the masses' complacent acceptance of extensive social and economic deprivation.

On rare occasions, the charitable sector feels constrained to produce evidence of its effectiveness. *Social Programs That Work* (Crane 1998)

---

6. For a few examples, see Grob (1983) on mental health, Patterson (1981), Katz (1986), and Stricker (2007) on twentieth-century poverty and social welfare. Also Mencher (1967), Lubove (1971), Trattner (1994), and Leiby (1978).

identifies nine presumably successful programs—five educational, two that address substance abuse, one to improve nutrition, and one to treat juvenile delinquency—several of which were supported with philanthropic money. However, none of the nine was rigorously evaluated. Crane acknowledges that "unfortunately it is impossible to be sure that the distinctions between the treatment and comparison groups are produced by the program and not by initial differences in the make up of the group" (16). Indeed, most of the research that Crane cites in support of the effectiveness of the programs is more remarkable for its departure from standard scientific practice than its adherence.

Yet even granting many mulligans for methodological flaws, Crane could come up with only nine programs. At least a few of them, in particular the Abecedarian project, if in fact it did succeed, represent extraordinarily rare instances of individual dedication, skill, and personal charm. But the point of the Crane project was to identify interventions that are widely relevant to contemporary problems. Greater research rigor borne of prudent skepticism would probably have led to a confession of philanthropy's futility in addressing social welfare problems, given its small, poorly funded, and personalized social interventions. Yet the charitable sector has supplanted skepticism with a convenient faith in its good heart and creative mind. Scientific philanthropy, the initial justification for much charitable giving, has never been taken seriously as an enterprise that is largely unwilling to test the effectiveness of its programs.

There are hardly any systematic, let alone scientifically credible, evaluations of the philanthropic programs supported by charities, business corporations, or foundations. None of the historical analyses of America's private provisions for the needy had the advantage of definitive studies but rather relied on newspaper and magazine accounts, administrative data and reports, diaries and memoirs, commission findings, and the like. There is a gulf between the library of instructions, injunctions, manuals, and other sources on how to conduct a program evaluation that are published by the charitable sector and its nearly uniform failure to follow its own advice and actually assess the outcomes of philanthropic service programs.

In a fashion typical of this literature, Wing (2004) provides instructions on "assessing the effectiveness of capacity-building initiatives" but does not offer a single instance of a successful assessment. Porter and Kramer (1999), lamenting the failure of foundations to evaluate their programs, can point only to a few in-house analyses; they do not reference a single publically available and credible program evaluation. Kramer and Bickel state that "U.S. foundations spend well over $100 million each year on the evaluation of the programs they fund" (2004, 51) but give no examples. Relying on administrative data, which impair program evaluation, Modesto (2003) actually assessed a faith-based welfare-to-work program, but without citing any other evaluation of similar programs; coincidentally he concluded that faith-based services provided no advantage for the poor. Steckel and Lehman (1997) chose "America's best nonprofits" on the basis of an anecdote. The few evaluations of philanthropic services that do exist are almost invariably case studies that draw on file data and are usually written by program officers.

Braverman, Constantine, and Slater (2004) list reasons for foundations' resistance to evaluation that are generally applicable to the rest of the philanthropic sector: reluctance to look foolish or ineffective, unwillingness to test assumptions about the good heart and good works, no sense of obligation that program accountability be evaluated, wariness of criticism, and so forth. In fact, few foundations spend money on evaluation, and when they do, the result is usually self-congratulatory, ritually praising good management practice and saluting "scientific philanthropy" and the business community that funded their endowments.[7]

The more rigorous evaluations of public programs (which frequently realize their services through contracts with nonprofit agencies), many of them reviewed in previous chapters, attest nearly unanimously, following a bit of secondary analysis, to program ineffectiveness.[8] By extension, it seems reasonable to conclude that less well funded and less accountable philanthropic services are even less effective, a conclusion sustained by the evidence, such as it is, of charitable services that attend to the poor.

In this case an absence may be proof of a presence: the failure to

7. Searches of the Social Sciences Citation Index, Eric, psychINFO, Sociofile, Google, and others, including dedicated Web sites such as the Nonprofit Sector Research Fund, using a variety of terms (charity, philanthropy, evaluation, outcome, effectiveness, and others) and even a variety of organizations (Red Cross, United Way, and others) in a variety of combinations, yield very few evaluations but a ton of instructions on how and why to conduct them.

8. Here the distinction between "nonprofit" and "charitable" has merit. Many nonprofits are established specifically for the purpose of receiving public grant money that carries a contractual agreement to cooperate with evaluations. Charitable and philanthropic organizations are under no such obligation and famously exercise their freedom in this respect.

evaluate charitable programs suggests that the quality and effectiveness of charitable services have been and remain peripheral concerns, hardly "philanthropy's new agenda [of] creating value" (Porter and Kramer 1999). Lacking evidence of programmatic success or even much effort to evaluate programs, philanthropy becomes a performance art of national values rather than a production function in human progress, that is, an attempt to achieve explicit, measurable, humane goals. By subordinating programmatic effectiveness to ritualistic affirmations of the American creed, social acceptability, rather than programmatic achievement, determines the fate of philanthropic services.

Typically, new social services develop in response to public awareness of an emerging problem. The transition from initial to more regular funding depends far more on a new service's conformity with community values—usually its promotion of individual responsibility along with the acceptance of an unambitious service role that abides pressures to minimize taxes—than on its actual ability to achieve its programmatic goals. Communal acceptance depends on attracting supporters, preferably of the more influential kind, maintaining administrative coherence, and adapting to existing patterns of service.

> Recruitment of support is enhanced when a program's symbolic value is great and its direct costs are low, e.g., for women's temporary shelters or Big Brother and Sister programs. Recruitment is very difficult when large new costs are required, e.g., for hospitals to serve poor people, jobs programs, higher cash welfare benefits, public housing. In short, a program's social acceptability is the major predictor of its success. Only rarely is a program's direct service benefits, its rational content, a primary factor in its destiny.
>
> Many social services were designed in just this way. Programs to treat drug and alcohol addiction, crime, mental disease, homelessness, battered women, foster children, socially deprived adolescents, poverty and so forth were established because of their low relative costs, their symbolic value and their fervent supporters. Few of these programs have ever been credibly evaluated. (Epstein 1992, 137)

Both the religious and the secular faces of American charity reflect similar values. America's civic religion neatly parallels its religious theology. Absent the desire to convert the sinner and the belief in God, the two sectors are ideologically indistinguishable, both sharing faith in gnomic (mystical) processes of knowing, chosenness, heroic individualism, and personal responsibility. Indeed, reformed Christian belief in a personal relationship with God, unmediated through a priestly caste, is consistent with the nation's belief in the immediacy of social knowledge as well. Mystical epiphanies certify religious truth and, in their extension to social welfare services, undergird the central role of personal experience rather than systematic, objective science as the source of program wisdom. In the same way that the truth of Jesus may be revealed to a believer through faith, the virtues of charitable and philanthropic programs are known through the mystical vehicles of revelation, spirit, and transcendent truth.

The exceptionalism of the American system, the virtues of its social institutions, and the wisdom of its tenets resist rational testing. In this climate, social welfare provisions are only incidentally temporal provisions to handle the complexities of social interactions and national purpose; they become ordained, divine, secular expressions of the nation's certitude in its correctness. The obviousness of religious and civic virtue animates American charity and philanthropy, explaining both the absence of rigorous evaluation and the highly personalistic style of poverty programs, that is, the preference for organized personal charity over publicly institutionalized provisions for need. Social welfare is transformed from the provision of material necessities to an opportunity for personal reformation and civic salvation, the return of the sinner to the communion of virtuous citizens.

Voluntary charitable services often contain components of both religious and secular faith. Habitat for Humanity Incorporated (HFHI), "an ecumenical Christian ministry . . . seeks to eliminate poverty housing and homelessness for the world, and to make decent shelter a matter of conscience and action."[9] Employing the assistance of volunteers as construction labor and the "sweat equity" of future owners, HFHI claims to have built more than 225,000 houses worldwide since its founding in 1976. Recipients of HFHI's largesse—"partners"—apply to a selection committee that assesses their level of need, their willingness to participate in building their home, and "their ability to repay the loan," since the "partner" is expected to bear many of the costs of construction. Thus HFHI shines with the glow of the American faith in self-

9. See http://www.habitat.org/how/factsheet.aspx.

help, volition, good deeds, enterprise ("sweat equity"), and a screening process to separate the worthy from the sinner. However, it does not address the depth of homelessness. Its implicit suggestion that the problem is amenable to private and voluntary resolution belies the persistence of millions in the United States alone who lack adequate housing and the fact that HFHI has built fewer than ten thousand homes per year worldwide. Rather than a sizeable answer to the housing problem, HFHI offers ceremonies of volunteerism that blend the civic with the religious and refresh the mythic civic virtues of sociability and neighborliness. In the typical fashion of charitable social services, HFHI subtly denies collective responsibility for social need. Quite pointedly, HFHI and charity in general supplant a public entitlement to minimal services with moral certification, and are apparently more concerned with identifying saints and sinners than with relieving material need. HFHI amounts to a sermon on citizen responsibility made graphic in the provision of a few houses.

Faith-based social services have always been endorsed, if not actually favored, in the United States, although the recent tolerance for funding frankly religious services with public money is novel, at least in contemporary America. Yet the religious sector has failed as badly as the public sector in administering social welfare. The religious sector and the nonprofit sector have long accepted public payments and private donations to care for the mentally and developmentally impaired as well as dependent children, overseeing the distribution of the widow's mite for vulnerable populations.

But religious agencies' obedience to policy orthodoxy and political tastes, along with an unseemly voracity for service contracts, often contradicts its religious values. Religious charitable organizations are prominent in their blatant failure to provide safe and nurturing environments for dependent children and their obliging silence about the deficits of care. The sorry plight of child foster care in the United States (and such precursors as the "orphan trains" and "contracting out") debunks the popular equation of nonprofit with humane while reaffirming the observation that religious organizations serve the popular will rather than constitute uniquely ethical expressions of a higher calling.[10] A humane

10. For commentaries on the quality of foster care in the United States, see Pelton (1989), Epstein (1999), Costin, Karger, and Stoesz (1996), and Bernstein (2001), among many others.

conscience, let alone a lofty religious sensibility, would welcome the objective evaluation of programs intended to relieve need. The retreat into romantic rectitude is not only moral backsliding but political convenience that undercuts the desirability of greater equality and ignores challenges to the nation's sense of its chosenness—the holy state of God's favorite people.

America's turn to religion for remedies to social problems is the natural consequence of its conviction that social problems result from deformed character, moral impairments, and the stubborn rejection of the American concept of virtue. The church's personalized attention to sin is fulfilled through a variety of formalized exhortations in programs for the poor. The mission to save and reform is realized as personal service in the range of child and family service agencies and general counseling clinics, many of which are church affiliated (e.g., Lutheran Social Services, Jewish Family Services, Catholic Charities, the Salvation Army, and so forth) and in secular nonprofit agencies.

The specialization of the charitable sector leaves material relief, minimal as it is, to the public sector. The attention to sin is also compatible with the reigning assumption of the 1996 policy changes in public assistance—that the relief of need through entitlements to public services undercuts individual enterprise, self-sufficiency, and dignity, engendering the problem it was intended to address. In this way many charities lament the provision of public care even while they accept government contracts for service. Boys and Girls Town, long identified as a Catholic charity, takes per diem subsidies from public agencies for its high-quality foster care—which it justifies as temporary treatment rather than long-term surrogate care—but then refuses to press for similar care for the far larger number of children who need it. The organization falls back on programs to teach family skills that do little more than preach to parents about their responsibilities to their children. It does not accept the wisdom of its own program: many children without parents need the high quality and very expensive surrogate families that Boys and Girls Town provides to its few charges.

The general sentiment that the churches are on the right track to social salvation has encouraged a proliferation of faith-based social services through "charitable choice" under President Clinton and then under President Bush's Office of Faith-Based and Community Initiatives. Billions of federal social service dollars have been funneled to faith-based organizations that merge their religious roles with secular programs such as child day care. Yet, whatever the confusion of public and private responsibility in fulfilling a role as a proxy for government, the justification for these programs has little to do with actually remedying social problems and thus attending to questions of effectiveness. DiIulio's (2003) artful equation of nonprofit, for-profit, charitable, and religious organizations as legitimate government contractors apparently endorses the pietistic romanticism of faith-based organizations; in fact, DiIulio promotes the remedy of faith even while he carefully separates the sacred and the secular in administering public social services. He avoids claiming that faith-based care is more effective than strictly secular care—an impossible task in the absence of credible evaluations—asserting only the eligibility of faith-based organizations to compete for public social service contracts on an equal footing with other organizations. None of the service contracts is committed to effective services or even decent care but only to current standards of acceptable care, that is, care that fulfills the specific requirements of the service contracts. The contracts are statements of national priorities and the popular consensus of what should be provided to specified populations of recipients.

In contrast, Olasky commends faith-based care as an effective remedy for poverty and other social problems specifically because of its religious content. His *Compassionate Conservatism* (2000) provided the blueprint for the Office of Faith-Based and Community Initiatives—DiIulio was its first director—and captures popular sentiment about the prominent role of faith in American citizenship. Compassionate conservatism—the application of conservative principles to philanthropy—defines personal change through faith as the key to resolving social problems.

> While on drugs eighteen years ago, [Nimo Colon] accidentally shot himself through the spine. Bitter and unable to perform much manual labor, he sold drugs and saw no meaning to life until God grabbed him twelve years ago. He is now in charge of a small weight room. . . .

> The crime drop-off came because of genuine inner change. "Make Jesus the center of life," Smith said, "and the other issues fall into place." Creating new jobs, he noted, was not nearly as important as creating new hearts: "There are a lot of job openings. Our focus is on changing people, on motivating them to change." (Olasky 2000, 115, 136)

Relying on anecdotes gathered on a tour in which he informally evaluated instances of religious compassion in the United States, Olasky
evokes the tenets of the American myth of charity: localism and person-
to-person charity, good hearts and dedicated reformers, individual responsibility, spontaneous epiphanies of morality, dedicated evangelism,
and fervent religious conversions. Yet Olasky offers no systematic, let
alone objective, evidence to sustain his contention that faith-based services cured addiction, restored sanity, provided jobs, improved incomes,
created housing, reduced crime, or prevented disease. Olasky's promotion of religious alternatives to secular care relies on the devices of the
sublime that subvert the question of their demonstrable effectiveness.
In this way charity becomes less a matter of relief and more one of
proselytizing social values through rituals of group solidarity that distin-
guish the saved from the sinner, the poor from the comfortable, the
good citizen from the bad. Religious charity, with its emphasis on personal conversion, is a pervasive American institution, a tenet of DiIulio's
"real moral majority," and a core impediment to addressing the material
deprivation and unequal treatment suffered by millions of Americans.

DiIulio observes that "the general public strongly supports the consti-
tutional balance that is reflected in charitable-choice laws. For example,
in opinion surveys conducted in 2001 and 2002 by the Pew Forum
on Religion and Public Life, wide majorities backed charitable-choice
legislation. They agreed that program beneficiaries 'should have a variety of options,' including religious providers, and that religious service
providers are 'more caring and compassionate' than nonreligious ones"
(2004, 76). Yet "charitable choice" is not simply a neutral series of services that may be packaged in different types of agencies; it is an option
for religious content as part of social service and the endorsement of
faith-based care. Charitable choice embodies the ideological preference
of the American people to see failure of the individual will as the primary reason for social and economic need.

It is ludicrous to count as assistance to the poor charitable services
that are little more than modernized sermons on sin, unless the assumption is made that poverty is the result of a character flaw. But even
in this case there is no evidence that proselytizing has ever been effective, at least not without a conquering army to back it up. Still, effectiveness is not the abiding justification for charity; the value of the mission
to the poor lies in the reaffirmation of social values through the ceremonies of conversion—a boon for the volunteer, the charity, and the

society that donates to it, but not for the recipient. The bits of material benefit that come along with charitable services—a house here and there, a basket of food, some second-hand clothing, a hot meal—seem to be payments to the poor for playing their role in this drama of social projection and soft scapegoating.

The enduring faith-based self-assurances of the United States are mysteries of social development. Only a few thousand Puritans emigrated to the American colonies, yet their rigid, exclusionary sense of salvation and their unquestioning faith in the virtue of their way of life have beguiled Americans ever since. Faith is a romantic assertion of special wisdom that transcends doubt and skepticism, rational tendencies that have been confined largely to science and technology. In romantic faith, "true knowledge is not worked out by man but worked in him; only the flood of grace brings it to him and gives him the quintessence of knowledge, the totality of insight. Knowledge here is not what instructs but what redeems" (Baeck 1970, 207).

The romantic will, often embellished with the little dramas of usurping elites, cunning special interests, and conspiracies of the mighty and the media, determines the shape of American social welfare. It has no need of proof because it has already beatified its purpose with inner knowledge. The call for objective testing seems blasphemous. For the romantic,

> the desire to yield to illusion, justifiable in art, here characterizes the entire relation to the world. In the deliberately sought-out twilight of longing and dream, the border lines of . . . life are effaced. Reality becomes mere mood; and moods, eventually, the only reality. Everything, thinking and poetry, knowledge and illusion, all here and all above, flows together into a foaming poem, into a sacred music, into a great transfiguration, an apotheosis. . . .
>
> Romanticism therefore lacks any strong ethical impulse, any will to conquer life ethically. It has an antipathy against any practical idea which might dominate life, demanding free, creative obedience for its commandments, and showing a clearly determined way to the goals of action. (Baeck 1970, 191–92)

The volunteer is a pillar of both secular and religious charity and often an ecstatic whose virtue is realized and faith expressed through unpaid personal benevolence. At the same time, ostensibly unpaid service (e.g., internships, board membership) that improves the volunteer's skills, social standing, or knowledge may confer a future financial or professional benefit that greatly diminishes the altruistic content of the activity; indeed, these sorts of unpaid activities are perhaps best seen as investments in professional training, public relations, and marketing. Very often, volunteers do not perform explicitly charitable services but rather engage in reciprocal service: in a given community, some are den mothers, some coach little league, some are candy stripers in hospitals—all activities provided to one's own, fairly intimate social group. At other times, a romantic ideal of service—altruism, good works, patriotism, religious zeal—motivates the reciprocating volunteer to wander past personal benefit into charity for others. In these cases, while some volunteers provide marketable services, the activities of many others may lack a palpable monetary value, either because the service is of little value to anyone but the volunteer, or because it is of such poor quality that no one would pay for it.

The many claims for the value of volunteers in social services typically ignore the deeply romantic impulses that propel personal charity and that require many agencies to develop volunteer programs. Volunteers are often accepted into an agency less for their direct contributions than because they are barometers of public acceptability—a Nielsen rating for charities—and vehicles of agency promotion, although more to funding sources and other sanctioning groups than to service recipients.

Drawing on survey data, E. Brown (1999) ingeniously estimates that volunteer activities in 1996 were worth at least $203 billion and as much as $410 billion when informal helping is considered. But Brown does not actually assess the quality of volunteer activities (or attempt to discount benefits by harm done), nor does she apportion the contributions among self-service, reciprocal service, and altruism. The estimates are very weak, and the question of true social contribution remains unanswered. Like Sherr (2008), the literature on volunteers constitutes little more than a performance manual for the American ritual of charitability. Volunteerism is apparently held in the same esteem as mother's love, too sacred to profane with systematic scrutiny.

While faith-based charities are often romantically pietistic, addressing need with the spontaneity of a moving spirit, charitable foundations are gravely liturgical. Foundations profess a commitment to rationality and insight—the application of scientific rigor to the melioration of social problems through effective programming. They display intellectual snobbery toward the public sector, often presenting themselves as the brains for the mule of government. Foundations are the well-tailored, well-mannered romantics of the charitable world but romantics nonetheless, especially absent any evidence that their programs do more than flatter the American conceit of exceptionalism. They have failed to demonstrate that their relatively small checkbooks buy progress in areas in which much greater public expenditures have failed.

The annual reports of philanthropic foundations are bare of rigorous assessments of their enterprises. Indeed, they continue to evaluate their programs in the manner of the Ford Foundation's reports on Mobilization for Youth, relying on the intuitions of presumably expert site visitors and review boards rather than more systematic and objective methods.

The Ford Foundation's initial funding, which allowed MFY to step a bit outside public tolerance for organizing the poor, offers philanthropies a cautionary tale. The questions that MFY raised about the lack of foundation accountability to American preferences were enough to deter many very modest intrusions of philanthropy into social politics. Subsequently, foundations directed more of their money to neutral projects well within the boundaries of popular taste: medical and social research, traditional social welfare programs, international development, and the arts. The foundations have become as lofty and vacuous as their pretensions to improve human civilization. Rather than take the risks of creativity, they are the guardians of America's social orthodoxy.

For all of their bombast about social responsibility and deep, deep concern, American corporations sustain only a small portion of the philanthropic sector. Despite a year in which corporate profits rose by 35.8 percent (in part as a result of corporate tax "relief"), their 2005 contribution of $13.77 billion (which was taken as expenses against profit, thus costing only about sixty-five cents for each contributed dollar and probably passed on to consumers in the form of price increases) amounted to only 5.3 percent of total charitable giving and 1.8 percent of corporate profit. Corporate charity is a classic oxymoron, a mawkish form of public relations whose business focus is guarded by the marketing executives who often head up company charities.

Like a Volkswagen bug with a Rolls-Royce grill, philanthropy is self-parody. It does not fund its many pretensions; it is customarily self-serving; its programs for those in need do not help; it is the voice of orthodoxy reaffirming traditional values; it pampers national vanity; and it makes little effort to assess its own behavior. Philanthropy performs rituals of American virtue as moralizing bedtime stories for a nation of romantics.

> Tell me a story, tell me a story
> Tell me a story, remember what you said
> You promised me you said you would
> You got to give in so I'll be good
> Tell me a story, then I'll go to bed
> ("Tell Me a Story," recorded by Jimmy Boyd and Frankie Laine)

Community Organization

Community organization in the United States fits well into a discussion of philanthropy, since a large number of its initiatives are typically funded through foundations and traditional charities.[11] Community organization as it has been practiced is usually an instance of social efficiency; it seeks to realize a large benefit from a small investment by employing knowledge of social conditions, human and organizational behavior, and social institutions to remedy social problems within the permissible limits of a society's dominant ethos.

The field makes the defining assumptions that a community can be guided to develop the will to profitably focus its resources on its problems. Presumably, populations in need have not realized their potential to remedy problems and achieve goals because they are disorganized or blocked from the political system by tradition, social circumstances, or invidious forces. Community organization offers an array of participatory and problem-solving techniques to reach consensus within a group of people, to develop a position of negotiation with dominant political forces, and to achieve the pleasures of democratic communion and sociability. It typically relies on the efforts of volunteers, that is, unpaid

---

11. Although community organization typically concerns decision making, whereas community development attempts more material goals, one usually entails the other. In the present discussion, the two terms are used synonymously. Community organization and community development are long-standing educational concentrations in social work, public administration, and the range of planning disciplines. Moreover, this analysis of community organization is restricted to the American experience. Foreign cultures, particularly in poor nations, present different contexts and have different symbolic meanings. Nonetheless, the foreign experience has been no more hopeful than the American (Epstein 1994).

community members, to develop and execute its interventions. Most recently the field has adopted Putnam's language of social capital—his myth of communal self-invention—as its social reality to increase the store of civic participation in troubled communities by way of reducing crime, increasing social integration, improving work performance, promoting self-help, and attacking urban blight.

Special knowledge is key to its ambition to be distinguished as a profession, since the techniques and goals of community organization are also the common property of democratic governance. Without recourse to the special lore of community organization and trained community organizers, communities organize their own systems for handling grievances, for addressing common problems, and for sharing resources; they negotiate and form power blocs to achieve favored ends; they develop leadership and expertise; they explore issues. The process of populations acting in forethought is as old as human civilization. Yet in reaching for professional standing, often on grounds of scientific respectability, the field claims to have accumulated objective, accurate information and replicable skills that improve the common processes of social development and governance. Moreover, in its attention to poverty and social isolation, community organization asserts an ethical core superior to democratic government's mechanical translation of social preference into public policy. The profession of community organization purports to improve the humanitarian conditions of society.

Yet there is little that is professional about community organization and little that is notably humanitarian. The field has been unable to amass a list of credible successes or to attribute apparent successes to its own efforts; its presumed achievements are often associated with other interventions, notably the infusion of substantial money for which it cannot take credit. Moreover, its professional authority rests on a small body of research and program evaluations that are anecdotal and customarily qualitative, marred by recurrent unreliability and bias.

The field took heed from projects like Mobilization for Youth and the early community action programs of the War on Poverty to stay within the political tolerance and social ethos of the nation. Community organization is a deeply obedient social institution with little ability or freedom to take on problems of social reform. Its activities are engendered by the culture. Revolutionaries do not train in schools of social work or other graduate programs; social and political revolutions are not mapped out by academic savants or agency staff. Rather than opposition and conflict, community organization, in its typical and current form, promotes the pillars of the American consensus, the themes of its romantic myths: social capital, assets development, consensus techniques, and coordination. It offers the inspiration of volunteerism and self-help, although professionally guided, as a substitute for greater material equality.

Community organization's characteristic strategy of handling problems outside the culture's customary grievance systems, service patterns, and social institutions intensifies the social isolation of deprived groups by identifying them as needy and pathological, that is, as disorganized and incapable of formulating effective leadership on their own. Community organization may also delay solutions by proceeding on the fiction that small communities of the poor, with professional assistance, have the power to remedy their own problems or force the existing system to accommodate their demands. Its romantic anthropological insistence that communities have latent talents, unique charms, and inalienable rights to be themselves replicates the common flaw of the diversity movement, which substitutes an imagined specialness—a stereotype of the other—for greater social equality in a shared culture. In this sense, community organization promotes the very inequality that may lie at the root of America's social problems.

The dearth of evaluative material or even clear theory concerning community organization suggests that American society, in the manner of its philanthropies, is unconcerned with the programmatic achievements of the field but rather more invested in its ceremonies of Americanism. Rather than a serious attempt to remedy social problems, community organization ritualizes fundamental democratic myths of self-help, autonomy, citizen power, and local knowledge, infusing all with a sublime romance of the American spirit. At its most contentious, community organization promotes a defiant populism that bolsters the recurrent American appetite for balkanized politics. It is telling that community organization, while embracing Enlightenment values, stands culturally for the reverse: clairvoyance over knowledge, myth over reality, spiritualism over material conditions, and social obedience over political competition and advocacy.

The Comprehensive Community Revitalization Program

The Comprehensive Community Revitalization Program in the South Bronx (CCRP) is typical of contemporary community revitalization projects, that is, service programs that attempt to improve both the physical and the social conditions of communities. CCRP was initially funded in 1991 with $3 million from the Surdna Foundation, subsequently receiving more than $9 million from twenty other foundations and corporations. During its seven years of operation in a community of half a million people, it leveraged more than $40 million in public and additional private funds for specific social service projects, in the end spending about $100 per resident of the South Bronx. CCRP sought to involve local residents in the creation of a comprehensive social service plan that would attack poverty and improve the conditions of their neighborhoods. Rather than pursue isolated projects, CCRP was dedicated to a comprehensive approach that would presumably derive increased benefit from the synergy of its different programs.

CCRP adopted the strategy of inducing long-established community development corporations in the South Bronx to go beyond their basic housing roles to address human service problems. These public service corporations were implementing large portions of New York City's $5 billion commitment to improve housing in the South Bronx. The problems of the South Bronx, one of the poorest neighborhoods in the nation, were both obvious—employment, health services, education, and so forth—and subtle, involving quality-of-life issues that might be met through the urban amenities of parks and community recreation. To these ends, CCRP provided technical assistance and financial resources for the community development corporations to involve local residents in planning activities.

CCRP did not seek to organize residents politically but rather worked through established lines of authority to create a traditional array of social services, convincing local community development corporations to augment their housing activities by pursuing "comprehensive" social services. It employed community organization techniques of participation to achieve these ends. Its essential coordinating function and its use of the community development corporations as "intermediaries" between residents and funding sources recall the logic behind the health and welfare councils of the 1950s and even Mobilization for Youth. CCRP is prominent for its reputed success among the large number of "comprehensive community initiatives" and local neighborhood development efforts collected under the Local Initiatives Support Corporation, all apparently inventions of the philanthropic world.

Yet it is difficult to confirm the success of the project or its lasting influence. Even its fundamental commitment to resident participation seems compromised by the enormous overlay of professionals who apparently made many of the basic design decisions. CCRP takes credit for increasing the availability of primary health care in underserved areas—"35,630 patient visits in 1997 is very impressive" (Spilka and Burns 1998, 16). However, this number of patient visits—sufficient to provide comprehensive primary care for about seven thousand people for one year—addresses only a tiny portion of the health care needs of the half-million residents of the South Bronx. CCRP had assisted the community development corporations to partner with "quality, stable well regarded providers who were seeking to open non-profit primary health care practices in the South Bronx" by finding suitable locations and funds to renovate facilities (Miller and Burns 2006, 5). CCRP never bothered to evaluate the quality of the medical care.

CCRP apparently "helped to catalyze several economic development projects": catering and child care programs, a thrift shop and a microloan program, a shopping center, "a home health care enterprise for AIDS/HIV patients," a training program in computer repair, and a printing business. The programs were funded by public and philanthropic grants. Rather than economic development, the programs appear to be instances of privatized public services. "Understanding that creating jobs and improving access to employment were the . . . toughest challenges . . . CCRP and the community development corporations addressed the problem directly from the beginning" (Spilka and Burns 1998, 16). After seven years, CCRP had achieved a total of only 382 job placements: 135 full-time positions with benefits, 75 full-time positions with no benefits, and 172 part-time positions, most without benefits. These few, often marginal, placements would probably have occurred without CCRP's efforts.

CCRP apparently contributed to the local quality of life: $6 million was spent on nine new or upgraded parks, local (but largely unspecified) attention to crime, and a specialized housing program for HIV patients. Finally, CCRP takes credit for improving the operations of the community development corporations: "With CCRP funding, technical assistance, partner brokering, and their own contacts and fundraising 'know-how,' the community development corporations grew substantially" (Spilka and Burns 1998, 19). That growth is accounted for by the listed programs in health, employment, economic development, and quality of life, and also by increased housing. However, the commitment to the South Bronx of urban development funds for housing preceded CCRP.

In the end, CCRP did not achieve an array of comprehensive services; it failed to provide extensive medical services, broad educational supplements, substantial employment or employment training, crime reduction, improved sociability, greater political influence, or more attention by city government to the embedded poverty of South Bronx residents. In short, it failed to address even a small amount of neighborhood need. None of the funders insisted on a serious evaluation to augment CCRP's own dutiful consultant report (Spilka and Burns 1998). The eight-year follow-up by its executive director is more memoir than evaluation, boasting great lessons for the field in the processes of community organization but lacking any evidence that those lessons produced measurable, important gains; moreover, it is not clear what remained in the South Bronx after the CCRP experts left (Miller and Burns 2006).

CCRP also failed to address seemingly obvious questions about persistent problems in the South Bronx, including the local quality of life, or the effectiveness of the community development corporations themselves. Indeed, CCRP's failure to produce remedies for urban problems through community organization recommends a search for alternative strategies that rely less on the questionable capacities of impoverished people living in impoverished areas to change their circumstances. Yet the commercial interests that funded CCRP—the banks and their foundations—are not in the business of encouraging social movements that seek to raise taxes and increase the public provision of adequate housing, health care, education, employment, and neighborhood amenities. Rather, they seemed content with a ceremony of concern that dramatized the splendors of self-reliance to a public content with large social and economic inequality. In a sense, CCRP and professional community organization generally serve as public entertainments, a bit of postmodern theater.

Consensus Organizing

Consensus organizing was initially branded by the Allegheny Conference on Community Development in Pittsburgh during the 1980s as a nonconfrontational strategy "to mobilize both community members and supporters," that is, resources (Gittell and Vidal 1998). However, consensus organizing eliminates the possibility of conflict in negotiation and thus constrains the ability of a community organization to develop power. The overarching commitment to consensus also forces the obedience of professional community organization to the national ethos and largely to the acceptance of contemporary conditions. Its goal is analogous to robbing labor unions of the ability to strike: "Consensus organizing frames its goal very differently from conflictual organizing. The objectives are to develop neighborhood leadership, organize community-based and controlled organizations, and facilitate respectful and mutually beneficial relationships between neighborhood-based leaders and organizations and the larger metropolitan-area support community" (52).

The Local Initiatives Support Corporation (LISC), one of the leading umbrella groups for community development in the United States, tested "the efficacy of a novel 'consensus organizing' approach in developing community-based capacity and forming new community development corporations" to pursue housing and other local development projects (Gittell and Vidal 1998, 2). The LISC demonstration was conducted in poor neighborhoods in three cities during the 1990s. It theorized that increasing trust and cooperation through consensus organizing would lead to material benefits that would improve the quality of life of residents in poor communities: housing, jobs, economic development, improved human services, and numerous others, including a sense of community: "Perhaps the greatest potential value of the Local Initiatives Support Corporation demonstration was its effort to strengthen the foundation on which community development depends by instituting processes to increase social capital bonds and bridges and fill structural holes in community political and social space to the benefit of local residents" (21).

The specific goals of the demonstration, which LISC called "intermediate outcomes," were to "(1) establish community-based and -controlled community development corporations with neighborhood leaders as board members; (2) foster beneficial financial, technical, and political contacts between residents of targeted neighborhoods and leading organizations and individuals in the support community; and (3) have community development corporations (and community development corporation board members) develop and then demonstrate their competency through the completion of housing development projects" (Gittell and Vidal 1998, 227–28).

After almost five years, the LISC demonstration had organized nineteen community development corporations in poor communities in the three target cities, although only eleven of them survived more than four years. The degree of shared control was problematic, with fewer than five board members taking charge in each of the more successful organizations. However, the project was able to raise only about $4.5 million locally, and most of the money apparently came from foundations and public development agencies. The committed funds were inadequate for even a single real estate project of modest size. A large community park costs more; a commercial center, or even five hundred units of housing, costs much more. Apparently the "support community," and notably local businesses, did not buy into the project's development plans. LISC conceded that "sustained, broadly based involvement was hard to achieve. . . . None of the local program directors lived up to initial expectations regarding the short-term demonstration program objective of active engagement of the private sector in community development, that is, broad-based participation with ongoing learning and bridge building" (Gittell and Vidal 1998, 117). More to the point, none of the community development corporations completed successful real estate programs—at least, no list of successful projects accompanies the evaluation, although the project claims some vague success in achieving its real estate objectives in one of the three demonstration cities. The strategy of cooperation among the community development projects also failed. While the private sector certainly appreciated the deferential, consensual style of community development, it showed little interest in learning "to interact constructively with volunteers" (118). Since private capital or at least external investment was pivotal—after all, poor communities by definition lack economic resources—consensus organizing apparently failed to achieve its most crucial goal. Moreover, the failure to achieve the secondary goal of building broadly participatory local agencies raises questions about the efficacy of any form of community organization.

The demonstration's grandiosity should have been punctured by the reality of the outcomes. Yet community organization projects seem impervious to their failures. As with the CCRP, the LISC demonstration drew important lessons for professional community organization from its experience—"how local factors, context, and implementation affect performance" (Gittell and Vidal 1998, 119)—in preserving faith in the value of consensus organizing, local control, economic development, and the rest of the romance of citizen empowerment. Yet the projects themselves belie the fundamental assumptions of community organiza-

tion and local development. Hard cash is required for economic development, and notably for housing. Neither the business community nor the
public sector would provide the cash, reprising the theme of American
indifference to poverty.

Basic material needs go unmet in the interminable chanting of community organizers about democratic process, citizen participation, and
the satisfaction of neighborliness. For all their professed good intentions, community processes of empowerment have not developed much
power. Apparently there was no deep pool of dissatisfaction from which
to draw organizational strength in the LISC demonstration communities. Community organization possesses no special insight, skill, or
power to create a political appetite without social support. The organizer's will is not sufficient, while consensus organizing looks like capitula-
tion to prevailing inequities. The fundamental satisfaction of Americans
with their society—the absence of manifest discontent in spite of many
attempts to organize oppositional voices—belies the appetite for changing the material distributions of Americans, either through the private
or the public sector.

There is apparently very little evidence to support an effective practice
of community organization. Ohmer and Korr (2006) reviewed the standard academic literature between 1985 and 2001 and came up with only
twenty intervention studies worldwide that met their very minimal standards of "quantitative or combined quantitative and qualitative" methodologies. Only nine of them employed "experimental or statistical
controls," and even those were deeply flawed. Seven of the twenty concerned international development. The remaining thirteen studies of
community organization in the United States were even less sophisticated than the evaluations of the LISC demonstration and CCRP. Some
of these thirteen studies were actually not evaluations of community
organization projects but weak speculative pieces that tested quantitative
models to predict the outcomes of organizing or sought to develop community health indicators; many were trivial, addressing leadership training programs, but only through the satisfaction of participants rather
than through more direct observation of their effectiveness; most of the
studies relied on unaudited surveys of community organization agencies
or participant interviews. The single most credible study, an evaluation
of organizing in one location over the course of seventeen years, was
reported in a doctoral dissertation that never made it into the standard,
peer-reviewed literature.

Mizrahi and Rosenthal (2001), one of the least impaired of Ohmer and Korr's studies, investigated coalitions of community organizations by applying a detailed interview instrument to "70 past and current coalition organizers and leaders" during focus groups. They reached the inane conclusion that, "second only to commitment to goal/cause/issue, competent leadership was the factor most often mentioned as critical to coalition success" (74). However, success was never defined, perceptions were never grounded, and thus the reports of participants could not be related to the actual outcomes of community organizations and their coalitions. At the same time, the methodology was too weak to sustain the reliability of the responses.

Wagenaar et al. (1999), another of the best Ohmer and Korr studies, claim that a community organization drive in fifteen randomly selected small communities succeeded in changing "alcohol-related behaviors among 18- to 20-year olds," as well as the alcohol tolerance of a variety of venders and community institutions. Again, however, their evidence is based on surveys, notably of the youths and venders. They offer no objective, independent data that drinking patterns actually changed or that the vendor and institutional changes were sustained.

Cummings and Glaser (2005), another among Ohmer and Korr's best, surveyed community-based organizations to compare the ability of community development corporations with community action agencies to "mobilize residents of low income neighborhoods to participate in redevelopment efforts" (267). They found no difference between the two types of development agencies. However, only 36 percent of their sample responded, and they could not verify the accuracy of any of the reported data. More tellingly, none of their inferences about "the political economy of community development" emerge credibly from the data, nor can they be tied to the agencies themselves rather than the agency environment. That is, community development agencies may be the creatures more than the creators of the political and social milieu.

The absence of credible information never subdued the transformative ecstasies of professional community organization. The National Association of Social Workers puts community organizing in "the forefront of community practice in the 21st century" with an onslaught of anecdotes about heroic overcoming that promise comprehensive community development, economic revitalization and self-sufficiency, political and social change, the empowerment of the poor and near poor, and improvements in housing, health, education, neighborhood sociability, and social services (Ewalt, Freeman, and Poole 1998, xii). There is hardly any concession to the routine historic failure of these attempts or to the difficulty of achieving material ends without concrete resources. Difficulties like incomplete understanding of "mechanisms," inadequate information, few resources, embedded social attitudes, and neighborhood inertia are magically resolved by the clairvoyance and life experience of "experts." The heroic will and skills of the professional community worker are apparently sufficient. Systematic, objective information is seen as an impediment to desire, which is implicitly the critical condition of reform. Each of the thirty-eight chapters in Ewalt, Freeman, and Poole (1998) dutifully reviews the relevant literature to draw uncritical inspiration from the testimonies of published savants: remedies for social problems do not cost much but rely on the will of the abused and oppressed to work together and on the timeless wisdom of American folkways.

It requires a romantic otherworldliness to ignore the influence of the broader culture—the popular consensus—in both creating and sustaining the deprivations that community organization is presumably dedicated to relieve: "Out of the authors' experience and research has come confidence that people, working together, can muster the strength to slow, or even stop, the decline of their local living places and bring them to renewed states of stability and viability. Well organized residents and the 'natural allies' they can garner are nearly always capable of reversing social and physical decline in their home community" (Murphy and Cunningham 2003, 25). Well-organized residents do indeed exist, especially in well-organized, responsively governed communities; many communities do revitalize themselves; commercial enterprises are constantly planned and executed; housing goes up and old structures are renovated; some impoverished people become wealthy. But these situations emerge naturally from the common participatory patterns of the culture. Professional community organization has not demonstrated a routine capacity to create well-organized residents but rather thrives on the confusion between natural occurrences and the field's efforts. Murphy and Cunningham only offer anecdote and journalism to sustain their claims, while ignoring the field's enormous number of failures. The assertion that the professional community organization process is nearly always successful is ludicrous; the authors' confidence is proof of nothing but the insularity of the devout.

The minuscule number of residents who typically participate in professional community organizing endeavors—only three hundred in the three LISC demonstration cities, a typical experience—suggests local indifference rather than support. It is rare that a community organization enrolls even 1 percent of local residents. Most often community revitalization projects are merely tolerated by local residents who remain skeptical about motives and the capacity to deliver on promises. For all its vaunted concern with locally derived projects and acceptance, professional community organization is usually a mission to deviant communities, not a local form that captures the enthusiasm of residents. The mission is usually funded by organizations that are alien to local residents and that proselytize an idealized vision of the transformative power of democratic synergy. That vision of local capacity defies the common experience of residents.

Community organization addresses the disorganization of the poor rather than the social conditions of the larger society that may have engendered the problem. By attending to the pathology of the poor—their disorganization—community organization propagates the orthodox values of the dominant culture. Community organization projects, recalling the War on Poverty's community action agencies, rarely if ever meet the pressing needs of residents, substituting neighborliness and good manners for jobs, income support, health care, housing, and the other material needs that bedevil the lives of the poor. If the budgets of professional community organization projects were allocated to resident groups, it is doubtful that they would devote them to community organization.

The cumulative history of community organization—an interminable catalogue of overblown promises and vacuous theorizing ending in failure—suggests a refutation of its central premise and Murphy and Cunningham's great confidence: small communities and neighborhoods lack the capacity and resources to remedy their own problems; even when organized into dedicated political blocs, they lack the power to wring large reallocations from public budgets.[12] This should be obvious. The sick cannot heal themselves, the unemployed with low skills typically cannot hire themselves, the disabled cannot earn a living, poor people cannot afford quality housing, poor minorities lack power. The

---

12. This may be a more plausible conclusion than Warren's (2001) triumphalism for twenty-five years of Alinsky-type organizing in the Southwest through the Industrial Areas Foundation.

resources of the fragile community organizer—desire, skill, time, dedication, a few dollars, and little political support—seem pitifully inadequate against the deprivations of troubled and needy communities and
the inertia and indifference of the society to their conditions. However,
the romantic soul was devised precisely to avoid the inconveniences of
reality. The theology of professional community organization has remained robust for more than fifty years, periodically refreshed with contemporary testimonials of conversion, witnessing of miracles, and
evidence of the power of faith.[13]

13. The literature on community organization is full of empty bombast. A review of fifty
years' worth of scholarship reveals almost no improvement over time. Each theory presents
a series of steps by which to achieve communal goals that replicate in one form or another a
prototypical professional problem-solving process, but fails to adduce evidence to demonstrate either the efficacy of the process or, more tellingly, its sustaining assumptions. Saul
Alinsky (1969, 1971), for example, wrote raucous polemics rather than chart books; he knew
how to vilify and curse. It has often been observed ironically that his vaunted early success—
Back of the Yards in Chicago—used its communal solidarity to keep minorities from moving
in. Warren (2001), as noted above, claims great success for Alinsky-style organizing in the
Southwest, but it seems that more than a quarter-century of effort should produce more than
a few social service programs. Communities Organized for Public Service, "a new model for
faith-based community building and political action," has had no notable political influence
(9). Poston (1953) and Lippitt, Watson, and Westley (1958) provided an early statement of the
stages of professionally planned change but gave little evidence that the stages were necessarily sequential. Ross (1967, 1958) illustrates the value of his "hypotheses about community
life" and his "principles relating to organization" with cameos of organizers and their projects. Perlman and Gurin (1972) endeavored to update Ross, but without improvement. Rothman (1974) attempted to address the problem of the literature on the field but unfortunately
as a believer rather than a skeptic, uncritically accepting the authority of very weak research.
Indeed, Rogers's first edition of Diffusion of Innovations (1962) did largely the same thing,
although he acknowledged a vast problem with both the literature and the variability of the
field's studies; still, none of the theories of professional community organization have
achieved the sophistication of his theory. Cox et al. (1979) provide an anthology of the conventional wisdom, a series of largely undocumented memoirs and polemics, notably one by
Alinsky that is, to use his own words, "conspicuous for its sterility" (426). Henderson, Jones,
and Thomas (1980) and Henderson and Thomas (1980) provide the British mirror image of
the American experience; more the conventional wisdom of public relations than an engineered technique, their listing of skills is intuitive, lacking any evidence. Mondros and Wilson (1994) take the organizer through the steps of empowerment—recruiting participants,
deepening participation, developing strategy, and so on, culminating in evaluation and feed-
back—but again without the ability to demonstrate the practical value of the process. Delgado
(2000) adapts the process to an urban setting with similar steps but covered in different
linoleum—assessment, mapping, engagement, intervention, evaluation. The many antholog-
ies of practice repeat the same formulas with the mechanical loyalty that comes through in
Rothman (1999). Vidal (1992) reports on perhaps the most systematic study of community
development agencies; it improved on the typical self-reported survey by sending site visitors
to 130 community development agencies in thirty cities. The sample favored older, larger,
and diversified agencies, excluding the more typical community organization project that
develops social services and resident support. Its principal conclusion seems obvious: "Ac-

Professional community organization is a romance of the rationalistic, adopting the cant and couture of rationality but not the substance.
Its processes appear to follow the logic of problem solving: identification
of a problem, early explorations, development of alternative solutions,
comparative analysis, selection, implementation, and evaluation. However, the absence of good information, the lack of appropriate resources,
and the commitment to the rituals of transformative democracy undercut even a protorational enterprise. Any nascent commitment to objectivity is overwhelmed by the folklore of populism, the myth of self-
creation, and a dysfunctional nostalgia for the sociability of small-town
life. The field seems to persist for these sentimental rituals, affirming a
national ethos that offers little to poorer and low-status groups.

The role of professional community organization in technology transfer gave the field its most plausible successes. The experience was
largely rural and initially emerged to improve the agricultural productivity of traditional farmers. The agricultural extension services of land
grant universities were largely dedicated to disseminating the innovations of agricultural science. Later, the same techniques were applied in
the third world, extending an initial concern with improving agricultural
productivity to transferring the technologies of small business development, assets development, and even sophisticated manufacture. The
theory of technology transfer may be the clearest statement of the community organization process, in large part because it begins with a specific, measurable goal: the transfer of a presumably effective technology
to improve living conditions for the recipient.

However, the elegance and impressive reach of the theory—notably
the work of Everett M. Rogers (2003)—is not matched by routine, sustained successes or credible tests of its effectiveness either in the United
States or abroad. For a technology to be successfully transferred, the
cultural and commercial conditions in which it was developed also need
to be transferred. More often than not, the transferred technology
withers without sophisticated markets, marketing skills, the ability to
accommodate economic changes, educational supports, and conducive
attitudes in the target population. In the United States, agricultural science engendered agribusiness, which superseded inefficient family

cess to external resources is critical to the success of organizations working toward the redevelopment of poor neighborhoods" (143). Its other conclusions, about the value that
community development corporations add to the revitalization process, are inappropriate
inferences from what is essentially survey data compiled by sympathetic site visitors.

farms and small agricultural entrepreneurs. Indeed, the new agricultural technologies required advanced skills and access to considerable
capital, both beyond the capacity of a community organization project
or its extension service. Traditional community organization, typically
applied to small communities of one sort or another, is incapable of
influencing the social forces that drive the society and economy and that
may even determine cultural adaptation.

Community organization is not a profession in the sense of a discipline with credible information and tested skills. The field presents
nearly insurmountable challenges to simple descriptive research, let
alone definitive tests of its interventions. It is destined to remain, at best,
a craft or even a folkway. It is nearly impossible to identify sampling
frames of communities or to conduct randomized experimentation;
even matched controls are impossible without definitive knowledge of
the determinants of local decision-making processes; measures are usually unreliable; the concepts defy easy specification. Yet the difficulties
of objective, systematic evaluation do not adequately explain the consistently subjective, partisan, thin polemics that characterize the literature
and pass as evaluations. The nature of the field rather than the nature
of its work may account for its literature.

Community organization is a denomination in the religion of democracy, as much a cult of political resurgence as a social welfare trade;
it demands unquestioning belief more than impartiality. Community
organizers are the cadres of social efficiency, motivated by a near-ecstatic
faith in creating great social and political change with tricks of organizational consent, with small programmatic catalysts, and with a frayed
promise to awaken the dormant potential of the citizenry. Objective valu-
ation of its efforts deteriorates into an issue of group solidarity. "Outside
evaluators, prized for their objectivity by funders and policymakers, may
be viewed with skepticism by program participants and staff for the
same reason: an outsider's objectivity can be equated with ignorance of
what's 'really' happening, and thus dismissed as not reflective of the
truth."[14] Truth, in this case, is a demand of pietism, not an objective
fact.

Still, the obstructiveness and insularity of community organization
projects would not be tolerated by a society concerned with their out-

14. See http://www.commbuild.org/html_pages/showresults.asp?search, 3 (accessed
July 2007).

comes or even threatened by their style. The little melodramas of community organization that reaffirm American myths of personal responsibility and communal self-reliance supersede the self-deceptions of staff in explaining the persistence of the field. Resistance, opposition, protest, defiance, and the rest of the turmoil of live social conflict occur only alongside a population that is both adequately frustrated with social conditions and free enough to act on its animosities. The ability to create frustration and animosity among a complacent population has yet to be demonstrated.

Community organization is typically not an extension of social institutions but instead is conducted as a mission to the disorganized margins of society. Rather than provide greater equality to deprived populations through jobs, education, income supports, and the rest, community organization is a strategy of draining change from the impoverished themselves. It implies the need to treat a pathological subculture rather than challenge the rigidities of social institutions and cultural priorities. Quite in line with its tacit role as professional pathologist, the dominant themes of the field—empowerment, consensus organizing, and social capital—suggest a commitment to social norms rather than to the needs of the aggrieved.[15] Confrontation and conflict, especially between cherished norms and marginalized populations, is socially unacceptable, even doomed, because of its unpopularity.

The field has always been bedeviled by the possibility that the society itself, rather than any temporary internal dislocation or incongruity, is the impediment to success. In service to traditional values of personal responsibility and deprived of evidence of substantial production functions in either physical or social development, professional community organization plays a ceremonial role in affirming American values. The field seems oblivious to its own paradox: despite the frequent revolutionary mood of organizers and theorists, community organization is obedient to the dominant ethos. After all, funding for community organization projects customarily flows from the very institutions—notably businesses, corporate philanthropies, and government—that drain considerable profit from the romance of American self-invention and personal responsibility.

---

15. Community organization supports Mills's (1943) characterization of the professional pathologist, even to the point of the idealized sense of rural virtue, now via Putnam and social capital.

Conclusion

The philanthropic sector and professional community organization are neither change agents nor independent voices of novel insight. They are orthodox social institutions that reflect the priorities of their donors, which are essentially agents of the accepted culture. The symmetry among philanthropy, community organization, and dominant social norms pays homage to the consistency of the United States itself. The symmetry of public and private policy—the failed War on Poverty and the deficient charitable sector—are tributes to the American consensus. Rather than any deep diversity or cleavage of values, the United States has produced a remarkably homogeneous citizenry, superficially different in body type and skin tone but very much the same in its beliefs, insights, social aspirations, and, most important, behavior. The culture wars have raged more among intellectuals and the copy-hungry media than among the people themselves. Indeed, the culture wars are probably more reality entertainment than a serious struggle among large, passionate social factions over serious matters with important consequences.

Transcendent idealism, the good-hearted volunteer, the amateur social worker, the Sunday philanthropist, and personal charity are pietistic expressions of a mystical relation to the sublime that is very much a defining element of the American religion, an immediacy of the divine spirit that enraptures the nation's civil religion and social policies. The conversion experiences of the enlightened volunteer and the professional community organizer validate epiphanies of social truth—blessings of wisdom—that are imperatives of social obligation. They also mark a boundary of both citizenship rights and virtue between the donor and the recipient.

Altruism may not quite exist as the selfless, competent, and true entity that it has come to mean. Volunteers serve personal ends. They are frequently incompetent, and volunteer services may often produce more harm than good. But the philanthropic sector promotes volunteerism and community self-help for their ceremonial value far more than for their substantive contributions. For each hands-on benefit that a personal volunteer may provide—handing out food packages, doling out the Thanksgiving mashed potatoes—a price is frequently paid in degradation, an overbearing sense of holiness that a recipient endures, along with the irritation of being put in one's place. For every hour of free accounting or legal advice a volunteer board member may provide, there is also a constrained role for the agency, perennially obedient to short budgets and obliging relations with donors from the private as well as the public sector. The volunteer, by the very nature of being self-motivated to provide a service, tends also to transmit the culture, with all of its assumptions of value and socialization that created the volunteer. It is a serious mistake to assume that through an act of will a volunteer can transcend the culture, that the charitable agency is a free agent rather than the consensual creation of a mass will, or that the philanthropic sector is an independent voice of goodness.

Critically, philanthropy and community organization are strategies separated from social institutions or, put another way, they participate in the social institution of separateness, maintaining the cultural and political isolation of marginal citizens. Both strategies justify their interventions under banners of targeting and service efficiency or as a necessary condition of social and political development and as a mechanism of social reform. Yet philanthropy and professional community organization, its frequent patron, are not in the habit of producing social change.

Community organization carries philanthropy's sense of social pathology, acting out its assumptions of self-renewal through self-help and self-invention with communities. The romantic assumption that democratic processes have failed and that the American consensus is thus fractured may simply be wrong: "Many Americans have simply lost faith in the ability of traditional forms of democratic politics to address the most critical questions facing their families and communities," M. R. Warren insists. "In response to our democratic malaise, Americans across the political spectrum have been looking for ways to revitalize American politics" (2001, ix).

In fact, Warren's faith is an errant belief in American dissatisfaction and political malaise. The consistent failure of professional community organization speaks to a very different reality that lacks a constituency for substantial social, economic, or political change in America. Instead, countless democratic decisions and personal choices have freely aggregated into the present situation of inequality and deprivation. Endlessly and openly described, they persist because of the consent of the American people. This enduring consent is institutionalized and scripts the role for philanthropy and community organization as dramatizations of the American consensus rather than as challenges to social complacency. The problem is not democracy but decency and desire.

CONCLUSION:
THE IRON SCULPTURE

Poverty, cultural deprivation, and nagging want endure in the United States because its citizens want it that way. The wealthiest nation ever, and wealthier now than it has ever been, has the resources to atone for its inequities. Yet Americans pretty much agree that people end up where they deserve to be, and thus they denigrate public provisions as moral hazards that encourage the evil ways of the poor. The poor are miscreants, the rich have contributed a lot, and those in between offer proportionate contributions and problems. The deserving exceptions among the poor are to be dealt with through private charity, discretionary but minimal public services, and supervision by the socially provident. The themes of heroic individualism and social efficiency have persisted through the history of American social welfare with the cold rigidity and indifference of an iron sculpture.

The U.S. government has based its antipoverty legislation on the fundamental assumption that its welfare provisions are both appropriate and wise. They fulfill the myth of American uniqueness blessed by a God who smiles on his most magnificent creation. Apparent deep cleavages among Americans—the so-called culture wars—are the inventions of media and intellectuals desperate for entertaining social narratives. However, the evidence flatly contradicts the notion of a deeply divided nation and reflects a startling agreement on basic values. The enormous range of preferences and frequently passionate instances of opposition are illusory. Rather than encourage differences, the national consensus is so deep as to be both unthreatened and indifferent to them.

The programs of the War on Poverty, notably including the personal social services that it devised, did not succeed on their own terms, let alone reduce poverty. American attention to poverty and related social problems has been a rain dance that never produced rain, imposing the empty credo of personal responsibility on populations in need of material relief, in spite of the ease with which the nation could have solved the problem of poverty through jobs, education, public assistance, health care, and other interventions. The social insurances have had only a modest effect on reducing poverty, and even less than that if the alternative is private intrafamilial transfers and perhaps even increased lifetime savings. In spite of enormous national wealth, many citizens live out their retirement years on inadequate incomes. Social services perpetuate Americans' approval of social and economic differences.

The War on Poverty programs reflected an underlying commitment to the core American value of personal responsibility. Staff members and the semiprofessions of social welfare remain the principal beneficiaries of the institutionalized spoils system of personal social services. The vaunted achievement of the Great Society in finally doing away with de jure racial discrimination through the Civil Rights Act and Voting Rights Act never came with the hard resources necessary to pay for the damage done by slavery and its aftermath, or for the great harm done by American society to other groups of Americans—Native Americans, Hispanics, immigrants, the traditional poor. The creation of formal procedural equality without substantive equality marks the indifference of Americans to basic rights of citizenship, an indifference to suffering, social isolation, and gross inequality as monumental as the nation's wealth.

Philanthropy and charity have always been woefully inadequate responses to economic and social need. Moreover, the charitable sector seems even more orthodox and less accountable than the public sector, papering over its rituals of goodness with avowals of great insight, imagination, and social responsibility. If anything, the consistent vacuity of the charitable sector pays tribute to the imprudence of allowing the dead to dictate the future through legacies and trusts. Professional community organization, one of the traditional activities of the helping professions, is a mission of conversion, a form of charity extended by the reigning American ethos to groups viewed as pathological and deviant.

In addition to its usefulness as social patronage, American social welfare passes on living fables of heroic individualism that ennoble the nation's insistence that citizens largely care for themselves or do without. Its divorce from programmatic effectiveness explains both the emptiness of provisions for those in need and the absence of rigorous research and program evaluations. In turn, the apparent indifference to program failure, and thus to social need, suggests that current arrangements are acceptable and that the policymaking system has largely rejected the processes of rationality. Social welfare and by extension social policy are engendered by mass agreement rather than by any distortion of democratic processes. Broadly democratic America has denied itself decent social welfare provisions.

The nation's technological and scientific prowess has not inspired social decision making, which remains tenaciously rooted in the mysteries of social preference. Science remains a totem of American social decision making, a debased form of social truth that lacks the true rigor of rational testing. The institutional distortion of objective truth has also compromised the social sciences. "Poverty knowledge," to use O'Connor's (2001) phrase, is not objective knowledge but a system of ideologically driven beliefs about appropriate citizen behavior that have become both enshrined as public policy and, most important, broadly socially adopted.

Poverty knowledge is just one hymn in the American hymnal of heroic individualism—ecstatic chosenness, a pietism of unique favor that is Darwinian if not actually celestial, and mystical processes of knowing. The rational enterprise in social decision making, the hope of the Enlightenment, has been supplanted in the United States by a far more primitive and privatistic set of values that seem to be a point of essentialism, embedded in the American experience, entwined in its being.

American decision making is largely impervious to rational argument but extraordinarily sensitive to the national will. The very openness of the nation, its near-universal enfranchisement, the absence of sanctioned oppression, its extraordinary freedoms, and the easy access to its own political institutions, including an abundance of information, belie the possibility that enduring social policy is manipulated, imposed, distorted, or even grandly cozened in the arms of saints or in a class of the wise and powerful. The War on Poverty and American social welfare, despite their failures and inadequacies, are popular. Consent is built into social policy by the acquiescence and choices of the masses, setting a boundary of the socially tolerable around the competition for leadership.

The process of decision making takes place through an ecology of detached roles and, because of its decentralization and embeddedness, is nearly impossible to control; the most powerful influence of individuals and plural interests are twigs on the path of national momentum. Rational social planning, including the notions of scientific philanthropy, purposive social work, engineered social welfare programs and social engineering generally, and scientific management, is a fiction of hubristic control, a stretch for objective and coherent authority to embellish the political and perhaps even the inevitable.

Histories of social welfare typically adopt the mythical hope of the Enlightenment for political and social destiny as a conscious process of social decision making that can be controlled, and that awareness and purpose guide policy choices. In contrast, a more accurate history of social welfare becomes a study of social habits, including enduring public policy, as the true imprint of national preference. The activities of politicians, lobbyists, the business sector, individual actors, and the rest, rather than the central scenes of the customary drama of policy, are relegated to supporting roles in explaining social choices. Lindblom's observation that business plays a favored role in American decision making is apt not because of business's financial prowess or cunning control of national power centers but because Americans prefer a large private sector and the entrepreneurial lottery game (Lindblom and Woodhouse 1993). Business is a favored national institution and free enterprise a favorite American myth; Americans approve of them, deferring to commercial elites in the deepest core of their expressed preferences for work, mating, style, local and national leadership, choice of career, and popular culture. Created through an ecology of detached role organizations, American social policy is the "spontaneous order" of an underlying consensus.[1] Social welfare policy has been consistently inadequate because the American consensus has been consistently ungenerous.

The Culture Wars

The influence of mass preferences on social decision making is circumscribed to the extent to which there are in fact "culture wars" over deep

---

1. "Spontaneous order" is how Hamowy (1987) describes the function of Smith's unseen hand. It stands for the unexplained but also suggests mystery and perhaps even the inexplicable.

divisions in American consent. The culture wars over American ideology as it justifies both legislated and social choices have raged over the origins, growth, and responsibilities of the modern state, and frequently over its provisions for social welfare, including Social Security and welfare in its narrow sense of public assistance. The core issue is whether the current American state, including its social welfare provisions, has the consent of the American people, that is, whether state ideology is endorsed by the governed.

The generosity, wisdom, and effectiveness of social choices are secondary to sovereignty and power, which in a democracy are matters less of civilization and progress than of legitimacy. The question whether the nation can afford its welfare provisions or whether they are effective in achieving their explicit goals seems ancillary to the question of social approval, that is, whether America's two-tier structure—social insurance for workers and public assistance for the nonworking poor—is the creation of predatory elites operating in defense of popular consent or whether it is broadly symmetrical with popular intentions and has widespread support.

Elites are legitimate if their positions have popular approval, expressed in elections as well in the more mundane and perhaps more important sphere of social appreciation and daily consent. In a similar way, state autonomy is exercised with little legitimacy when it is exercised against popular wishes through unrepresentative interests that thwart mass preferences—perhaps a pluralism of elites that creates the illusion of selfless public service while actually pursuing fundamental interests that are hostile to the welfare of the masses.

Popular consent is central to theories of modern democracy; it legitimizes both political leadership and the subsequent choice of policies. Governance would seem to become increasingly problematic, and policies more diffuse and blunted, as citizen attitudes become intensely divisive and hostile to existing social policy, let alone to the basic role or functions of any government. Yet popular consent, except as a ritual of democracy, remains a submerged theme and is often even ignored in prevailing expositions of policy formulation. In fact, debates about political power typically center on the characteristics and geography of political influence and political leadership more than on the degree of consent for any posited structure of decision making. On the one side, the pluralists argue that power is widely shared and that the state is autonomous, free of any allegiance to or control by illegitimate elites (Skocpol 2000,

1995, 1992; Weir, Orloff, and Skocpol 1988). Skocpol, for one, has an enormous affection for a tutelary elite, gold guiding tin, at the center of the state's autonomy—this elite constitutes a guardian class of higher education and civic sensibility in noble service to its epiphanies of the public's need. While Skocpol's sense of state autonomy is customarily defined negatively as freedom from class dominance, it often embraces the autonomy of the state in a positive sense of direct accountability to itself—the free space of public service—with only long-term, ultimate accountability to the governed.

On the other side, Domhoff, following the scholarly tradition that in the United States most notably includes Floyd Hunter and C. Wright Mills, offers class control as an explanation of American politics. Domhoff argues that political power is exercised by relatively few—often by the commercial and social elite of a self-perpetuating capitalist class— and largely for their own advantage in opposition to democratic interests and, occasionally, even the voiced preferences of the masses (Domhoff 1996, 1990, 1967; Domhoff and Dye 1987; Mills 1956; Hunter 1953).

Both Domhoff and Skocpol seem to prefer to avoid condemnations of the American people as institutionally predatory and mean-spirited, or even as Mencken's "booboisie." Both Marx and Mao held tenaciously to political reeducation in order to remedy false consciousness and preserve the virtue of the masses. Ascribing to the masses a false consciousness instead of inherent inferiority or moral blame avoided the contradiction of advocating revolution on behalf of people who were unworthy of it. Yet Gordon's (1992) gendered observation of a masculine influence over the social insurances and a feminine provenance for relief (ADC, then AFDC, now TANF, along with other relief programs for dependent children, the disabled, and so forth) might well be reinterpreted as broad social approval then and now for standing policy: women, even the most intelligent and socially conscious of them, as well as men, even the most unthinking and self-serving, never escaped the institutionalized biases of their culture; they did not even appear to reach for a loftier logic of social welfare. Thus, if socialization rather than any rational process of self-reflection is the common root of social policy, then the autonomy of the state and its guardian class become vanities of American democracy dominated by the myth of individualism. In a similar way, elite dominance may be strongly limited by the requisite deference of those at the desks of power to sublime popular consent.

These two lines of analysis—pluralism and "class dominance"—range through the discourse of four separate ideologies relevant to American policy: old liberalism, new liberalism, Old Right and New Right (Lowi 1995). Lowi's remaining two ideologies—Old Left and New Left—along with Marxian analyses, generally fall outside America's political attention. To simplify, what animates American political discourse concerning the role of the state is competition between free market policies (old liberalism), regulation and compensation for the risks of capitalism (new liberalism), and popular social conservatism (old conservatism, largely the religious Right, looking to government to protect social order and morality but also including powerful elements of the new conservatism, including the neoconservative rejection of social welfare compensation). Each ideology embraces a different mixture of Lowi's earlier types of state function: distributive (the patronage state, not the market), regulatory, and redistributive (Lowi 1964). Using this vocabulary, American social policy has moved decidedly toward the conservative social agenda and the old liberalism's preference for the free market, becoming less regulatory while increasingly substituting distributive grants (patronage, in Lowi's terms) for redistributive rights, notably evidenced by the 1996 reform of welfare and the drift of the policy discussion concerning the future of the social insurances.

The United States rejects the mystical as an explanation of decision making as much out of cultural style—an insistence on the concrete in policy discourse—as out of the professional and disciplinarian interests of the analysts and their constituencies. Yet without a true science to measure policy effects, to identify the contingencies of leadership, and, more broadly, to describe the popular will, social decision making is returned to the default position: the social will is mystically constructed through unknown processes, perhaps of social interaction, by which large populations of people with self-perceived common stakes reach a consensus over policy choice. Culture is largely elaborated through the tacit behavioral consent of its members, only occasionally expressed through elections that inexplicably coordinate its institutions and their actors; the institutions can be described, but the processes of social creation (including the creation of consent) remain hidden within the semievolved consciousness of the human animal. Hegel, shorn of God's specific provenance and taken as a social scientist at a very rudimentary point of description in theory development, may be more to the point than any evangelist of the Enlightenment pursuing truth in an academic department of political science, sociology, or economics. The mystical—a comforting ignorance such as tradition, exceptionalism, God's favor, or, most emphatically, capitalism's spontaneous order—may be the only remaining, yet still unsatisfying, explanation for policy. The mystical becomes relevant as a consequence of the near impossibility of identifying the determinants of social policy, that is, of adjudicating between the influence of masses and elite or demonstrating the force of other factors.

The efforts of the social sciences to ground political theory—the discussion of legitimacy, governmental form, policy goals, and influence—have been frustrated by the near impossibility of disentangling the role of leadership from the preferences of followership, except when clear conflicts emerge over important policies. The question remains open whether the masses are led through coercion, manipulation, and misinformation to submit to a predatory leadership, or whether power is exercised with popular consent. However, it is only a pressing matter in the presence of popular discontent with the structures and processes of social decision making, that is, a culture war in fact.

Over the past few decades, social scientists have estimated the degree of social consensus in America, significantly including the degree of support for social welfare policies. Yet the recent dispute over the existence of "the culture wars" has proceeded from the possibility that political polarization may undermine the ability to govern. Hunter wants "rational discourse" to supplant the "emotivism" that undercuts "the very possibility of serious and sustained moral reflection and argument . . . the kind democracies require to stay vital" (1994, 216). Certainly he is not unique in appropriating rationality to justify his own preferences, this time for a vague "modesty in politics" built upon self-generated common values that nurture the culture through "communities of moral discourse" (228, 235). Also following Hunter's anecdotal style of analysis, Gitlin (1995) suggests that America is riven by the politics of identity, which seem to be producing irreconcilable differences. "The core of the culture wars thesis is the claim that the component issues generate cumulative social divisions because each is structured in the opposition between two distinct religio-moral world views: the orthodox and the progressive. . . . As a consequence, culture war conflicts are fertile sources for political mobilization and social conflict. . . . [They] discourage compromise and tend, instead, toward intense divisions and escalating conflicts, ultimately leading to violence" (Downey 2000, 91).

The culture war advocates often draw their proof of polarized American attitudes sufficient to undermine a common core of civic beliefs from intuitive, qualitative interpretations of the public discourse of opinion elites (Hunter 1991, 1994; Gitlin 1995). In response, social scientists, relying upon attitude surveys to estimate the size of social cleavages, point out that except for the issue of abortion, polarization is insubstantial and has actually been decreasing for the past twenty years. Not surprisingly, the two sides of the culture war debate, while seeming to agree on the perils of intense conflict, make different assumptions about the American policy process by way of justifying the relevance of their very different findings, that is, the relative influence of elite opinion versus mass opinion, the power of leadership to determine events rather than to occupy roles largely constrained by institutional forces. Still, the authority of all the conclusions is vulnerable to the quality of the data and research methods that sustain them.

Hunter (1991, 1994) confined his discussion of polarization largely to the "body" issues, that is, abortion, but also sexuality and women's rights. While Hunter ignored general attitudes in focusing on elite opinion, he consistently assumed that opinion elites—those who appeared to speak for the different sides of issues—were also important actors, both in the sense of determining social policy and in sustaining the course of a dispute by recruiting support for their points of view. Gitlin (1995) made the same implicit assumptions about identity politics. Yet the failure to demonstrate that opinion elites form mass opinion or are capable of mobilizing general political support for conflict strengthens the possibility that even apparently intense disputes, such as those over abortion and sexuality, are frequently rhetorical, especially when a broader consensus may cushion policy radicalism, preventing fervent conflicts from threatening political stability. Indeed, while painful for some, intense dispute, especially as it becomes overexposed in the media, may serve more as entertainment than as political threat, providing a catharsis that actually displaces serious aggression.

The social scientists, notably DiMaggio, Evans, and Bryson (1996), seemed to minimize the presence of intense polarization by describing a general and growing American consensus in which abortion seemed to be an outlier. Indeed, Mouw and Sobel (2001) have even questioned the degree of cleavage over abortion (although Evans, Bryson, and DiMaggio 2001 insist that their initial estimates are accurate). Across a variety of social issues (crime and justice, race and poverty, gender, abor-

tion and sexuality, political orientation), groups (age, educational attainment, race, gender), and measures of polarization (dispersion,
bimodality, constraint, and consolidation), DiMaggio, Evans, and Bryson
(1996) reported a large, consistent, and seemingly stable American consensus. Their data minimize the intensity of the cleavage over abortion,
suggesting an abiding tolerance for the "pro-choice" position; the most
populated differences occur between the liberals and the center, rather
than between the extremes of liberals and conservatives. DiMaggio,
Evans, and Bryson's American consensus has been generally corroborated by similar analyses that have also refuted the existence of large
polar camps (Lindaman and Haider-Markel 2002; Brooks and Cheng
2001; Miller and Hoffman 1999; Hoffman and Miller 1998; Evans
1997; Williams 1997).

A detailed summary of attitudes toward social welfare by income
class—a curious omission in a literature focused on social rivalries—
further strengthens the argument for a strong American consensus. The
differences in attitudes toward the provision of welfare and the welfare
state between the wealthiest and the poorest deciles of Americans average only a little over twenty percentage points across more than thirty
years of recent opinion polls (Epstein 2004). The same consistency
among income classes also holds up across gender and race, undermining the view of a society riven by class differences. In the United States,
income classes are only income groups.[2]

2. On the one hand, Hunter (1994) and Gitlin (1995) assume that political divisiveness
is adequately tested by the opinion of elites in narrow but intense disputes. On the other
hand, many social scientists assume the determinative influence of mass opinion (in contrast
to actual preferences expressed as behavioral choices) and their ability to accurately and reliably define it. They assume that people are aware of their attitudes to begin with and then
report them accurately. It remains surprising that very little attention has been paid in analyses of the culture wars to the possibility of response falsification, except as an afterthought
in DiMaggio, Evans, and Bryson (1996). At the same time, the search for the underlying
substance of reported attitudes has not addressed the instrumental possibility that bi- and tri-
modalities express the confusion of respondents rather than informed polar commitments.
Nevertheless, while the social sciences are confident that "the distribution of social attitudes
is essential to mitigating, sustaining, or intensifying conflicts" (Downey 2000, 91), they have
demonstrated no ability to predict intense violence, let alone revolution (Kuran 1995), from
reported attitudes. Existing patterns of polarization in American society, even when expressed as intense differences of opinion, may not reflect an "underlying cultural fragmenta-
tion" (Renshon 2000, 214). To the contrary, they may signal an underlying consensus that
encourages political accommodation through regulated contests over ideology and power. In
the same way, Hunter's (1991) ominous sense of domestic rivalries has not predicted subsequent perils to American governance separate from the near-permanent and characteristic
violence of the culture itself. American millenarianism (Hunter's "Puritan theology") fails to
predict either the awakening or the content of the nation's extremism.

With a taste for critiques of journalism and for anecdote, the culture wars speak past evidence of an American consensus, invoking stereotypes as evidence and substituting their own "emotivism" for "rational" discourse. In spite of the limitations of the culture war dispute—elusive qualitative analysis of elites and the unreliability of opinion data—the American consensus appears to have been consistently supportive of America's bifurcated social welfare system while hostile to the very essence of the welfare state: the provision of economic security and greater cultural parity for socioeconomically marginal groups. Americans appear to be intensely antipathetic toward welfare narrowly construed as public assistance for the destitute (Schiltz 1970; Shapiro, Patterson, and Young 1987; Weaver, Shapiro, and Jacobs 1995).

At the same time, Americans appear overwhelmingly to endorse a government role in securing the general social welfare; they offer consistent support for Social Security (that is, old age, survivors, disability, and health insurance—OASDHI): "the public has consistently supported increasing or at least maintaining existing spending levels for Social Security" (Baggette, Shapiro, and Jacobs 1995, 437). At the same time, the public is more or less evenly divided over questions of the government's domestic role and basic social philosophy. However, there is a marked preference for Lowi's regulatory functions of the state rather than an enhanced role in redistribution, especially to produce greater equality among income groups. The consensus on OASDHI does not, however, necessarily translate into a preference for generous sharing, since a large proportion of Americans seem fatalistically to accept the possibility that benefits will decline over time and that at least a portion of the program should be privatized. Americans do not place a high priority on the program ("the salience of Social Security as a national issue has historically been very low"), even while they say they are willing to "spend more" for greater benefits, although these benefits are apparently to be funded through regressive Social Security taxes rather than progressive federal income taxes (Baggette, Shapiro, and Jacobs 1995, 421).

Yet the support is treacherous, in that polled preferences for expenditures over taxes have not translated into electoral support for candidates who campaign for larger government; to the contrary, voters have expressed a massive rejection of what so-called conservatives have successfully branded "tax-and-spend liberalism." Indeed, the consistency of support for OASDHI may boil down to a preference for the very limited provisions of the present program. The preference for policy minimal-

ism—social efficiency—supersedes the wisdom of greater income security provided through increased public programs, in spite of a large
reported desire to increase benefits. In the same way, the reported support for an enhanced government role may in fact come down to support
for the present role, with all of its parsimony and limitations. Some
degree of response falsification is also suggested by the fact that "most
people have considered themselves to be very well or fairly well informed about how the Social Security system works," a preposterous
contention except as a catechism of citizenship. While most Americans
may be aware that they are paying Social Security taxes for their own
future benefit, it is doubtful that more than a few are aware that the
program does not truly provide insurance but operates more like an
intergenerational welfare plan. They are, however, probably quite aware
of its severe limitations, given that they receive periodic estimates of
their own retirement benefits and are usually aware of what parents and
relatives are receiving. It is telling that tax expenditures for relatively
wealthy Americans through tax credits, bigger 401(k)s, and larger IRAs
far outstrip relief to poorer retirees through more generous OASDHI
checks or even an adequate Medicare drug assistance program.

The few attempts to demonstrate either support for increased social
welfare services or deep changes in American attitudes toward social
welfare fail to credibly document their arguments. Cook and Barrett's
(1992) survey seemed to deny the massive evidence of a conservative
shift *during* the Reagan presidency. However, Cook and Barrett's actual
response rate was very low; many of its crucial questions were worded
conveniently; it did not rotate the order of its questions and thus suffered from many halo effects. Indeed, a similar survey by Public Agenda
(1995) seems more consistent with sixty-five years of reported antagonism toward welfare. Public Agenda reported virtually no difference between the deep hostility toward welfare voiced by whites, blacks, and
welfare recipients themselves. Even during the Great Depression and
shortly thereafter, Schiltz (1970) reports that large pluralities of public
relief recipients were often against extending social welfare to uncovered
groups (at that time primarily domestics and farm workers).

Nevertheless, the supposition of mass support for an increased welfare state in both the narrow and broad senses was boosted by the
Demos Common Wealth Project (Demos 2002). Drawing on more than
twenty polls conducted between 1996 and 2001, the Demos report
found considerable support for work training, day care, the Earned In-

come Tax Credit, and national health insurance, programs that are presumably necessary to move people off public assistance and into jobs. On the basis of these polls, the report challenges the conventional conclusion of widespread antagonism toward the poor, which in this case also implies welfare recipients. "This review of public opinion over the last five years reveals that the public's views are both more complex and supportive than is generally assumed. . . . [Thus] it appears that a policy agenda based on core values of fairness, equality of opportunity and government—as well as personal—responsibility could ratchet up wide support" (1). The report's explanatory invention—its hypothetical construct—is a new widespread appreciation for the travails of poorer workers that has "blurred the old distinctions between the 'welfare poor' and the 'working poor.'" Accepting the polled responses literally and naively, the report sidesteps the possibility that lower-paid work maintains its customary stigma—an enforced penance for laziness and improvidence and a sign of social, intellectual, and economic inferiority. In the same way, attitudes toward lower-paid work may now be voiced with the polite deference of contemporary discourse, the obligatory but superficial sympathy of the better off for those who struggle, as well as the mystifying but characteristic self-denigration of the poor and near poor. The Demos project at no point questioned the credibility of its polls or raised the possibility that its newly discovered national value, which blurs the distinction between working and welfare poor, is a reflexive, prosocial response that masks true beliefs.

Support for program changes to AFDC, expanded public health insurance, and increased public retirement benefits have been variously reported over the years but, paradoxically, together with great antagonism toward recipients of public welfare. The consistent finding of conflicting attitudes in the Demos report, as well as in most other published sources, is either glossed over, reinterpreted as actual compatibility, or reconciled by arbitrarily elevating one attitude over others. The possibility of massive response falsification—in part due to citizens' report of ritualistic values rather than decisive preferences—has naturally been subordinated to the value of opinion polls themselves as important vehicles of the public will.

It is difficult to decide whether respondents are antagonistic toward the perceived inefficiencies of the welfare programs or toward the notion of welfare itself. Yet consistent negative attitudes toward welfare recipients—the perception of their moral unworthiness—and a consistent preference for notions of personal responsibility over social responsibility, offer an interpretive key. The long-standing hostility toward the narrow popular understanding of welfare takes on far broader meaning when seen as antagonism toward social welfare itself. Tellingly, the antagonism becomes concrete in the high level of political support for the increasingly conservative direction of American social welfare policy since 1968, which continues past the welfare reforms of 1996 and their 2005 reauthorization.[3]

Unfortunately, the culture war debate is conducted primarily through opinion survey data. In contrast, detached role theory points to the more reliable evidence of freely chosen patterns of behavior. Yet both the chosen and the verbalized converge on the conclusion of an enormous underlying consent in the United States for its meager social welfare provisions and, more broadly, for current social institutions and patterns of leadership. Both sources reprise the troubling conundrum that America's democratic preferences may not be welcoming, generous, or tolerant.

An Ecology of Detached Roles

American social welfare is an organic immanence—a dimension of American life—built on citizen choices that are made both consciously and intuitively. Social welfare and social policy in general are not discrete, purposive plans proposed to the society after much deliberation and then sanctioned through the formal procedures of voting and legislation, although deliberative democracy is the myth of coherence that is imposed on the process. Rather, social welfare is an impelled expression of core preferences that is engendered in much the same manner as other cultural institutions of American life, such as the English lan-

---

3. Teles (1998) explains this political shift as the result of a sea change in American attitudes toward social welfare since 1961. Unfortunately, he fails to mention that 1961 as well as 1948 were startling exceptions to the rule in the context of sixty-five years of polling that consistently reports that only tiny percentages of Americans support increasing welfare spending. Moreover, Schiltz (1970) attributes the 1961 poll results to a quirk in the wording of the questionnaire. The very limited provisions of the American welfare state, from its inception in the 1930s to the present, may reflect persistent and pervasive antagonism to the public provision of generous social welfare, which is to say, any sort of effective social welfare. Rather than the hijacking of public policy by a conservative, business-dominated elite, a stingy social welfare policy is quite consistent with American values.

guage, popular entertainment as well as high art, folklore, baseball, family life, and food. Enduring social institutions are built from daily use.

U.S. social policy expresses collective preferences and patterned, habitual social behaviors—the nation's mores—that grow from the ways in which Americans perceive and act on whatever it is that constitutes their social environment. Social policy goes beyond questions of popularity and evanescent fashion; it also lies beyond the reach of rationality. Enduring American social policies are embedded as the collective will of an increasingly homogeneous society. American social welfare policy is a positive construction in the manner of its formal laws, stating preferences rather than wisdom, decency, or interpretations of the Ten Commandments. American social welfare is the way America wills it to be. It is a cultural form, and culture cannot be controlled, fantasies of dominance and collective paranoia notwithstanding. It is the people's religion. For American social welfare to change, the American people would have to change the way they interpret experience.

Rather than a rational or even a considered process, American social welfare is formed in the body of the culture, accepted through the huge variety of paths worn deep by use, of practiced habits, of burnished familiarities and all the little satisfactions and fears that impel collective behavior. Despite the formal appearance of public policy, social preferences emerge as "spontaneous orders" of seated national preferences. The determinants of formal social choices, such as the War on Poverty and the other public provisions for citizens in need, as well as the activities of the charitable sector, are found within the routine social existence of the population. Public policy in an open society such as the United States is the collective embodiment of private, individual choices.

The semblance of a deliberative process, even adorned with popular discussion and critical analysis, is typically confused with broad consideration. Yet the policymaking process is not deliberative in the sense that the citizenry sorts through the evidence and then decides on appropriate policy. Instead, national priorities are set through the competition and negotiation of detached role organizations that draw their sanction from individual priorities. Every choice a citizen makes increases or decreases the valence of a particular role and thus the influence of the organization that represents that role. Within an array of choices that are limited, for example by income and time, a person's emphasis on a particular activity or purchase of a particular product enhances the market standing and social standing of that activity and product relative to all others. In this way, when families spend time with their children and allocate a relatively large portion of their income to them, the general strength of children's political claim to national resources increases; that is, the general priority of children changes as a function of their individual importance, measured in part as time and attention that are freely allocated to them by their parents in preference to competitive activities and interests. Role organizations are often unelected, but they are still sanctioned intermediaries between citizen choice and social policy.

Similarly, as individuals use their income and time to amuse themselves through spectator entertainment, athletic participation, and personal efforts to develop these sorts of skills and knowledge, other activities receive less attention and fewer resources. These preferred activities, in turn, gain increasing policy importance through the enhanced influence of organizations dedicated to recreation. Even seemingly small choices signify preferences and have policy effects: the preference for fast food shifts traditional family functions to the commercial sector and enhances its standing; time shifted to television viewing and away from reading improves the standing of entertainment industries over schooling. In their best practice, sociology and anthropology document the preferences of a people by describing their free behavioral choices.

Consistent individual choices aggregate in important collective meanings. The decline of labor unions, and along with it the fading political importance of lower-paid workers, expresses the choice of workers to go it alone. The insistence that workers are not pursuing their best interests—in itself a political judgment rather than a rational conclusion—is quite distinct from the fact that they have stated their preference by not joining unions. Similarly, the increase in the age of first marriage, the high divorce rate, and the declining fertility rate; the racial resegregation of America; the continuing popularity of private transportation over public transportation and detached housing and suburban living over dense urban neighborhoods; the preference for tribal identities of race, ethnicity, sex, and gender; the extraordinary prevalence of obesity, violence, and mood-altering drugs, and similar choices of the population impel social policy.

The daily choices of individuals as they go about their lives sanction organizations that are constrained by a relatively narrow obligation to function on behalf of their defining roles. The obligation is often formally stated in charters, but more often it develops de facto as limited organizational resources are allocated to core role constituencies. Role organizations depend on and represent individual role choices in political competition with other role organizations; in this way, role organizations are deeply dependent on particular roles and become directly accountable to individuals through their choice of roles rather than through a formal sanctioning process. In this sense, the role decisions of individuals become politically detached from the individuals themselves and assigned, by dint of acting in the role, to the organizations that represent those choices. Thus the fundamental principle of a democratic society lies in the freedom of the individual to allocate his or her own roles. Public elections are relatively rare opportunities to correct deviations from national preference, that is, to assure that power distribution remains consistent with the popular will. Elections and much of the machinery of government are ill equipped to handle the complexity of preferences and the multitude of specific policy choices. Rather, the system of detached role organization operates smoothly, without the encumbrances of formal planning and review, to translate the will of the nation into both private institutions and public law.

Seen through the lens of detached role organization, participatory democracy loses its rustic fantasy of daily citizen oversight through town meetings and intimate knowledge of policy. Direct participation in an open society fluidly transforms personal choices into social policy. The way citizens live their lives becomes policy. Thus an informed citizenry is less important than an open system in which role organizations digest information in competition with each other. It is critical that information be available, but the expectation of broad citizen awareness is unnecessary, and is actually impossible in light of the complexity of modern society and the overwhelming amount of information it has generated.

Quite obviously, the democratic process of role representation has been distorted and undermined at times by commercial monopolies, stolen elections, misleading information, errant leadership, bribery, cronyism, and the like. But, typically, deviant forms are brought back into conformity through criminal prosecution and new legislation, but most powerfully as the loss of individual support leads to the triumph of competitive role organizations.

Many policies do not endure, but this does not necessary suggest that mass preferences are dormant or defied. Rather, periods of changing preferences or threats to stable policy tend to experiment with new forms. The meager provisions of the War on Poverty were retrenched over the following decades as popular antagonism toward poorer and lower-status Americans grew, and, substantially, as Americans embraced more tightly their traditional forms of handling the deviant and the needy through church and neglect. The War on Poverty experimented with a new type of popular leadership that failed in proportion as it seemed to depart from American tradition. After the conflicts of its early years, the War on Poverty simply re-created traditional American programs for the poor and rejected any obligation to press a contrarian agenda. Community action became outreach for community services. The question of why America refused to change is probably unanswerable. But the fact that it did not because it did not wish to is perhaps the overriding point of historical analysis. The acceptance of traditional forms—that is, doing very little about poverty through the public sector—is symmetrical with a widely popular choice of individualism, if not actually indifference to need.

Because of the openness of American society, the lack of change itself measures a preference that is witnessed in both enduring public legislation and the sociological and anthropological instances of citizen inertia. The telling point is that the poor themselves did not flock to participate in oppositional groups during the War on Poverty or, afterward, in any of the urban renewal efforts of community organization. As with the unions, the defined beneficiaries of change freely neglected to challenge the dominant American ethos or to accept the new forms of representation.

The same sorts of role choices have been reflected in American social movements since the civil rights and Great Society years. Even then, however, civil rights eclipsed economic rights. The signal achievement of the extension of the voting franchise to blacks was not accompanied by a second Reconstruction. There were no forty acres and a mule, let alone the massive and sustained expenditures necessary to equalize educational levels, income, the availability of jobs, and access to housing, health care, and mental health services, to name a few areas of racial disparity. The near-universal extension of the voting franchise resolved one of the deep contradictions of American society. However, occurring without much attention to the actual conditions of citizenship—Berlin's positive liberty—the universal franchise has substituted indifference for abuse. Indeed, it is worth considering whether heroic individualism necessarily imposes a destiny of social atomization.

Since the War on Poverty era, the reformist urge has been channeled into consumer affairs, women's and gay rights, Christian fundamental-ism, and environmental protection, all causes that largely seek proce-dural reforms rather than substantive equality. Each of these movements accepts the basic fairness of American socioeconomic stratification, seeking only procedural parity for particular populations. Even the union movement, in becoming more syndicalist (e.g., "UAW–Daimler Chrysler," in one slogan), has given up its role as the economic embodi-ment of a broad advocacy for lower-paid and lower-status citizens. The active pressures for change are exerted on behalf of the traditional middle-class project, markedly neglecting problems of inequality. That neglect is broadly popular, uncontradicted by the actions of the poor and lower-paid citizens themselves.

Each reform movement is largely a collection of associated role orga-nizations that draw their influence from particular activities of citizens. Participation is the clearest form of sanction. Each movement is rooted in particular choices of citizens that give priorities to their roles in con-sumption, gender and sexual orientation, work, and health. The ecology movement has never come to grips with its own policies—the hardships that restricting the supply of energy and land, to take two examples, will have on poorer populations. Indeed, this lack of attention to the redistributive effects of environmental conservation is encouraged by a society that largely ignores the needs of its poorer citizens. Those who would save the planet from global warming have not proposed steps to save poorer and lower-status humans from the burdens of their enthusi-asms. The choice of these role organizations to abandon redistributive social welfare is built from the quotidian behavioral choices of the popu-lation itself. Indifference to need is built into the American way of life. Perhaps it is even a biblical legacy, as Noah had no plan to save all the beasts, only representative pairs of each species.

Movements that directly challenge American economic stratification have not found constituencies because concerns about economic depri-vation receive little individual attention as Americans go about their lives: few urban riots or protests; little expression of concern with poverty and the poor in local, intimate organizations such as churches, political clubs, and the like; a failing union movement; few charitable donations to the poor; little attention in popular media to economic hardship; scant concern for the homeless; lower crime rates even as inequality increases; and, for what it is worth, an avalanche of polled data suggesting a startling homogeneity of attitudes among Americans despite their economic, gender, regional, age, ethnic, and racial differences.

A Final Word

Popular romantic preferences determine the rights that come with citizenship. But why these particular preferences, and why they are so Puritanical, remains a mystery. Tawney and Weber, differing over the direction of the relationship between capitalism and religious conviction (actually, social ideology), may have missed the yearning for material plenty as the underlying cause of both. Technological innovation, the source of wealth, endorsed the utility of science and by extension the culture of science, which is probably the model for the open society. Freedom is tolerated for its bounty via science and technology but certainly not for its irritating conflicts and the price it exacts in human obsolescence. Science and the scientific culture, broadly conceived as the Enlightenment hope, stand in opposition to detached role organizations. However, the noble cause lost.

Industrialization and economic growth account for the major reduction of poverty in the United States as elsewhere. At first glance, the remedy for poverty would seem to lie in market participation, jobs, pay, productivity gains, and greater efficiency. However, the market does not distribute benefits proportionate to social contributions and effort, nor does it provide for those who cannot work or who cannot earn an adequate income. Since the 1970s the great gains of economic growth have not been shared fairly. The amount of underlying poverty in the United States has remained stubbornly high, while the amount relieved through public programs has remained stubbornly low. While there is a clear national preference to gain income through the market, it will probably become increasing difficult to do so, especially in light of low wages, international competition, limits on skill levels, limits on training, and enduring human tragedy that limits work participation. The problem of relative poverty is much worse; huge numbers of citizens are isolated from participation in the basic institutions of American culture by psychological, medical, educational, social, and economic barriers.

Yet industry and business are not equipped with heart or head to provide social welfare. They function best as economic institutions—competitive, efficient, profit-driven, and bountiful sources of public revenue. If inequality and other social problems amenable to financial resolution are to be addressed in the United States, the vehicle will have to be social policy, notably public remedies. Either Americans will accept a pervasive range of public roles in redistribution—public jobs, enhanced public and higher education, national health insurance, livable wages secured through some type of negative income tax, and the like—or the society will become even more stratified. Either the current rules of citizenship will give way to greater sharing, or the nation will pay an enormous price in human suffering for its rhapsodies of individual self-sufficiency. Then again, an infinite capacity for self-deception may ease the transition to greater sharing by maintaining the fiction of self-invention, heroic individualism, and the rest; the vast landscape of the irrational is not without a fertile anarchic beauty.

Mass preference and thus mass consent are customary sidelines in historical analyses that treat them as concessions to popular democracy, ornaments for their theories of class dominance and competition among interest groups. The alternative seems more plausible: the national will, expressed through the choices of the American people rather than through their very unreliable opinions, is the central structural element in the social policymaking process. However, the national will is an instance of culture and politics that supplants reason with tradition, received values, and aggregate preferences; the national will is not amenable to rational planning, let alone sectarian manipulation. Instead of the hidden hand of the market, a different kind of mysticism—citizen consensus—has determining influence over social policy.

Current social welfare provisions still maintain the principles of poor relief that prevailed in the early nation. The evolution from the Puritan's shiny hat buckle to the Gucci loafer is about as much of a change as the American civic religion permits. Tocqueville's 1835 attitude toward social need remains maddeningly popular, explaining the American reluctance to invest deeply in its own citizens and to address its deficits with more than the fear of the devil.

> I am deeply convinced that any permanent, regular administrative system whose aim will be to provide for the needs of the poor will breed more miseries than it can cure, will deprave the population that it wants to help and comfort, will in time reduce the rich to being no more than the tenant-farmers of the poor, will dry up the sources of savings, will stop the accumulation of capital, will retard

the development of trade, will benumb human industry and activity, and will culminate by bringing about a violent revolution in
the State, when the number of those who receive alms will have
become as large as those who give it, and the indigent, no longer
being able to take from the impoverished rich the means for providing for his needs, will find it easier to plunder them of all their
property at one stroke than to ask for their help. (Tocqueville 1997)

Tocqueville's attitude is ever refreshed in the continuing retreat of
the American consciousness from public provision for poorer and lower-
status Americans that even at its most generous, in 1973, was patently
inadequate. The denial of full citizenship, especially in the context of
enormous economic growth, perpetuates the superstitions and the fantasies of self-invention, autonomy, God's favor, good hearts, hard work,
and insight. Autonomous actors, concerned elites, predatory elites, special interests, the genius of democracy, unseen hands, conspiracies of
the wealthy, the media, the alien, the insidious, and spontaneous orders
have no messianic destiny to interfere with the American dance maca-
bre. The worst to be said is that history is prologue; the best is that there
is always hope. But hope is a recourse of desperation and a confession
of moral bankruptcy.

TABLES

Table 1 Social Security Beneficiaries 65 or Older, 2004

Ratio of Social Security[a] to Total Income[b] (%)	Number of Beneficiaries	Percentage of Beneficiaries	Median Annual Social Security Amount (dollars)			Percentage in Poverty[d]
			Total	Retired Workers	Other[c]	
1–9[e]	792,534	2.6	3,800	3,919	2,371	0.6
10–19	1,634,332	5.3	9,799	9,828	8,539	0.8
20–29	2,121,912	6.9	11,200	11,479	9,535	0.8
30–39	2,394,276	7.8	11,695	11,839	10,399	0.8
40–49	2,409,209	7.9	11,599	11,599	10,531	1.6
50–59	2,597,949	8.5	11,599	11,635	10,399	2.4
60–69	2,109,668	6.9	11,599	11,599	11,395	3.6
70–79	2,138,403	7.0	11,018	11,052	10,200	6.1
80–99	*6,937,378*	*22.7*	*10,699*	*10,764*	*10,399*	*9.0*
80–89	2,208,257	7.2	11,071	11,119	10,579	8.2
90–99	4,729,121	15.5	10,459	10,531	10,303	9.3
100	7,458,922	24.4	9,043	8,959	9,199	18.2

SOURCE: Social Security Administration, drawing on U.S. Census Bureau, Current Population Survey, public-use file of the March 2005 Annual Social and Economic (ASEC) Supplement, http://www.census.gov/cps.

NOTE: Persons with zero income or with negative total income, earnings, or income from assets are excluded. All calculations are weighted using the March Annual Social and Economic (ASEC) Supplement person weights. The table does not include 3,083,960 nonbeneficiary persons.

[a] Social Security includes retired-worker benefits, dependents' or survivor benefits, disability benefits made by the Social Security Administration prior to deductions for medical insurance, and railroad retirement insurance checks from the U.S. government. "Medicare" reimbursements are not included. In addition, fewer than twenty persons received transitionally insured benefits, a special type of retirement benefit, in 2004. For further information on types of Social Security benefits, see the Social Security Administration's *Annual Statistical Supplement to the Social Security Bulletin* (2005), 18–19.

[b] Total income includes earnings, unemployment compensation, workers' compensation, Social Security, Supplemental Security Income, public assistance, veterans' payments, survivor benefits, pension or retirement income, interest dividends, rents, royalties, income from estates and trusts, educational assistance, alimony, child support, cash assistance from outside the household, and other miscellaneous sources. It is income before deductions for taxes or other expenses and does not include lump-sum payments or capital gains. Noncash benefits, such as food stamps or energy assistance, are not included.

[c] "Other" includes disabled (adult or child); widowed; spouse; surviving child; dependent child; benefits

received on behalf of surviving, dependent, or disabled child(ren); other (adult or child); and respondents reporting more than one reason for receiving Social Security. These individual categories were too small to support distributions by reason for receiving benefits.

[d]The Census Bureau uses a set of income thresholds that vary by family size and composition to determine who is poor. If a family's total income is less than that family's threshold, then that family, and every individual in it, is considered poor. The poverty thresholds do not vary geographically, but they are updated annually for inflation using the Consumer Price Index (CPI-U). The official poverty definition counts money income before taxes and excludes capital gains and noncash benefits (such as public housing, Medicaid, and food stamps). Poverty statistics are based on a definition developed by Mollie Orshansky of the Social Security Administration (SSA) in 1964 and revised in 1969 and 1981 by interagency committees. This definition was established as the official definition of poverty for statistical use in all executive departments in 1969 (in Bureau of the Budget, Circular no. A-46) and was reconfirmed in the Office of Management and Budget Statistical Policy Directive no. 14.

For further details, see the section "Changes in the Definition of Poverty" in U.S. Census Bureau, Current Population Reports, series P-60, no. 133. The poverty thresholds are increased each year by the same percentage as the annual average Consumer Price Index (CPI). The poverty thresholds are currently adjusted using the annual average CPI-U (1982–84 = 100). For further information on how the poverty thresholds were developed, and subsequent changes in them, see Gordon M. Fisher, "The Development and History of the Poverty Thresholds," *Social Security Bulletin* 55, no.4 (1992): 3–14.

[e]Includes persons with at least $1 in income but less than 1 percent of income from Social Security.

Table 2   Social Security Beneficiary Aged Units[a] 65 or Older, 2004

Ratio of Social Security[b] to Total Income[c] (%)	Number of Beneficiary Units[d]	Percent of Beneficiary Units[d]	Percentage of Nonmarried Beneficiary Units with Total Income Below $15,000	Percentage of Married Couple Beneficiary Units with Total Income Below $25,000	Median Annual Social Security Amount ($)
1–9[d]	754,707	3.2	8.4	0.9	5,011
10–19	1,540,979	6.5	6.0	2.2	12,799
20–29	1,732,194	7.3	6.6	3.8	13,199
30–39	2,045,661	8.6	9.4	6.2	13,799
40–49	2,024,083	8.6	13.7	8.6	14,400
50–59	2,135,385	9.0	21.1	13.1	14,000
60–69	1,877,057	7.9	27.5	19.0	14,800
70–79	1,788,200	7.6	48.0	34.3	13,999
80–99	*4,710,897*	*19.9*	*75.2*	*68.8*	*13,231*
80–89	1,716,684	7.3	68.1	57.0	13,399
90–99	2,994,213	12.7	79.1	76.3	13,200
100	5,052,911	21.4	91.2	92.4	10,699

SOURCE: Social Security Administration, drawing on U.S. Census Bureau, Current Population Survey, public-use file of the March 2005 Annual Social and Economic (ASEC) Supplement, http://www.census.gov/cps.

NOTE: Aged units with zero total income or with negative total income, earnings, or income from assets are excluded. All calculations are weighted using the March ASEC Supplement person weights. The table does not include 2,229,046 nonbeneficiary aged units.

[a]Aged units are married couples living together and unmarried persons. Persons outside the marital unit

and their income are excluded. The age of a married couple is the age of the husband, unless he is under fifty-five years old; otherwise, the age of the married couple is the age of the wife.

[b]Social Security includes retired-worker benefits, dependents' or survivor benefits, disability benefits made by the Social Security Administration prior to deductions for medical insurance, and railroad retirement insurance checks from the U.S. government. "Medicare" reimbursements are not included. In addition, fewer than twenty persons received transitionally insured benefits, a special type of retirement benefit, in 2004. For further information on types of Social Security benefits, see the Social Security Administration's *Annual Statistical Supplement to the Social Security Bulletin* (2005), 18–19.

[c]Total income includes earnings, unemployment compensation, workers' compensation, Social Security, Supplemental Security Income, public assistance, veterans' payments, survivor benefits, pension or retirement income, interest, dividends, rents, royalties, income from estates and trusts, educational assistance, alimony, child support, cash assistance from outside the household, and other miscellaneous sources. It is income before deductions for taxes or other expenses and does not include lump-sum payments or capital gains. Noncash benefits, such as food stamps or energy assistance, are not included.

[d]Includes persons with at least $1 in income but less than 1 percent of income from Social Security.

REFERENCES

Aaron, H. 1978. *Politics and the Professors: The Great Society in Perspective*. Washington, D.C.: Brookings Institution Press.

Acs, G., and P. Loprest. 2007. *Final Report: TANF Caseload Composition and Leavers Synthesis Report*. Washington, D.C.: Urban Institute.

Alinsky, S. 1968. "The War on Poverty—Political Pornography." In *Poverty: Power and Politics*, ed. C. I. Waxman, 172–206. New York: Grosset and Dunlap.

———. 1969. *Reveille for Radicals*. New York: Vintage Books.

———. 1971. *Rules for Radicals*. New York: Random House.

Altman, D. 2001. Review of *Bowling Alone: The Collapse and Revival of American Community*, by Robert D. Putman. *Gay and Lesbian Worldwide Review* 8 (2): 39.

Anderson, P. R. 1973. "Job Corps and Neighborhood Youth Corps: A Critical View." *Humbolt Journal of Social Relations* 1 (1): 8–16.

Auspos, P. 1988. *Maine: Final Report on the Training Opportunities in the Private Sector Program*. New York: Manpower Demonstration Research Corporation.

Baeck, L. 1970. *Judaism and Christianity*. New York: Atheneum.

Baggette, J., R. Y. Shapiro, and L. R. Jacobs. 1995. "The Polls—Poll Trends: Social Security—an Update." *Public Opinion Quarterly* 59:420–42.

Barber, B. R. 2000. "The Crack in the Picture Window." *The Nation*, August 7, 29–34.

Barber, G. M., et al. 2003. "Welfare Reform in Kentucky: A Five-Year Evaluation by the Kent School of Social Work, University of Louisville." *Insights on Southern Poverty* 1 (2): 6–8.

Bassi, L., et al. 1984. *Measuring the Effect of CETA on Youth and the Economically Disadvantaged*. Washington, D.C.: Urban Institute.

Bebbington, P., S. Johnson, and G. Thornicroft. 2002. "Community Mental Health Care: Promises and Pitfalls." In *Psychiatry in Society*, ed. N. Sartorius et al., 131–70. New York: John Wiley and Sons.

Beck, B. M. 1969. "Community Control: A Distraction, Not an Answer." *Social Work* (October): 14–20.

Becker, E. 1973. *The Denial of Death*. New York: Free Press.

Bellin, S. S., and H. K. Geiger. 1970. "Actual Public Acceptance of Neighborhood Centers by Urban Poor." *Journal of the American Medical Association* 214 (12): 2147.

Bentler, P. M., and J. A. Woodward. 1978. "A Head Start Revolution: Positive Effects Are Not Yet Demonstrable." *Evaluation Review* 2 (3): 493–510.

Bernstein, N. 2001. *The Lost Children of Wilder: The Epic Struggle to Change Foster Care.* New York: Pantheon Books.

Blavatsky, H. P. 1972. *Dynamics of the Psychic World.* Wheaton, Ill.: Theosophical Publishing House.

Bosworth, B. P., G. Burtless, and S. E. Anders. N.d. "Capital Income Flows and the Relative Well-Being of America's Aged Population." Unpublished paper. Washington, D.C.: Brookings Institution.

Bould, S. 1970. "Citizen Participation in Social Policy: The End of the Cycle." *Social Problems* 17 (3): 313–25.

Brager, G. 1963. "Organizing the Unaffiliated in a Low-Income Area." *Social Work* (April): 34–40.

———. 1969. "Commitment and Conflict in a Normative Organization." *American Sociological Review* 34 (4): 482–91.

Brandon, W. 1977. "Politics, Administration, and Conflict in Neighborhood Health Centers." *Journal of Health Politics, Policy, and Law* 2 (1): 79–99.

Braverman, M. T., N. A. Constantine, and J. K. Slater. 2004. *Foundations and Evaluation: Contexts and Practices for Effective Philanthropy.* San Francisco: Jossey-Bass.

Brooks, C., and S. Cheng. 2001. "Declining Government Confidence and Policy Preferences in the U.S.: Devolution, Regime Effects, or Symbolic Change?" *Social Forces* 79 (4): 1343–75.

Brown, E. 1999. "Assessing the Value of Volunteer Activity." *Nonprofit and Voluntary Sector Quarterly* 28 (1): 3–17.

Brown, M. K. 1999. *Race, Money, and the American Welfare State.* Ithaca: Cornell University Press.

Bryant, T. E. 1970. "Goals and Potential of the Neighborhood Health Centers." *Medical Care* 8 (2): 93–94.

Burtless, G. 1989. "The Effect of Reform on Employment, Earnings, and Income." In *Welfare Policy for the 1990s,* ed. P. H. Cottingham and D. T. Ellwood, 103–45. Cambridge: Harvard University Press.

———. 2007. "What Have We Learned About Poverty and Inequality? Evidence from Cross-National Analysis." *Focus* 25 (1): 12–17.

Carter, R. K. 1971. "Clients' Resistance to Negative Findings and the Latent Conservative Function of Evaluation Studies." *American Psychologist* 6:118–24.

Center on Philanthropy. 2006. *Giving USA, 2006.* Indianapolis: Center on Philanthropy at Indiana University.

———. 2007. *Patterns of Charitable Giving by Income Group, 2005.* Indianapolis: Center on Philanthropy at Indiana University.

Chertow, D. 1974. "Literature Review: Participation of the Poor in the War on Poverty." *Adult Education* 26 (3): 184–207.

Citro, C. F., and R. T. Michael. 1995. *Measuring Poverty: A New Approach.* Washington, D.C.: National Academy Press.

Clark, K., and J. Hopkins. 1968. *A Relevant War Against Poverty: A Study of Community Action Programs and Observable Social Change.* New York: Harper and Row.

Clotfelter, C. T. 1992. *Who Benefits from the Nonprofit Sector?* Chicago: University of Chicago Press.

Cloward, R. A., and I. Epstein. 1965. "Private Social Work's Disengagement from the Poor: The Case of Family Adjustment Agencies." In *Proceedings of the Eighth Annual Social Work Day Conference*, 1–54. Buffalo: State University of New York at Buffalo.

Cloward, R. A., and L. E. Ohlin. 1962. *Delinquency and Opportunity*. New York: Free Press.

Cnaan, R. A., W. J. Sinha, and C. C. McGrew. 2004. "Congregations as Social Service Providers: Services, Capacity, Culture, and Organizational Behavior." *Administration in Social Work* 28 (3–4): 47–68.

Coleman, J. 1957. *Community Conflict*. Glencoe, Ill.: Free Press.

Cook, F. L., and E. J. Barrett. 1992. *Support for the American Welfare State*. New York: Columbia University Press.

Cook, T. D., and W. R. Shadish. 1982. "Metaevaluation: An Assessment of the Congressionally Mandated Evaluation System for Community Mental Health Centers." In *Innovative Approaches to Mental Health Evaluation*, ed. G. J. Stahler and W. R. Tash, 221–53. New York: Academic Press.

Costin, L. B., H. J. Karger, and D. Stoesz. 1996. *The Politics of Child Abuse in America*. New York: Oxford University Press.

Cox, F. M., et al. 1979. *Strategies of Community Organization*. Itasca, Ill.: F. E. Peacock.

Crane, J. 1998. *Social Programs That Work*. New York: Russell Sage Foundation.

Crews, F. 1993. "The Unknown Freud." *New York Review of Books*, November 18, 1993, 55–66.

Culhane, D. P., S. Metraux, and T. R. Hadley. 2002. "The Impact of Supportive Housing for Homeless People with Severe Mental Illness on the Utilization of the Public Health, Corrections, and Emergency Shelter Systems: The New York–New York Initiative." *Housing Policy Debate* 13 (1): 107–63.

Cummings, S., and M. Glaser. 2005. "Neighborhood Participation in Community Development: A Comparison of Strategic Approaches." *Population Research and Policy Review* 4 (3): 267–87.

Currie, J., and D. Thomas. 1995. "Does Head Start Make a Difference?" *American Economic Review* 83 (3): 341–64.

———. 2000. "School Quality and the Longer-Term Effects of Head Start." *Journal of Human Resources* 35 (4): 755–74.

Curtis, R. L., Jr., and L. A. Zurcher. 1971. "Voluntary Associations and the Social Integration of the Poor." *Social Problems* 18 (3): 339–57.

Dahl, R. A. 1976. *Democracy in the United States: Promise and Performance*. Chicago: Rand McNally.

Danziger, S. H., and R. H. Haveman. 2001. *Understanding Poverty*. Cambridge: Harvard University Press.

Davidson, R. H. 1969. "The War on Poverty: Experiment in Federalism." *Annals of the American Academy of Political and Social Science* 385 (September): 1–13.

Davies, G. 1996. *From Opportunity to Entitlement: The Transformation and Decline of Great Society Liberalism*. Lawrence: University Press of Kansas.

Dawes, R. M. 1994. *House of Cards: Psychology and Psychotherapy Built on Myth*. New York: Free Press.

DeFillipis, J. 2002. "Symposium on Social Capital: An Introduction." *Antipode* 34 (4): 790–95.

Delgado, M. 2000. *Community Social Work Practice in an Urban Context.* New York: Oxford University Press.

Demos. 2002. "New Opportunities: Public Opinion on Poverty, Income Inequality, and Public Policy, 1996–2001." http://www.demos-usa.org/Pubs/POReport/.

Diamond, P. 2004. "Social Security." *American Economic Review* 94 (1): 1–24.

Diamond, P. A., and P. R. Orszag. 2004. *Saving Social Security: A Balanced Approach.* Washington, D.C.: Brookings Institution Press.

DiIulio, J. J., Jr. 2003. "Government by Proxy: A Faithful Overview." *Harvard Law Review* 116:1271–84.

———. 2004. "Getting Faith-Based Programs Right." *Public Interest* 155 (Spring 2004): 75–88.

DiMaggio, P., J. Evans, and B. Bryson. 1996. "Have Americans' Social Attitudes Become More Polarized?" *American Journal of Sociology* 102 (3): 690–755.

Dineen, T. 1996. *Manufacturing Victims.* Montreal: Robert Davies.

Dodenhoff, D. 1998. "Is Welfare Really About Social Control?" *Social Service Review* (September): 310–36.

Domhoff, G. W. 1967. *Who Rules America?* Englewood Cliffs, N.J.: Prentice Hall.

———. 1990. *The Power Elite and the State: How Policy Is Made in America.* Hawthorne, N.Y.: Aldine de Gruyter.

———. 1996. *State Autonomy or Class Dominance.* Hawthorne, N.Y.: Aldine de Gruyter.

Domhoff, G. W., and T. R. Dye. 1987. *Political Elites and Organizations.* Newbury Park, Calif.: Sage Publications.

Downey, D. J. 2000. "Situating Social Attitudes Toward Cultural Pluralism: Between Culture Wars and Contemporary Racism." *Social Problems* 47 (1): 90–111.

Dubey, S. N. 1970. "Community Action Programs and Citizen Participation: Issues and Confusions." *Social Work* (January): 76–84.

Dufresne, T. 2000. *Tales from the Freudian Crypt.* Stanford: Stanford University Press.

Elinson, J., and C. E. Herr. 1970. "A Sociomedical View of Neighborhood Health Centers." *Medical Care* 8 (2): 97–103.

Ellard, C. J. 1974. *An Investigation of the Influence of the In-School Neighborhood Youth Corps on Employment and Earning in Houston, Texas.* Springfield, Va.: National Technical Information Service.

Ellwood, D. T., and M. J. Bane. 1994. *Welfare Realities: From Rhetoric to Reform.* Cambridge: Harvard University Press.

English, G. 1972. "The Trouble with Community Action . . ." *Public Administration Review* (May–June): 224–31.

Epstein, W. M. 1992. "Professionalization of Social Work: The American Experience." *Social Science Journal* 29 (2): 153–66.

———. 1993. *The Dilemma of American Social Welfare.* New Brunswick, N.J.: Transaction Publishers.

———. 1994. "Economic Development and Social Welfare in the Third World: The End of Romance." *Journal of International and Comparative Social Welfare* 4:107–37.

———. 1995. *The Illusion of Psychotherapy*. New Brunswick, N.J.: Transaction Publishers.

———. 1997. *Welfare in America: How Social Science Fails the Poor*. Madison: University of Wisconsin Press.

———. 1999. *Children Who Could Have Been: The Legacy of Child Welfare in Wealthy America*. Madison: University of Wisconsin Press.

———. 2002. *American Policy-Making: Welfare as Ritual*. Boulder, Colo.: Rowman and Littlefield.

———. 2004. "Cleavage in American Attitudes Toward Social Welfare." *Journal of Sociology and Social Welfare* 31 (4): 175–99.

———. 2006a. *Psychotherapy as Religion: The Civil Divine in America*. Reno: University of Nevada Press.

———. 2006b. "Response Bias in Opinion Polls and American Social Welfare." *Social Science Journal* 43 (1): 99–110.

Erlanger, H. S. 1978. "Lawyers and Neighborhood Legal Services: Social Background and the Impetus for Reform." *Law and Society* (Winter): 253–74.

Etzioni, A. 2001. "Survey Article: On Social and Moral Revival." *Journal of Political Philosophy* 9 (3): 356–71.

Evans, J. H. 1997. "Worldviews of Social Groups as the Source of Moral Value Attitudes: Implications for the Culture Wars Thesis." *Sociological Forums* 12 (3): 371–404.

Evans, J. H., B. Bryson, and P. DiMaggio. 2001. "Opinion Polarization: Important Contributions, Necessary Limitations." *American Journal of Sociology* 106 (4): 944–59.

Ewalt, P. A., E. M. Freeman, and D. L. Poole. 1998. *Community Building: Renewal, Well-Being, and Shared Responsibility*. Washington, D.C.: NASW Press.

Fleischman, J. L. 2007. *The Foundation: A Great American Secret*. New York: Public Affairs.

Ford, R., and P. Ryan. 1997. "Intensive Case Management for People with Serious Mental Illness—Site 2: Clinical and Social." *Journal of Mental Health* 6 (2): 181–91.

Frankfurt, H. G. *On Bullshit*. Princeton: Princeton University Press.

Frieden, B. J., and M. Kaplan. 1975. *The Politics of Neglect: Urban Aid from Model Cities to Revenue Sharing*. Cambridge: MIT Press.

Friedman, L. 1977. "The Social and Political Context of the War on Poverty: An Overview." In *A Decade of Federal Antipoverty Programs: Achievements, Failures, and Lessons*, ed. R. H. Haveman, 21–47. New York: Academic Press.

Gale, D. E. 1995. *Understanding Urban Unrest: From Reverend King to Rodney King*. Thousand Oaks, Calif.: Sage Publications.

Garces, E., D. Thomas, and J. Currie. 2002. "Longer-Term Effects of Head Start." *American Economic Review* 92 (4): 999–1012.

Gates, C. T. 2003. "The Civic Landscape." *National Civic Review* 92 (1): 67–73.

Geomet, Inc. 1972. *Study to Evaluate the OEO Neighborhood Health Center Program at Selected Centers*. Rockville, Md.: Geomet.

Gilbert, N. 1970. *Clients or Constituents: Community Action in the War on Poverty*. San Francisco: Jossey-Bass.

Gilder, G. F. 1981. *Wealth and Poverty*. New York: Basic Books.

Ginsberg, M. I. 1969. *Economic Opportunity Amendments of 1969: Hearing Before the Senate Subcommittee on Employment, Manpower, and Poverty.* 93d Cong., 2d sess., May 8, 81–89. Washington, D.C.: U.S. Government Printing Office.

Ginzberg, E., R. P. Nathan, and R. Solow. 1984. "The Lesson of the Supported Work Demonstration." In *The National Supported Work Demonstration,* ed. R. G. Hollister Jr., P. Kemper, and R. A. Maynard, 305–19. Madison: University of Wisconsin Press.

Gitlin, T. 1995. *The Twilight of Common Dreams.* New York: Henry Holt.

Gittell, R., and A. Vidal. 1998. *Community Organizing: Building Social Capital as a Development Strategy.* Thousand Oaks, Calif.: Sage Publications.

Glazerman S., P. Z. Schochet, and J. Burghardt. 2000. *National Job Corps Study: The Impacts of Job Corps on Participants' Literacy Skills, Final Report.* Princeton: Mathematica Policy Research.

Gordon, L. 1992. "Social Insurance and Public Assistance: The Influence of Gender in Welfare Thought in the United States, 1890–1930." *American Historical Review* 97 (1): 19–54.

———. 1994. *Pitied But Not Entitled.* New York: Free Press.

Grob, G. N. 1983. *Mental Illness and American Society, 1875–1940.* Princeton: Princeton University Press.

Grogger, J., and L. A. Karoly. 2005. *Welfare Reform: Effects of a Decade of Change.* Cambridge: Harvard University Press.

Grogger, J., L. A. Karoly, and A. L. Klerman. 2002. *Consequences of Welfare Reform: A Research Synthesis.* Santa Monica, Calif.: Rand Corporation.

Gross, M. L. 1978. *The Psychological Society.* New York: Random House.

Gustman, A. L., and T. L. Steinmeier. 2001. "Retirement and Health." *Social Security Bulletin* 64 (2): 66–91.

Haar, C. M. 1975. *Between the Idea and the Reality: A Study of the Origin, Fate, and Legacy of the Model Cities Program.* Boston: Little, Brown.

Haggstrom, W. C. 1965. "Poverty and Adult Education." *Adult Education* 3:145–48.

Hamowy, R. 1987. *The Scottish Enlightenment and the Theory of Spontaneous Order.* Carbondale: Southern Illinois University Press.

Haveman, R. H., ed. 1977. *A Decade of Federal Antipoverty Programs: Achievements, Failures, and Lessons.* New York: Academic Press.

Hayes, R. L., W. K. Halford, and F. T. Varghese. 1995. "Social Skills Training with Chronic Schizophrenic Patients: Effects on Negative Symptoms and Community Functioning." *Behavior Therapy* 26:433–49.

Helms, J. 1974. *Economic Opportunity Legislation: Hearing Before the Senate Subcommittee on Employment, Poverty, and Migratory Labor Committee on Labor and Public Welfare.* 93d Cong., 2d sess., August 8, 320–25. Washington, D.C.: U.S. Government Printing Office.

———. 1986. *Men and Marriage.* Gretna, La.: Pelican Publishing.

Henderson, P., D. Jones, and D. N. Thomas. 1980. *The Boundaries of Change in Community Work.* London: Allen and Unwin.

Henderson, P., and D. N. Thomas. 1980. *Skills in Neighborhood Work.* London: Allen and Unwin.

Hessler, R. M., and C. S. Beavert. 1982. "Citizen Participation in Neighborhood

Health Centers for the Poor: The Politics of Reform, Organizational Change, 1965–77." *Human Organization* 41 (3): 245–55.

Hoffman, J. P., and A. S. Miller. 1998. "Denominational Influences on Socially Divisive Issues: Polarization or Continuity?" *Journal for the Scientific Study of Religion* 37 (3): 528–46.

Hollister, R. G., Jr., P. Kemper, and R. A. Maynard, eds. 1984. *The National Supported Work Demonstration*. Madison: University of Wisconsin Press.

Holloway, F., and J. Carson. 1998. "Intensive Case Management for the Severely Mentally Ill: A Controlled Trial." *British Journal of Psychiatry* 172:19–22.

Horwitz, A. V. 2007. "Science or Scientism." *American Journal of Child and Adolescent Psychiatry* 46 (8): 1092–93.

Humes, E. 2006. *Over Here: How the GI Bill Transformed the American Dream*. New York: Harcourt.

Hunter, F. 1953. *Community Power Structure*. Chapel Hill: University of North Carolina Press.

Hunter, J. D. 1991. *Culture Wars: The Struggle to Define America*. New York: Basic Books.

———. 1994. *Before the Shooting Begins: Searching for Democracy in America's Culture Wars*. New York: Free Press.

Jacobs, B. 1981. *The Political Economy of Organizational Change*. New York: Academic Press.

Jantti, M., et al. 2006. "American Exceptionalism in a New Light: A Comparison of Intergenerational Earnings Mobility in the Nordic Countries, the United Kingdom, and the United States." IZA Discussion Paper no. 1938. Bonn, Germany: IZA.

Johnson T., M. Gritz, and M. K. Dugan. 2000. *National Job Corps Study: Job Corps Applicants' Programmatic Experiences, Final Report*. Seattle: Batelle Memorial Institute.

Kaitz, E. M., and H. H. Hyman. 1970. *Urban Planning for Social Welfare*. New York: Praeger.

Katz, M. B. 1986. *In the Shadow of the Poorhouse: A Social History of Welfare in America*. New York: Basic Books.

Kelleher, M. J. 2001. "The Professional Ideology of Social Pathologists Transformed: The New Political Orthodoxy in Sociology." *American Sociologist* (Winter): 70–88.

Ketron, Inc. 1980. *The Long-Term Impact of Win II: Longitudinal Evaluation of the Employment Experiences of Participants in the Work Incentive Program*. Wayne, Pa.: Ketron, Inc.

Key, V. O. 1961. *Public Opinion and American Democracy*. New York: Knopf.

Kramer, R. M. 1969. *Participation of the Poor: Comparative Community Case Studies in the War on Poverty*. Englewood Cliffs, N.J.: Prentice Hall.

Kramer, R. M., and W. E. Bickel. 2004. "Foundations and Evaluation as Uneasy Partners in Learning." In *Foundations and Evaluation: Contexts and Practices for Effective Philanthropy*, ed. M. T. Braverman, N. A. Constantine, and J. K. Slater, 51–75. San Francisco: Jossey-Bass.

Kuran, T. 1995. "The Inevitability of Future Revolutionary Surprises." *American Journal of Sociology* 100 (6): 1528–51.

Lamb, W., et al. 1970. *National Evaluation of Community Action Programs, Report No. 2: The Culture of CAP.* Cambridge, Mass.: Barss, Reitzel and Associates.

LaPiere, R. T. 1965. *Social Change.* New York: McGraw-Hill.

Lappe, F. M., and P. M. Dubois. 1997. "Building Social Capital Without Looking Backward." *National Civic Review* 86 (2): 119–29.

Lasch, C. 1978. *The Culture of Narcissism: American Life in an Age of Diminishing Expectations.* New York: W. W. Norton.

Layard, R. 2005. *Mental Health: Britain's Biggest Social Problem.* http://www.strategy .gov.uk/downloads/files/mh layard.pdf (accessed August 15, 2006).

Lee, V. E., et al. 1990. "Are Head Start Effects Sustained? A Longitudinal Follow-Up Comparison of Disadvantaged Children Attending Head Start, No Preschool, and Other Preschool Programs." *Child Development* 61 (2): 495–507.

Lee, V. E., and S. Loeb. 1995. "Where Do Head Start Attendees End Up? One Reason Why Preschool Effects Fade Out." *Educational Evaluation and Policy Analysis* 17 (1): 62–82.

Lehman, A. F., et al. 1997. "A Randomized Trial of Assertive Community Treatment for Homeless Persons with Severe Mental Illness." *Archives of General Psychiatry* 54 (11): 1038–43.

Leiby, J. 1978. *A History of Social Welfare and Social Work in the United States.* New York: Columbia University Press.

Lemkau, P. V. 1971. Letter to the editor. *American Journal of Public Health* 61 (12): 2337–38.

Lerman, J. A., and C. Danielson. 2004. *Why Did the Welfare Caseload Decline?* Santa Monica, Calif.: Rand Corporation.

Lerman, P. 1975. *Community Treatment and Social Control: A Critical Analysis of Juvenile Correctional Policy.* Chicago: University of Chicago Press.

Leuchtenburg, W. E. 1963. *Franklin D. Roosevelt and the New Deal, 1932–1940.* New York: Harper and Row.

Levitan, S. A. 1969. "The Community Action Program: A Strategy to Fight Poverty." *Annals of the American Academy of Political and Social Science* 385 (September): 63–75.

Levitan, S. A., and B. H. Johnston. 1975. *Job Corps: A Social Experiment That Works.* Baltimore: Johns Hopkins University Press.

Lieberman, J. A., et al. 2005. "Effectiveness of Antipsychotic Drugs in Patients with Chronic Schizophrenia." *New England Journal of Medicine* 353 (12): 1209–23.

Lieberman, R. P., et al. 1998. "Skills Training Versus Psychosocial Occupational Therapy for Persons with Persistent Schizophrenia." *American Journal of Psychiatry* 155:1087–91.

Lilienthal, S. O., S. J. Lynn, and J. M. Lohr, eds. 2003. *Science and Pseudoscience in Clinical Psychology.* New York: Guilford Press.

Lindaman, K., and D. P. Haider-Markel. 2002. "Issue Evolution, Political Parties, and the Culture Wars." *Political Research Quarterly* 55 (1): 91–110.

Lindblom, C., and E. J. Woodhouse. 1993. *The Policy-Making Process.* Englewood Cliffs, N.J.: Prentice Hall.

Lindner, E. W. 2006. *Yearbook of American and Canadian Churches, 2006.* Nashville: Abingdon Press.

Lippitt, R., J. Watson, and B. Westley. 1958. *Planned Change: A Comparative Study of Principles and Techniques*. New York: Harcourt, Brace and World.

Lloyd, J. R. 2001. Review of *Bowling Alone: The Collapse and Revival of American Community*, by Robert D. Putnam. *New Statesman* 130 (4539): 56.

Lowi, T. 1967. "Public Philosophy: Interest Group Liberalism." *American Political Science Review* 61 (1): 5–24.

———. 1995. *The End of the Republican Era*. Norman: University of Oklahoma Press.

Lubove, R. 1968. *The Struggle for Social Security: 1900–1935*. Cambridge: Harvard University Press.

———. 1971. *Poverty and Social Welfare in the United States*. New York: Holt, Rinehart and Winston.

Macmillan, M. 1997. *Freud Evaluated: The Completed Arc*. Cambridge: MIT Press.

Magat, R. 1979. *The Ford Foundation at Work: Philanthropic Choices, Methods, and Styles*. New York: Plenum Press.

Maller, C., et al. 1986. *Evaluation of the Economic Impact of the Job Corps Program: Third Follow-Up Report*. Princeton: Mathematica Policy Research.

Manski, C. F., and I. Garfinkel, eds. 1992. *Evaluating Welfare and Training Programs*. Cambridge: Harvard University Press.

Marder, S. R., et al. 1996. "Two-Year Outcome of Social Skills Training and Group Psychotherapy for Outpatients with Schizophrenia." *American Journal of Psychiatry* 153:585–92.

Marris, P., and M. Rein. 1982. *Dilemmas of Social Reform: Poverty and Community Action in the United States*. Chicago: University of Chicago Press.

Marx, A. J., M. A. Test, and L. L. Stein. 1973. "Extrahospital Management of Severe Mental Illness: Feasibility and Effects of Social Functioning." *Archives of General Psychiatry* 29:505–11.

Masters, S. 1981. "The Effects of Supported Work on the Earnings and Transfer Payments of Its AFDC Target Group." *Journal of Human Resources* 16 (4): 600–636.

Mazumder, B. 2005. "Fortunate Sons: New Estimates of Intergenerational Mobility in the United States Using Social Security Earnings Data." *Review of Economics and Statistics* 87 (2): 235–55.

McConnell, S., and S. Glazerman. 2001. *National Job Corps Study: The Benefits and Costs of Job Corps*. Princeton: Mathematica Policy Research.

McKey, R. H., et al. 1985. *The Impact of Head Start on Children, Families, and Communities: Final Report of the Head Start Evaluation, Synthesis and Utilization Project*. Washington, D.C.: U.S. Government Printing Office.

Mead, L. M. 1986. *Beyond Entitlement: The Social Obligations of Citizenship*. New York: Free Press.

———. 1997. *The New Paternalism: Supervising Approaches to Poverty*. Washington, D.C.: Brookings Institution Press.

Melzer, D., et al. 1991. "Community Care for Patients with Schizophrenia One Year After Hospital Discharge." *British Medical Journal* 303:1023–26.

Mencher, S. 1967. *Poor Law to Poverty Program: Economic Security Policy in Britain and the United States*. Pittsburgh: University of Pittsburgh Press.

Mettler, S. 2007. *Soldiers to Citizens: The GI Bill and the Making of the Greatest Generation*. New York: Oxford University Press.

Midgley, J., and M. Sherraden. 1997. *Alternatives to Social Security: An International Inquiry*. Westport, Conn.: Auburn House.

Miewald, C. 2003. "Making Experience Count in Policy Creation: Lessons from Appalachian Kentucky." *Journal of Poverty* 7 (1–2): 163–81.

Miller, A., and T. Burns. 2006. *Going Comprehensive: Anatomy of an Initiative That Worked*. Local Initiatives Support Corporation. http://www.knowledgeplex .org/showdoc.html?id=437741.

Miller, A. S., and J. P. Hoffman. 1999. "The Growing Divisiveness: Culture Wars or a War of Words?" *Social Forces* 78 (2): 721–52.

Mills, C. W. 1943. "The Professional Ideology of Social Pathologists." *American Journal of Sociology* 49:165–80.

———. 1956. *The Power Elite*. New York: Oxford University Press.

Mizrahi, T., and B. B. Rosenthal. 2001. "Complexities of Coalition Building: Leaders' Successes, Strategies, Struggles, and Solutions." *Social Work* 46 (1): 63–78.

Modesto, K. F. 2003. "Taken on Faith? Preliminary Findings of an Outcomes Evaluation of a Faith-Based Welfare to Work Program." Unpublished paper.

Mondros, J. B., and S. M. Wilson. 1994. *Organizing for Power and Empowerment*. New York: Columbia University Press.

Morehead, M. A., R. S. Donaldson, and M. R. Seravalli. 1971. "Comparisons Between OEO Neighborhood Health Centers and Other Health Care Providers of Ratings of Quality of Health Care." *American Journal of Public Health and the Nation's Health* 61 (7): 1294.

Moss, S. 1964. Memo from Simon F. Moss to Henry Saltzman, Ford Foundation Public Affairs Division, August 18, Ford Foundation archives, New York.

Mouw, T., and M. E. Sobel. 2001. "Culture Wars and Opinion Polarization: The Case of Abortion." *American Journal of Sociology* 106 (4): 913–43.

Moynihan, D. P. 1969. *Maximum Feasible Misunderstanding: Community Action in the War on Poverty*. New York: Free Press.

Mueser, K. T., et al. 1998. "Models of Community Care for Severe Mental Illness: A Review of Research on Case Management." *Schizophrenic Bulletin* 24 (1): 37–74.

Murphy, P. W., and J. V. Cunningham. 2003. *Organizing for Community Controlled Development: Renewing Civil Society*. Thousand Oaks, Calif.: Sage Publications.

Murray, C. 1983. *Losing Ground: American Social Policy, 1950–1980*. New York: Basic Books.

Murray, M. 1997. *And Economic Justice for All: Welfare Reform for the Twenty-first Century*. Armonk, N.Y.: M. E. Sharpe.

Myers, D., and A. Schirm. 1999. *The Impacts of Upward Bound: Final Report on Phase I of the National Evaluation*. Washington, D.C.: Mathematica Policy Research.

Myers, D., et al. 2004. *The Impacts of Regular Upward Bound: Results from the Third Follow-Up Data Collection*. Washington, D.C.: Mathematica Policy Research.

National Council of the Churches of Christ in the USA. 2006. *The Yearbook of American and Canadian Churches*. New York: National Council of Churches in the USA.

Nelson, R. H. 2002. *Economics as Religion: From Samuelson to Chicago and Beyond.* University Park: Pennsylvania State University Press.

Nolan, J. L., Jr. 1998. *The Therapeutic State: Justifying Government at Century's End.* New York: New York University Press.

O'Connor, A. 2001. *Poverty Knowledge: Social Science, Social Policy, and the Poor in Twentieth-Century U.S. History.* Princeton: Princeton University Press.

O'Connor, B. 2004. *A Political History of the American Welfare System.* Lanham, Md.: Rowman and Littlefield.

Oden, S., L. J. Schweinhart, and D. P. Weikart. 2000. *Into Adulthood: A Study of the Effects of Head Start.* Ypsilanti, Mich.: High/Scope Press.

Ohmer, M. L., and W. S. Korr. 2006. "The Effectiveness of Community Practice Interventions: A Review of the Literature." *Research on Social Work Practice* 16 (2): 132–45.

Olasky, M. 2000. *Compassionate Conservatism.* New York: Free Press.

Orshansky, M. 1968. "Recounting the Poor—a Five-Year Review." *Social Security Bulletin* (April): 2–19.

Ozgediz, S. 1973. *Survey and Analysis of the In-School NYC Programs: Final Report.* Springfield, Va.: National Technical Information Service.

Pantell, R. H., R. Reilly, and M. H. Liang. 1980. "Analysis of the Reasons for the High Turnover of Clinicians in Neighborhood Health Centers." *Public Health Reports* 95 (4): 344–50.

Parrott, S., L. Schott, and E. Sweeney. 2006. *Implementing the TANF Changes in the Deficit Reduction Act: Win-Win Solutions for Families and States.* Washington, D.C.: Center on Budget and Policy Priorities.

Patterson, J. T. 1981. *America's Struggle Against Poverty in the Twentieth Century.* Cambridge: Harvard University Press.

Pelton, L. H. 1989. *For Reasons of Poverty: A Critical Analysis of the Public Child Welfare System in the United States.* New York: Praeger.

Perlman, R., and A. Gurin. 1972. *Community Organizing and Social Planning.* New York: John Wiley and Sons.

Peterson, P. E. 1970. "Forms of Representation: Participation of the Poor in the Community Action Program." *American Political Science Review* 64 (2): 491–507.

Pilling, S., et al. 2002a. "Psychological Treatments in Schizophrenia: I. Meta-Analyses of Family Intervention and Cognitive Behavior Therapy." *Psychological Medicine* 32:763–82.

———. 2002b. "Psychological Treatments in Schizophrenia: II. Meta-Analyses of Randomized Controlled Trials of Social Skills Training and Cognitive Remediation." *Psychological Medicine* 32:783–91.

Piven, F. F., and R. A. Cloward. 1971. *Regulating the Poor: The Functions of Public Welfare.* New York: Vintage Press.

Plotnick, R. D., and F. Skidmore. 1975. *Progress Against Poverty: A Review of the 1964–1974 Decade.* New York: Academic Press.

Polsky, A. J. 1991. *The Rise of the Therapeutic State.* Princeton: Princeton University Press.

Porter, M. E., and M. R. Kramer. 1999. "Philanthropy's New Agenda: Creating Value." *Harvard Business Review* (November–December): 121–30.

Poston, R. W. 1953. *Democracy Is You: A Citizen's Guide to Action*. New York: Harper.

Prioleau, L., M. Murphy, and N. Brody. 1983. "An Analysis of Psychotherapy Versus Placebo Studies." *Behavioral and Brain Science* 6:275–310.

Public Agenda. 1995. *The Values We Live By: What Americans Want from Welfare Reform*. New York: Public Agenda.

Putnam, R. D. 2000. *Bowling Alone: The Collapse and Revival of American Community*. New York: Simon and Schuster.

Renshon, S. A. 2000. "Political Leadership as Social Capital: Governing in a Divided National Culture." *Political Psychology* 21 (1): 199–226.

Reynolds, R. A. 1976. "Improving Access to Health Care Among the Poor: The Neighborhood Health Center Experience." *Milbank Memorial Fund Quarterly: Health and Society* 54 (1): 47–82.

Riccio, J., D. Friedlander, and S. Freedman. 1994. *GAIN: Benefits, Costs, and Three-Year Impacts of a Welfare-to-Work Program*. New York: Manpower Demonstration Research Corporation.

Rieff, Philip. 1966. *The Triumph of the Therapeutic*. London: Chatto and Windus.

Rogers, E. M. 2003. *Diffusion of Innovations*. New York: Free Press.

Ross, M. 1958. *Case Histories in Community Organization*. New York: Harper and Row.

———. 1967. *Community Organization: Theory, Principles, and Practice*. New York: Harper and Row.

Rothman, J. 1974. *Planning and Organizing for Social Change: Action Principles from Social Science Research*. New York: Columbia University Press.

———. 1999. *Reflections on Community Organization*. Itasca, Ill.: F. E. Peacock.

Rotolo, T., and J. Wilson. 2004. "What Happened to the 'Long Civic Generation'? Explaining Cohort Differences in Volunteerism." *Social Forces* 82 (3): 1091–1121.

Rubin, L. B. 1969. "Maximum Feasible Participation: The Origins, Implications, and Present Status." *Annals of the American Academy of Political and Social Science* 385 (September): 14–29.

Salamon, L. M., and S. van Evern. 1973. "Fear, Apathy, and Discrimination: A Test of the Three Explanations of Political Participation." *American Political Science Review* 67 (4): 1288–1306.

Sardell, A. 1983. "Neighborhood Health Centers and Community-Based Care: Federal Policy from 1965 to 1982." *Journal of Public Health Policy* 4 (4): 484–503.

Schiltz, M. E. 1970. *Public Attitudes Toward Social Security: 1935–1965*. Washington, D.C.: U.S. Department of Health, Education, and Welfare.

Schochet P. Z., J. Burghardt, and S. Glazerman. 2001. *National Job Corps Study: The Impact of Job Corps on Participants' Employment and Related Outcomes*. Princeton: Mathematica Policy Research.

Seacat, M. S. 1977. "Neighborhood Health Centers: A Decade of Experience." *Journal of Community Health* 3 (2): 156–70.

Seidler, M. 1969. "Some Participant Observer Reflections on Detroit's Community Action Program." *Urban Affairs Quarterly* 5 (2): 183–205.

Shapiro, R. Y., K. D. Patterson, and J. T. Young. 1987. "The Polls: Public Assistance." *Public Opinion Quarterly* 51:120–30.

Shaviro, D. 2001. *Making Sense of Social Security*. Chicago: University of Chicago Press.

Sherr, M. E. 2008. *Social Work with Volunteers*. Chicago: Lyceum Books.

Skinner, C. 1995. "Urban Labor Markers and Young Black Men: A Literature Review." *Journal of Economic Issues* 29 (1): 47–56.

Skocpol, T. 1992. *Protecting Soldiers and Mothers: The Political Origins of Social Policy in the United States*. Cambridge: Belknap Press of Harvard University Press.

———. 1995. *Social Policy in the United States: Future Possibilities in Historical Perspective*. Princeton: Princeton University Press.

———. 2000. *The Missing Middle*. New York: W. W. Norton.

Slemrod, J. 1989. "Are Estimated Tax Elasticities Really Just Tax Evasion Elasticities? The Case of Charitable Contributions." *Review of Economics and Statistics* 71 (3): 517–22.

Smail, D. 2005. *Power, Interest, and Psychology*. Ross-on-Wye, UK: PCCS Books.

Smeeding, T. 2006. "Poor People in Rich Nations: The United States in Comparative Perspective." *Journal of Economic Perspectives* 20 (1): 69–90.

Smith, M., and S. Lipsky. 1995. *Nonprofits for Hire: The Welfare State in the Age of Contracting*. Cambridge: Harvard University Press.

Smith, M. L., G. V. Glass, and T. I. Miller. 1980. *The Benefits of Psychotherapy*. Baltimore: Johns Hopkins University Press.

Somers, G. G., and E. W. Stromsdorfer. 1970. *A Cost-Effectiveness Study of the In-School and Summer Neighborhood Youth Corps*. Madison: University of Wisconsin Industrial Relations Research Institute.

Sparer, G., and A. Anderson. 1972. "Cost of Services at Neighborhood Health Centers." *New England Journal of Medicine* 286 (23): 1241–45.

Sparer, G., G. B. Dines, and D. Smith. 1970. "Consumer Participation in OEO-Assisted Neighborhood Health Centers." *American Journal of Public Health and the Nation's Health* 60 (6): 1091–1102.

Sparer, G., and J. Johnson. 1971. "Evaluation of OEO Neighborhood Health Centers." *American Journal of Public Health* 61 (5): 931–42.

Spilka, G., and T. Burns. 1998. "Final Assessment Report: The Comprehensive Community Revitalization Program in the South Bronx." Philadelphia: OMG Center for Collaborative Learning.

Steckel, R., and J. Lehman. 1997. *In Search of America's Best Nonprofits*. San Francisco: Jossey-Bass.

Stein, L. I., and M. A. Test. 1980. "Alternative to Mental Hospital Treatment III: Social Cost." *Archives of General Psychiatry* 37:392–97.

Stoesz, D., and H. J. Karger. Forthcoming. *The Future of Social Work Education*. New Brunswick, N.J.: Transaction Publishers.

Strange, J. H. 1972a. "Citizen Participation in Community Action and Model Cities Programs." *Public Administration Review* (October): 655–69.

———. 1972b. "Community Action in North Carolina: Maximum Feasible Misunderstanding; Mistake, or Magic Formula?" *Publius* 2 (2): 51–73.

Stricker, F. 2007. *Why America Lost the War on Poverty—and How to Win It*. Chapel Hill: University of North Carolina Press.

Sundquist, J. L. 1969a. "Co-Ordinating the War on Poverty." *Annals of the American Academy of Political and Social Science* 385 (September): 41–49.

———. 1969b. *On Fighting Poverty: Perspectives from Experience.* New York: Basic Books.

Teles, S. M. 1998. *Whose Welfare? AFDC and Elite Politics.* Lawrence: University Press of Kansas.

Tilson, H. H. 1973. "Stability of Physician Employment in Neighborhood Health Centers." *Medical Care* 11 (5): 384–400.

Tocqueville, A., de. 1997. *Memoir on Pauperism.* Chicago: Ivan R. Dee.

Torrens, P. R. 1971. "Administrative Problems of Neighborhood Health Centers." *Medical Care* 9 (6): 487–97.

Trattner, W. I. 1994. *From Poor Law to Welfare State: A History of Social Welfare in America.* New York: Free Press.

Tyrer, P., and J. Morgan. 1995. "A Randomized Controlled Study of Close Monitoring of Vulnerable Psychiatric Patients." *Lancet* 345 (8952): 756–59.

Tyrer, P., et al. 1998. "Randomised Controlled Trial of Two Models of Care for Discharged Psychiatric Patients." *British Medical Journal* 316:106–9.

U.S. Bureau of Labor Statistics. 2005. Division of Information Services. *Volunteering in the United States: 2005.* December 9. http://www.bls.gov/opub/ted/2002/dec/wk5/art03.htm.

U.S. Census Bureau. 1968. *Statistical Abstract of the United States: 1968.* Washington, D.C.: U.S. Department of Commerce.

———. 1979–2002. "Historical Poverty Tables—Poverty by Definition of Income." http://www.census.gov/hhes/www/poverty/histpov/rdp05.html.

———. 2001. "Poverty in the United States: 2000." September. P60–214. Washington, D.C.: U.S Department of Commerce.

U.S. Comptroller General. 1974. *A Restructured Neighborhood Youth Corps Out-of-School Program in Urban Areas.* Washington, D.C.: U.S. General Accounting Office.

U.S. Congress. House. 1966. Committee on Banking and Currency. *Demonstration Cities and Metropolitan Development Act of 1966.* Public Law 89–754. 89th Cong., 2d sess. Washington, D.C.: U.S. Government Printing Office.

———. 1998. Committee on Ways and Means. *Overview of Entitlement Programs: Background Material and Data on the Programs Within the Jurisdiction of the Committee on Ways and Means.* 105th Cong., 2d sess. Washington, D.C.: U.S. House of Representatives.

———. 2004. *Overview of Entitlement Programs: Background Material and Data on the Programs Within the Jurisdiction of the Committee on Ways and Means.* 108th Cong., 2d sess. Washington, D.C.: U.S. House of Representatives.

U.S. Congress. Senate. 1965. Committee on Labor and Public Welfare, Select Committee on Poverty. *Expand the War on Poverty: Hearings Before the Select Committee on Poverty.* 89th Cong., 1st sess., June 28–29. Washington, D.C.: U.S. Government Printing Office.

———. 1967. Committee on Labor and Public Welfare, Subcommittee on Employment, Manpower, and Poverty. *Examination of the War on Poverty: Staff and Consultant Reports on Community Action Program, Middle Atlantic United States and North-Central United States.* 90th Cong., 1st sess., September. Washington, D.C.: U.S. Government Printing Office.

———. 2005. Committee on Finance. *Personal Responsibility and Individual Devel-*

opment for Everyone Act (PRIDE). 109th Cong., 1st sess., March 30. Washington, D.C.: U.S. Government Printing Office.

U.S. Department of Health and Human Services. 1998. Assistant Secretary for Planning and Evaluation. *Aid to Families with Dependent Children: The Baseline*. http://aspe.hhs.gov/HSP/AFDC/afdcbase98.

———. 1999. *Mental Health: A Report of the Surgeon General*. Rockville, Md.: U.S. Department of Health and Human Services.

———. 2004. Administration for Children and Families, Head Start Bureau. *Report to Congress on Head Start Monitoring: Fiscal Year 2004*. Washington, D.C.: Administration on Children, Youth, and Families.

———. 2005. Administration for Children and Families. *Head Start Impact Study: First Year Findings*. Washington, D.C.: Administration on Children, Youth, and Families.

———. 2006. *Head Start Program Fact Sheet*. Washington, D.C.: Administration on Children, Youth, and Families.

———. 2008. Health Resources and Services Administration. Proposed Budget. In author's possession.

U.S. Department of Labor. 2003. "Organizations for Which Volunteers Work." *MLR: The Editor's Desk* (January 2).

———. 2005. *Volunteering in the United States*. December 9. Washington, D.C.: U.S. Department of Labor.

———. 2008. Bureau of Labor Statistics. "Comparative Real Gross Domestic Product Per Capita and Per Employed Person: Sixteen Countries, 1960–2007." ftp://ftp.bls.gov/pub/special.requests/ForeignLabor/flsgdp.txt.

U.S. General Accounting Office (GAO). 1969. *Review of Economic Opportunity Programs*. Washington, D.C.: U.S. Government Printing Office.

———. 1978. *Are Neighborhood Health Centers Providing Services Efficiently and to the Most Needy?* HRD-77–124. Washington, D.C.: U.S. Government Printing Office.

———. 1998. *Job Corps: Links with Labor Market; Improved But Vocational Training Performance Overstated*. GAO/HEHS-99–15. Washington, D.C.: U.S. Government Printing Office.

Vanecko, J. J. 1969. "Community Mobilization and Institutional Change: The Influence of the Community Action Program in Large Cities." *Social Science Quarterly* 50 (3): 609–30.

———. 1970a. *Community Organization in the War on Poverty: Evaluation of a Strategy for Change in the Community Action Program*. Washington, D.C.: U.S. Department of Commerce.

———. 1970b. "Resources, Influence, and Issue Resolution in Large Urban Political Systems: The Case for Urban Renewal." PhD diss., University of Chicago.

Vidal, A. 1992. *Rebuilding Communities: A National Study of Urban Community Development Corporations*. New York: Community Development Research Center, New School for Social Research.

Wagenaar, A. C., et al. 1999. "Communities Mobilizing for Change on Alcohol: Lessons and Results from a Fifteen-Community Randomized Trial." *Journal of Community Psychology* 27 (3): 315–26.

Wagner, D. 2000. *What's God Got to Do with It? A Critical Look at American Charity*. New York: New Press.

Walther, R. H., and M. L. Magnusson. 1975. *A Longitudinal Study of Selected Out of School NYC—Two Programs in Four Cities: Final Report*. Washington, D.C.: George Washington University, Manpower Research Projects.

Warren, M. R. 2001. *Dry Bones Rattling: Community Building to Revitalize American Democracy*. Princeton: Princeton University Press.

Weaver, R. K., R. Y. Shapiro, and L. R. Jacobs. 1995. "The Polls—Trends: Welfare." *Public Opinion Quarterly* 59:606–27.

Weir, M., S. Orloff, and T. Skocpol. 1988. *The Politics of Social Policy in the United States*. Princeton: Princeton University Press.

Weisbrod, B. A., M. A. Test, and L. I. Stein. 1980. "Alternative to Mental Hospital Treatment II: Economic Benefit-Cost Analysis." *Archives of General Psychiatry* 37:400–405.

Weiss, C. H. 1970. "The Politicization of Evaluation Research." *Journal of Social Issues* 26 (4): 57–68.

Weissman, H. H., ed. 1969a. *Community Development in the Mobilization for Youth Experience*. New York: Association Press.

———. 1969b. *Employment and Educational Services in the Mobilization for Youth Experience*. New York: Association Press.

———. 1969c. *Individual and Group Services in the Mobilization for Youth Experience*. New York: Association Press.

———. 1969d. *Justice and the Law in the Mobilization for Youth Experience*. New York: Association Press.

Westinghouse Learning Corporation. 1969. *The Impact of Head Start: An Evaluation of the Effects of Head Start on Children's Cognitive and Affective Development*. Washington, D.C.: Clearinghouse for Federal Scientific and Technical Information.

White, J. 2001. *False Alarm: Why the Greatest Threat to Social Security and Medicare Is the Campaign to "Save" Them*. Baltimore: Johns Hopkins University Press.

Wholey, J. S. 1986. "The Job Corps: Congressional Uses of Evaluation Findings." In *Performance and Credibility: Developing Excellence in Public and Nonprofit Organizations*, ed. J. S. Wholey, M. A. Abramson, and C. Ellavita, 245–55. Lexington, Mass.: Lexington Books.

Williams, R. 1997. *Cultural Wars in American Politics: Critical Reviews of a Popular Myth*. New York: Aldine de Gruyter.

Wing, K. 2004. "Assessing the Effectiveness of Capacity-Building Initiatives: Seven Issues for the Field." *Nonprofit and Voluntary Sector Quarterly* 33 (1): 153–60.

Wittgenstein, L. 1980. *Remarks on the Philosophy of Psychology*. Vol. 2. Chicago: University of Chicago Press.

Wolfe, A. 1996. *Marginalized in the Middle*. Chicago: University of Chicago Press.

———. 1998. *One Nation, After All*. New York: Viking Press.

Ylvisaker, P. N. 1963. *Community Action: A Response to Some Unfinished Business*. New York: Ford Foundation.

Zigler, E., and J. Valentine, eds. 1979. *Project Head Start: A Legacy of the War on Poverty*. New York: Free Press.

Zilbergeld, B. 1983. *The Shrinking of America: Myths of Psychological Change.* Boston: Little, Brown.

Ziliak, J. P. 2005. "Understanding Poverty Rates and Gaps: Concepts, Trends, and Challenges." *Foundations and Trends in Microeconomics* 1 (3): 127–99.

Zill, N., et al. 2001. *Head Start FACES: Longitudinal Findings, Third Progress Report.* http://www.eric.ed.gov/ERICDocs/data/ericdocs2sql/content_storage_01/ 0000019b/80/17/1b/9d.pdf (accessed July 2007).

Zurcher, L. A. 1969. "Stages of Development in Poverty Program Neighborhood Action Committees." *Journal of Applied Behavioral Science* 5 (2): 223–65.

Zwick, D. I. 1972. "Some Accomplishments and Findings of Neighborhood Health Centers." *Milbank Memorial Fund Quarterly* 50 (4): 387–420.

INDEX

Abecedarian project, 185
ACORN, 6
Adam and Eve, 53
ADC, 220
affirmative action, 1
AIDS study, 176
Aid to Families with Dependent Children
  (AFDC), 8, 38, 126, 138, 142–44, 165,
  167, 220, 227
Alinsky, Saul, 35, 56, 105, 208
Alinsky-style organization. *See* community
  organization
Allegheny Conference on Community De-
  velopment in Pittsburgh, 201
American Association of Retired Persons
  (AARP), 158
America's myth, 6. *See also* romanticism
Americorps program, 1
Amish, 11
Anderson, A., 114, 253
Anderson, P. R., 84, 241
anomie, 12, 69

Back of the Yards in Chicago, 208
Baltimore, Maryland, 121
Bangladesh, the People's Republic of, 18
Bassi, L., 141
Beck, B. M., 34, 69
Becker, E., 128
Big Brothers/Big Sisters program, 42, 187
Boston, Massachusetts, 45
Boyd, J., 196
Boys and Girls Club, 182
Boys and Girls Town, 131, 190
Brager, G., 69, 71
Brown, E., 194
Bryson, B., 223–24

California Youth Authority, 89, 120
Catholic Charities, 190

Catholic Church, 183
Center on Philanthropy, 180–83
child welfare, xii, 169
China, 18
Christian fundamentalists, 176
citizenship, xv, 18–19, 21, 34, 44, 53, 58, 101,
  102, 162, 191, 212, 236
  consent, xiv, 14, 16, 17, 74, 108
  values, xi, xii, 2, 3, 8, 10, 13, 16, 20, 35, 125
Civilian Conservation Corps, 80
Civil Rights Act, 1, 51, 175, 176, 216, 232
  legislation, 19, 43, 111, 112
  organizers, 35, 56, 57, 59, 63
Cloward, Richard, 26, 27, 33, 34, 36, 37, 39,
  44, 57, 71, 107, 108, 184
  and Lloyd Ohlin 1962, 24, 38, 39, 41, 44
Cognitive Behavioral Therapy (CBT), 122,
  123
Columbia University School of Social Work,
  24, 39
  professional social work, 24, 25
Commission on Juvenile Delinquency, 80
community action agency (CAA), 58, 59, 60,
  61, 62, 63, 64, 65, 66, 67, 69, 70, 71,
  72, 73, 74, 101
Community Action Associates, Inc., 69
Community Action Program (CAP), 7–8, 19,
  23, 33, 36, 45, 55–62, 65–69, 71–72, 74–
  77, 79 114, 197, 232
community development. *See* community
  organizing
Community Development Block Grant Project, 76
community organizing, 1, 3, 7–8, 25, 30, 33–
  34, 36, 40, 50, 57, 59, 64, 69–70, 72,
  126, 201–5, 207, 208, 211
  agencies, 34
  Alinksy-style, 7, 207, 208
  block associations, 25, 31
  campaigns, 31

community organizing (*continued*)
  history of, 7
  mobilization, 33, 40, 65, 222
  organizers, 25, 34, 35, 36
community treatment, 118–19, 124–27, 133
  counseling, 8, 24, 25, 66, 80, 93, 102, 126, 127, 128, 168, 190
  Hinckley solutions, 6
Comprehensive Community Revitalization Program in the South Bronx (CCRP), 198, 199, 200, 201
Comprehensive Health Planning Act, 112
Concentrated Employment Training Act program (CETA), 141–42
Cook, F. L., 226
Crane, J., 184–85
Culhane, D. P., 133–35
Cummings, S., 205
Cunningham, J. V., 206
Currie, J., 95–97

Daimler Chrysler, 233
Debs, E., 73
Deficit Reduction Act, 167
Delgado, M., 208
Democratic Party, 70
Demos Common Wealth Project, 225–26
Denmark, 154
Department of Health, Education, and Welfare, 114
detached role theory, 228
  ecology, xi, xiii, xiv, xv, 10, 218, 233
  organizations, xi, xii, xiii, 13, 14, 15, 16, 61, 72, 229, 231, 234
Diamond, P. A., 160, 162
DiIulio, J. J., 191–92
DiMaggio, P., 223–24
Domhoff, G. W., 220
Du Bois, W. E. B., 51

Earned Income Tax Credit, 164, 169, 226–27
economic growth, 2–5, 48, 119, 234, 236
education, xii, 4, 6–7, 20, 25–26, 31, 37–39, 46, 48, 52, 56, 63, 74, 80, 82, 85, 89–90, 92–95, 99, 102, 111, 118, 138, 145, 149, 152–53, 168, 172, 183, 196, 199, 201, 205, 211, 216, 235
Edwards, J., 46
employment, 4, 6, 28, 31, 35, 37, 46, 48, 52, 72, 81–82, 89–90, 103–4, 106, 112, 116, 119, 135–39, 141–44, 146, 166, 152, 170–72, 199–201

training, 19
  vocational counseling, 25
England, 133
English, G., 70, 244
enlightened rationalism, 22
Etzioni, A., 12, 245
Europe, 11
Evans, J. H., 223–24, 244, 245
Ewalt, P. A., 206, 245

faith-based programs, 1, 8, 18, 80, 131, 168, 186, 189, 190–94, 197
federal government, 26, 45, 50, 59, 60, 114, 136, 166, 172, 180
Fichte, J., 7
Freeman, E. M., 206
free market, 7, 14
Freud, S., 7
Frieden, B. J., 76–77
Friedlander, D., 144–45
Friedman, L., 56, 79, 105
food stamps, 1, 6, 52, 136, 151, 153, 164, 165, 167, 169, 237, 238, 239
Ford, R., 121
Ford Foundation program, 22, 24, 27, 44, 45, 46, 47, 48, 49, 50, 53, 59, 95, 195
  consultants, 27, 35, 66
  Gray Areas Project, 23, 95
  support, 27
Foster Grandparents program, 104

Geiger, H. K., 113
GI Bill, 52, 105, 176
Gide, A., 19
Gilbert, N., 69–70
Ginsberg, M. I., 60
Gitlin, T., 222–24
Glass, G. V., 128
global warming, 2, 233
Gordon, L., 164, 220
Gray Areas Projects, 8, 23, 45, 47, 48, 59, 61, 148
  resident, 50
  street, 49
  success, 46, 95
Great Awakening, 6
Greater Avenues for Independence program (GAIN), 144, 145, 146
Green, E., 60
Grogger, J., 170–71
Gustman, A. L., 156
Gypsies, 11

Habitat for Humanity Incorporated (HFHI), 188, 189
Hadley, T. R., 133–35
Haiti, 18
Halford, W. K., 122
Hayes, R. L., 122
Head Start program, 19, 43, 55, 56, 58, 61, 65, 87, 95, 96, 97, 98, 99, 100, 101
   African American children, 96
   impact study, 97, 98
"Healthy Marriage Promotion" program, 168
hedonism, 12
Hegel, F., 7, 221
Helms, J., 60
Henderson, P., 208
Herr, C. E., 113
Hollister, R. G., 139
housing, xii, 1, 14, 25, 31, 35, 57, 77, 81, 89, 92, 111, 125, 134, 135, 136, 152, 164, 172, 176, 187, 188, 189, 199, 200, 201, 202, 204, 205, 206, 207, 230, 232, 238
   associations, 31
   development, 52, 78
   homelessness, 1, 135, 136, 152, 188, 189
   homeless policy, 133
   housing clinics, 31
   organization of tenants, 31
   Section 8, 136
   slums, 31
   transitional, 133
HUD program, 76
Hutterites, 11
Hyman, H. H., 77,

individualism, 1
   heroic, 2, 3, 5, 6, 15, 21, 35, 50, 55, 74, 76, 111, 126, 127, 167, 173, 188, 205, 206, 216, 232, 235
Industrial Areas Foundation, 56, 207
inequality
   income, xii, 154, 201
   egalitarian, 22
   social, xi, 2, 3, 4, 21, 23, 44, 51, 95, 100, 148, 155, 173, 174, 198, 213, 233
innovation, 14, 45, 49, 149
   technological, 3, 7, 11, 34
In-School NYC program, 103
IRS, 181, 183

Jacobs, B., 62, 68, 76, 225
Jacobs, L. R., 63–64
Jewish Family Services, 190

Jews, 11
Job Corps program, 19, 25, 80, 141
   Corpsmember, 83
   graduates, 83
   high school dropout, 80
John Birch Societies, 109
Johnson, J., 113–14
Jones, D., 208
Just Say No to Drugs program, 1, 6

Kaitz, E. M., 77
Kaplan, M., 76–77
Karoly, L. A., 170–71
Katz, M. B., 106, 148, 184
Kennedy, J. F.
   Committee on Delinquency and Youth Crime, 22, 23, 24, 47
   See also U.S. history: Kennedy administration; War on Poverty: Kennedy administration
Kentucky, 172
Ketron, Inc., 138, 139
Keynesian economics and construct, 21
Klerman, A. L., 170–71
Knights Templar, 109
Korr, W. S., 204–5
Kramer, R. M., 69, 185, 186, 187
Kuran, T., 224

Laine, F., 196
LaPiere, R. T., 109
Layard, R., 133
Lee, R., 46
Lee, V. E., 98
legal aid program, 23, 24
Legal Aid Society, 26
Legal Services program, 104
Lehman, A. F., 121
Lehman, J., 186
Lerman, J. A., 170–71
Lerman, P., 120
Leuchtenburg, W. E., 162–63
Levitan, S. A., 55, 59–60, 84
Lewis, J., 73
Liang, M. H., 114
liberal, 2, 5, 7–9, 14, 17, 20–22, 34, 36, 49, 58, 67, 109, 148–49, 158, 160, 163, 165–66, 169, 174, 221, 224
liberal Democratic Congress, 67
Lieberman, J. A., 124
Lieberman, R. P., 122
Lilienthal, S. O., 128, 130
Lindblom, C., 218

Lindsey, John (New York mayor) , 60
Lippitt, R., 208
Local Initiatives Support Corporation (LISC), 202, 203, 204, 207
Lohr, J. M., 128, 130
Lukoff, Irving, 30
Lutheran Social Services, 190
Luxembourg Income Study, 153
Lynn, S. J., 128, 130

Magnusson, M. L., 103
Maller, C., 81–85, 87
Manpower Development and Training Act programs, 63, 65, 69, 80, 84, 89, 103, 136, 137
Manpower Demonstration Research Corporation (MDRC), 137, 139, 142, 144, 145
Mao Zedong, 220
Marder, S. R., 122
Marx, Karl, 108
Masons, 109
Mathematica, Inc., 90, 91, 92
Maynard, R. A., 139
Medicaid, 1, 6, 52, 111, 163, 164, 176, 238
medical care, 6, 52, 111, 175, 236, 239
Mendota Mental Health Institute, study, 119
Mental Retardation Facilities and Community Mental Health Centers Construction Act, 117
Metraux, S., 133–35
Miller, T. I., 128
Mills, C. W., 220
Mizrahi, T., 205
Mobilization for Youth program (MFY), 8, 23, 24–44, 47, 50, 59–61, 66–67, 71, 73, 113, 114, 119, 148, 195, 197
    art program, 30
    board member, 30
    community staff, 27
    diversion program, 28
    enrollees, 37
    gang violence, 23
    juvenile delinquency, 8, 25, 28, 37–38
    program failure, 37
    programs, 38
    recidivism, 28
    services, 37
    slum youth, 30
Model Cities program, 1, 8–9, 19, 40, 61, 69, 73–79
Modesto, K. F., 186
Mondros, J. B., 208

Morgan, J., 121
Mouw, T., 223
Moynihan, D. P., 61, 105–6, 108
Murphy, P. W., 206–7
Murray, C., 20, 148, 165
Myers, D., 90–94

Nathan, R. P., 140
National Association of Manufacturers, 109
National Association of Mental Health, 132
National Association of Neighborhood Health Centers, 113
National Association of Social Workers, 205
National Council of the Churches of Christ, 183
National Job Corps study, 85, 86, 87
National Opinion Research Center's Permanent Community Sample, 64
National Organization for Women, 175
National Research Council, 154
National Welfare Rights Organization, 33
Nation of Islam, 174
    Million Man March, 174
Native Americans, 11
Nazi Germany, 18
neighborhood health centers, 19, 25, 29, 112, 113, 114, 115, 116, 117
Neighborhood Youth Corps, 25, 56, 102, 103, 136, 141
New Career program, 56
New Frontier programs, 20, 21. See also United States history
New Haven, Connecticut, 45–48, 50, 95
New York City, 24, 33, 55, 199
    agencies, 27
    Board of Education, 33
    Human Resources Administration, 60
    Lower East Side, 24, 32, 33, 36; 1964, rent strikes, 31
    shelter system, 134, 135
    Welfare Department, 32
Nietzsche, F., 7
    Nietzschean will, 35
No Child Left Behind, 1
Nonprofit Sector Research Fund, 186
North Carolina, 45
NY/NY experiment, 134–36

Oakland, California, 45
O'Connor, A., 217
Office of Economic Opportunity (OEO), 20, 23–24, 35, 40, 45, 50, 55–58, 60–62, 65,

67–68, 72, 74, 76–77, 79–80, 101, 104–6, 113, 148
reauthorization hearings, 34
Ohmer, M. L., 204–5
Olasky, M., 191–92
Old Left, 70
on-the-job training program (OJT), 142–43
Operation Mainstream program, 56, 104
opportunity theory, 23, 25, 29, 37–39, 41, 43, 81
Oregon, 60
Orszag, P. R., 160
    Diamond-Orszag proposal, 160

Patman, Wright, 78
Patterson, J. T., 106, 148
Peace Corps, 1, 42
Personal Responsibility and Work Opportunity Act, 165. *See also* Temporary Assistance for Needy Families (TANF)
Philadelphia, Pennsylvania, 45
Pilling, S., 122, 123
Piven, F. F., 37, 71, 105, 107–8, 184
Porter, M. E., 186–87
postmodern theory, 7, 35, 42
Poston, R. W., 208
poverty, xi, xii, 2, 4, 8, 18–20, 22–24, 26, 34, 35, 41–44, 46–48, 50–52, 55–56, 58–65, 67, 69, 70, 73–75, 78–79, 82, 94–95, 99–101, 108, 110, 112–13, 115, 117, 126, 136, 140, 144–45, 147–49, 152, 153–54, 156–58, 160, 165–66, 169, 172–76, 180, 182, 184, 187–88, 191–92, 197, 199, 201, 204, 215, 223, 232, 234, 237, 238
    economic deprivation, 19
    poor, 9, 25, 31, 33, 36, 37, 39
productive function
    and ceremonial function, 168, 179
    ritual, 1, 3, 5, 32, 43, 95, 100–101, 105, 110, 113, 127, 129, 141, 174, 187, 192, 194, 196, 198, 209, 216, 219, 227
psychotherapy, 6, 8, 24, 27, 126–33, 243, 245, 249, 253, 268
public policy, xii, xiii, 10, 14, 16, 19, 23, 151, 177, 212, 217, 229
Putnam, Robert, 25, 46, 50, 197, 211

Rand Corporation, study, 170
Red Cross, 186
"Responsible Fatherhood Initiatives" program, 168
Rogers, Everett M., 208, 209

romanticism, xii, 2, 6, 73, 113, 174, 191,193
    civil religion, 7, 21, 212
    Emersonian ideals, 15
    exceptional destiny, 2, 5, 20, 195, 222, 188
    myth, 2, 5–6, 9, 15, 18, 23, 55, 64, 74, 80, 117, 160, 167, 179, 189, 192, 197, 198, 209, 211, 215, 216, 218, 220, 228
    populist romance, 22
    predestination, 11
    Puritan, 2, 5, 19, 126, 193, 224, 235
    self-invention, 6, 15, 41, 55, 105, 127, 179, 197, 211, 213, 235, 236
Roosevelt, Theodore, 49
Rosenthal, B. B., 205
Ross, M., 208
Rothman, J., 208
Rural Loan program, 56
Russell Sage Foundation, 95
Russia, 18

Salvation Army, 190
Sardell, A., 113
Schiltz, M. E., 226, 228
Senate Committee on Labor and Public Welfare's Subcommittee on Employment, 69
Settlement House, 30, 41, 48, 117
    Henry Street, 41
Skocpol, T., 220
Slater, J. K., 186
Slemrod, J., 183
Smail, D., 128
Small Business Loan program, 56
Smith, Adam, 17, 95
Smith, M., 128, 191, 218
Sobel, M. E., 223
social attitude, cleavages, xiii, 215, 223
social capital, 2, 7, 50, 89, 197, 198, 202, 211, 246, 248, 252
    harmony, 2, 81
social efficiency, xii, 3, 5, 6, 7, 23, 40, 44, 45, 51, 52, 53, 70, 74, 78, 79, 99, 215, 226
social institutions, 3, 7, 10, 11, 16, 50, 52, 71, 72, 81, 89, 152, 180, 188, 196, 198, 211, 212, 213, 228, 229
social insurance, xii, 1, 6, 8, 21, 57, 110, 151, 155, 164, 216, 219, 220, 221, 225
    disability, xii, 1, 162, 225
    health, xii, 1, 163, 225, 227, 235
    old age, xii, 1, 6, 155, 225
    survivors, xii, 1, 225

social policy making, xiv, 8, 10, 12
  autonomous actors, xi, xvi, 61, 236
  autonomous government, xii, 8, 14
  class dominance, xiv, 9, 15, 16, 220, 221,
    235
  contract with America, 1
  elites, xii, xiii, xiv, 1, 10, 14, 47, 106, 107,
    109, 159, 174, 193, 218, 219, 223, 224,
    225, 236
  goals, 2, 3, 5, 8, 16, 17, 20, 22, 23, 24, 25,
    26, 30, 36, 37, 43, 44, 48, 49, 50, 51, 56,
    59, 61, 69, 72, 75, 76, 94, 99, 100, 104,
    108, 125, 132, 137, 145, 166, 187, 193,
    196, 187, 202, 208, 219, 242
  institutions, xii, 11, 20, 29
  intellectuals, xii, 15
  linear decision making process, 15
  logic, 21
  market-oriented, 2
  open political system, 10
  open society, xi, xiv, 10–12, 14–18, 109,
    146–47, 174, 231, 234
  participatory democracy, xiii, 16
  personal deviance, 2
  pluralism, 1
  political cohesion, 2; problems, 22; sys-
    tem, 12; process, 17
  rational, xii, 11, 16, 17, 22, 23, 58, 87, 149,
    167, 209, 217, 229, 235
  social decision making, xiii, xiv, 11, 12, 15,
    21, 23, 25, 77, 105, 106, 109, 152, 210,
    213, 217, 218, 221, 222, 231
  stakeholders, 9, 12, 13, 92
  time-ordered process, 13
  uncoerced choice, xii, 10, 147
social science, 15, 16, 23, 38, 44, 50, 58, 60,
    81, 87, 105, 106, 108, 137, 186, 217, 224,
    148, 222
  case studies, 28, 30, 39, 52, 68–69, 87,
    90, 101, 116, 146, 171, 186
  control group, 29, 37, 85–86, 91–92, 119,
    138, 156
  credible evidence, 4, 11, 21–22, 31, 43, 87,
    126–27, 132, 186
  data, xi, xiv, 10, 21, 27, 29–30, 52, 60, 63–
    65, 68–69, 78, 83, 86–88, 91–92, 96–
    97, 103, 108, 110, 114–16, 120–22, 132,
    140–41, 143, 158, 163, 171, 181, 183, 185–
    86, 194, 205, 209, 223–25, 228
  empirical evidence, 34
  empirical tests, 16
  evaluation design, 28, 30, 38

experimental group, 28
opinion poll, 2, 9, 10, 70, 85, 96, 158, 159,
    169, 224, 227, 228
outcomes, 16–17, 27, 31, 33, 37, 44, 47, 52,
    59, 76, 68, 80–82, 86–87, 89, 90–95,
    97, 101, 103–6, 108–9, 111, 113, 120–23,
    135, 138–39, 146–47, 185, 202–5
  qualitative, 39, 197, 204, 223, 225
  randomized design, 16–17, 97, 129, 171
  scientific evidence, 8, 11, 27, 43, 123, 126–
    27, 130, 132, 186
  survey, xii, 10, 12, 64, 68–69, 83, 90, 96,
    102, 130, 157–58, 181, 183, 186, 192, 194,
    204, 208–9, 223, 228, 141, 205, 226
Social Security Act, 1, 6, 141, 153, 155–56,
    158–64, 172, 174, 219, 225–26, 237–39
Social Security Administration, 157
social welfare, xii, 1, 4, 6, 18, 26, 33
  adequacy, 6
  bifurcated system, 8, 164, 225
  central theme, xi
  equality, 8
  factional, xii
  ideology, 3, 17, 174, 219, 221, 224, 234
  individual and family services, 24–25,
    28–29
  interventions, 4, 22, 34, 38, 39
  program inadequacy, 101, 124, 136, 146,
    151, 158–60, 163, 173
  progressive agenda, 9, 77
  redistribution of wealth, 39
  socioeconomic stratification, 5–6, 8–9, 14,
    23, 44, 111, 131–32, 146, 159, 173–75, 233
  strategy, 2, 23
  urban renewal, xii, 9, 76–79, 232
  welfare state, 8, 52, 53, 108, 167, 225
social work, 34, 36, 39, 127, 168, 205, 218,
    222, 244, 248, 250
  caseworkers, 25, 28–29, 32
  professional, 2
  students, 25
society, xiii, 2–9, 14–16, 18, 20, 23, 29, 40–
    42, 50, 56–57, 62, 70–72, 74, 81, 101–11,
    125, 128, 131, 135, 139–40, 152, 159, 166,
    175–76, 162, 193, 197, 204, 207–8,
    210–11, 224, 228–29, 232–33, 235
  central institutions, 6, 152, 155
  dominant culture, 43, 70, 207
  market-oriented, 2
  modern, 2–3, 6, 8, 20, 44, 125, 152, 219,
    231
  moral climate, 7

open, xi, xiv, 10–12, 14–18, 109, 146–47,
    174, 231, 234
social conditions, 12–13, 15, 100, 121, 126,
    132, 152, 174, 196, 199, 207, 211
Solow, R., 140
Somers, G. G., 103
Special Impact program, 56
state workfare experiments, 137, 144–45
    Maine experiment, 142
Steckel, R., 186
Steinmeier, T. L., 156
Stockholm syndrome, 15
Stromsdorfer, E. W., 103
Sundquist, L., 46–47, 78
Supplemental Security Income (SSI), 6, 135,
    153, 156, 163–64, 237
Supported Work program, 89, 139, 140
Sviridoff, Mitchell, 47
Synanon, 30

Teles, S. M., 228
Temporary Assistance for Needy Families
    (TANF), 5, 6, 8, 151, 154, 164, 165, 166,
    168, 169, 167, 170, 171, 172, 173, 174,
    220, 241, 251
    and Reform of 1996, 63
    2006 reauthorization of, 63
Thomas, D., 96–98, 208
Thomas, Tenny, 182
Training Opportunities in the Private Sector
    program (TOPS), 142–44
TransCentury, Inc. (consulting firm), 68
Trilateral Commission, 109
twentieth century, 18, 35, 117, 184, 251
Tyrer, P., 121

Unemployment Insurance program, 82
United States, xi, xvi, 1–3, 10, 12, 14–15, 17,
    18, 51, 101, 104, 107, 109, 118, 124,
    151–54, 157–58, 163, 173–74, 176, 189,
    192–93, 196, 202, 204, 209, 212, 215,
    217, 220–21, 224, 228–29, 234–35
    apartheid, 112
    complacent, xv, 128, 184, 211
    consensus, xii, xiii, 11–12, 14–16, 18–21,
        57, 70–71, 78–79, 107, 109, 137, 148,
        163, 173–74, 198, 204, 206, 212–13, 215,
        218, 221, 223–25, 235
    conservatism, 9, 21, 162, 191, 221
    cultural bounds, xiii; choice, xi, xxi, 9, 11–
        14, 39, 149, 152, 163,174, 177, 213, 221,
        224, 228, 229; condemnation, xi
    culture, xiv, 9–12, 14–17, 23–24, 38, 43, 57,

    70, 73, 88, 92, 106, 117, 132, 145, 152,
        155, 174, 176, 197–98, 206–7, 213–15,
        218, 220–21, 222–25, 228–29, 234–35
    economic growth, 2–5, 19, 48, 173, 234,
        236
    experience, 21
    first amendment rights, 36
    government, xiv, 1
    hyper-democracy, 12–13, 212
    indifference, xi, 2, 9, 40, 95, 111, 204, 215–
        17, 232–33
    July 4th, 151
    lower class, 24, 39, 71
    middle class, 19, 20, 34, 71, 175, 233
    national ethos, 14, 53, 65, 109, 111, 177,
        202, 209, 216
    preferences, xiii, 2–3, 6, 12, 14–16, 42, 49,
        51, 53, 61, 72–73, 76, 78, 100, 102,
        107–9, 124, 147, 151, 169, 174, 195, 214–
        15, 219, 220, 228–29, 234–35
    social movements, 14, 107, 176, 201,
        232–33
    system, xv, 2, 4, 8–10, 12, 14–15, 25, 32–33,
        35–36, 40–41, 46, 51, 56, 59, 61, 63, 73,
        77, 92, 105, 108, 112, 114, 117, 118, 124,
        127, 134, 136, 147, 153, 154, 156, 159,
        160–62, 168, 176, 188, 196, 216–17,
        225–26, 231, 235
    values, xii–xiii, xiv, 1, 3, 5, 8, 9–10, 12–13,
        15, 19, 22, 42, 72–73, 108–9, 111, 126,
        132, 147, 158–59, 162, 179, 195, 215, 217,
        227, 231, 235
Upward Bound program, 43, 56, 58, 65, 90–
    95, 101
    and Hispanic students, 92
U.S. Census Bureau, 104, 153, 157, 163, 172,
    237–38, 254
U.S. Comptroller General, 103, 254
U.S. Congress, House, 75, 78, 169, 254
U.S. Department of Education, 90
U.S. Department of Health and Human Ser-
    vices, 95, 97–98, 112, 133
U.S. Department of Housing and Urban De-
    velopment, 75
U.S. Department of Labor, 45, 87–88, 90,
    173, 255
U.S. General Accounting Office (GAO), 65,
    66–68, 72, 87–88, 103, 113–16
U.S. history
    Clinton administration, 137, 166, 190
    Great Depression, xv, 51, 155, 226
    Kennedy administration, 49, 68

U.S. history (*continued*)
  McCarthy era, 36
  New Deal, 166, 172
  Newt Gingrich Contract, 46
  Nixon and Carter administrations, 1, 7, 41, 61
  Reagan administration, 46, 61, 133, 141, 226
  slaves, 18, 88
  Vietnam War, 176
  World War II, xi–xii, xv, 2–3, 41, 51, 105, 157, 161
U.S. Senate, 34, 60, 69, 168, 246, 254

Vanecko, J. J., 64–65, 76
Varghese, F. T., 122
Vidal, A., 208
Volunteers in Service to America (VISTA), 1, 42, 56, 101, 104
voter registration program, 25, 31
Voting Rights Act, 1, 19, 51, 57, 175, 216

Wagner, D., 184
Walther, R. H., 103
War on Poverty, xi–xii, 1–2, 4–6, 16, 19–23, 36, 40–41, 44, 50–53, 57–58, 61, 67–68, 72, 74–75, 78–79, 84, 87, 101, 104–6, 109, 111, 118, 126, 146, 131, 133, 147, 148–49, 154, 163–66, 168–69, 175–76, 197, 207, 212, 216–17, 229, 231–32
  community action plan, 33, 232
  and the Great Society, xii, 7, 20, 52, 58, 112, 175, 216, 232
  Jacksonian democracy, 22

Johnson administration, xii
Kennedy administration, 47
  New Frontier, 20–21
1970s, 19–20
1960s, xii, 20, 39
  Nixon, 1, 20, 61
Warren, M. R., 208, 213
Washington, D.C., 45, 68
Watson, J., 208
Weber, M., 234
WEET program, 142–43
Weissman, H. H., 26, 29–31, 32, 34–35, 37
Welfare Department, 26, 29, 32
  New York City department, 32
  1966 organizing, 32
  system, 32, 33
Westinghouse Learning Corporation, 96, 256
Westley, B., 208
White House, Executive Office of the President, 67, 105
Wilson, S. M., 208
Wing, K., 185
work experience program, 56, 138, 140, 142
Work Incentive program (WIN), 138–39, 141
Work Study program, 56, 104

Yearbook of American and Canadian Churches, 182
  Council of Churches, 182–83
Ylvisaker, Paul, 46
YMCA, 184

Zilbergeld, B., 128
Zwick, D. I., 113

www.ingramcontent.com/pod-product-compliance
Lightning Source LLC
Chambersburg PA
CBHW021855020426
42334CB00013B/344